Tagalog Dictionary

PALI LANGUAGE TEXTS: PHILIPPINES

Social Science Research Institute
University of Hawaii

Howard P. McKaughan
Editor

TAGALOG DICTIONARY

TERESITA V. RAMOS

University of Hawaii Press
Honolulu

499.
2

The work reported herein was performed pursuant to a contract with the Peace Corps, Washington, D.C. 20525. The opinions expressed herein are those of the author and should not be construed as representing the opinions or policies of any agency of the United States government.

94 93 92 91   12 11 10 9

Library of Congress Catalog Card Number 71–152471
ISBN 0–87022–676–2
Manufactured in the United States of America

PREFACE

This dictionary forms one of three volumes on Tagalog. The other two are <u>Tagalog for Beginners</u> by Miss Ramos and Videa de Guzman and <u>A Synopsis of Tagalog Structures</u> by Miss Ramos. These form a part of a larger series under the name of <u>PALI Language Texts</u>: <u>Philippines</u> edited by the undersigned.

The entire series has been developed under the auspices of the Pacific and Asian Linguistics Institute of the University of Hawaii through a contract with Peace Corps (PC 25-1507).

It is the hope of the author of this dictionary and the editor of the series that this will be an aid to learners of Tagalog. It is our hope also that these learning materials will help foster the people to people friendship traditional between our countries. It should be noted that authors of texts in the series are from both the Philippines and the United States. Their working together in the development of these materials mirrors the close ties that can result from Americans learning Philippine languages.

Howard P. McKaughan
Editor

1. General

This dictionary is a compilation of about 4,000
Tagalog roots, affixes, stems (affix + root), and a
few compounds and idioms. Entries have been chosen
from Tagalog for Beginners which accompanies this
dictionary, Panganiban's Talahuluganang Pilipino-
Ingles, and from the compiler's native stock of
Tagalog words. They form in the judgement of the
compiler, the high frequency words that are necessary
for a non-Tagalog speaker to be able to communicate
effectively in day-by-day conversational situations.
Roots with certain affixes have been entered as well
as roots alone. This is because affixes in Tagalog
are very productive in word formation. Some stems
have meanings that cannot be predicted from the root
alone. For example, karamdáman, n., 'sickness, ail-
ment', comes from the root damdám which by itself does
not occur in the language. With the suffix -in (dam-
dámin, n.), the combination takes on the meaning of
'feeling, emotion, sensation'; with the compound affix
ma--in (maramdámin, adj.) the word means 'overly sen-
sitive'; and with the prefix mag- (magdamdám, v.),
it means 'to feel bad about'. Similar meanings are
given as subentries of the root word; in this case,
damdam. When a meaning can not be predicted, the
word base with the affixes is entered separately
(cf. karamdaman).

Most of the entries, however, are root words.
The general format of each entry is as follows:

> [Entry] [(country of origin)] [part of speech]
> [/affix/] [(irregular spelling)]
> [gloss]   [--syn., synonyms] [--var.,
> variant forms] [sentence illustrating
> the use of the entry, usually verb
> forms] [English free translation].

An example of an entry follows:

> dílat   n.   act of opening of the eyelids.
>   --syn. múlat.

> adj.   (dilát) wide-open eyes; wide-eyed.
>
> v.   /-um-/ to open (as of the eyes). Dumílat ka. You open (your eyes).
>
>   /i-/ to open one's eyes; to raise one's eyelids. Idílat mo ang mga mata mo. You open your eyes.
>
>   /mang-:pang-, -an/ Pinangdilátan niya ako. She glared at me.

Every entry (except for a very few) is followed by a symbol which identifies the part of speech of the item. The following symbols are used for such identification.

adj.	adjective
adv.	adverb
conj.	conjunction
dem.	demonstrative
int.	interrogative
intj.	interjection
mkr.	marker
n.	noun
num.	numeral
part.	particle
prep.	preposition
pron.	pronoun
p.v.	pseudo verb
qnt.	quantifier
v.	verb

Af. is used to identify an affix.

A root can have noun forming, adjective forming and verb forming affixes. When the root has different derivations, the order is usually the n. (noun) at the top of the list with the v. (verb) at the end.

Many foreign words have been assimilated and have become part of the language. Many of these entries have their origins identified by the abbreviations of the countries from which they were borrowed.

For example:

<u>kirí</u> (Ch)	Chinese
<u>basketból</u> (Eng)	English
<u>hákot</u> (Mal)	Malay
<u>lasáp</u> (Sk)	Sanskrit
<u>relohéro</u> (Sp)	Spanish

In this dictionary, borrowed words are entered with their original affixes if they so occur rather than by the root only because such affixes are not as productive in forming words as the Tagalog affixes are.

Following the part of speech, an entry may have an affix or affixes enclosed in slashes. If there are two affixes, the first one is the actor-focus affix and the second one, separated from the first by a colon, is usually the goal-focus affix; e.g. /mag-:i-/. The definition of the entry comes next followed by a synonym or a variant. Verb entries are often illustrated by a Tagalog sentence.

Sometimes when an affix is attached to a root the spelling of the word changes. A letter may be added or dropped, or the stress may shift to another syllable. When these changes occur, the word is spelled out and enclosed in parentheses following the affixes enclosed in slashes.

2. Selection of the Entries

a. Nouns

The compiler of this dictionary has chosen nouns that a learner will most likely meet and use early in common situations in the Philippines. High frequency nouns such as words referring to parts of the body, flora and fauna, food, colors, numbers, units of measure, means of transportation, clothes and shelter etc. are thus included in the dictionary. Terms useful to a visitor as he goes to market, to the office, to school, to the doctor, to the post office, to the store, to the movies, to the laundry, to the tailor or seamstress, to the barber shop or beauty salon etc. are also included.

b. Adjectives

Common descriptive base words used with the nouns above are listed with their affixes indicated between slashes if any.

c. Verbs

The Tagalog verb form has been found to be the most difficult part of the language to learn. To help the student use the right affix, all verb roots are followed by actor and goal focus affixes (if they may occur) and occasionally locative focus affixes for intransitive verbs. Of all the lists, the verb list is the most exhaustive, having about 1000 entries and illustrated by as many sentences. It is in this detailed listing of the verbs and their most common affixes that this dictionary, it is believed, makes its major contribution to a faster control of the language by a student.

d. Particles

Little words which are untranslatable by themselves but which have various meanings when in context (that is, when used in sentences) are included in the dictionary. Examples of these are the particles naman, man, pa, na, and nga'. These particles occur very often in conversations. To use the language without them will result in stilted Tagalog.

3. Phonology

The consonant phonemes of Tagalog are: p, t, k, b, d, g, ', m, n, ng, y, l, r, s, h, w, and y. Most of the consonant sounds have the same phonetic value as English consonant sounds. However, the stops p, t, k are unaspirated; r is flapped and t, d, n, s and l are dentals.

Tagalog vowel sounds are a̲, e̲, i̲, o̲, u̲. A̲ is a low central vowel, e̲ is a mid central vowel, i̲ is a high front vowel, o̲ is a mid back vowel and u̲ is a high back vowel. The Tagalog vowel sounds are not to be equated with English vowel sounds. They are the 'same-but-not quite' types of sounds. The closest sounds to the five vowel sounds of Tagalog follow.

a	the a̲ in f̲a̲ther
i	the i̲ in mar̲i̲ne
u	the o̲o̲ in m̲o̲o̲n
e	the e̲ in b̲e̲d̲
o	the o̲ in h̲o̲pe

Originally there were only three vowel sounds in Tagalog. E̲ was a variant sound of i̲, and o̲ of u̲. In most words these sounds still fluctuate freely, e.g. baba̲e̲ ~ baba̲i̲ 'woman', bal̲o̲t̲ ~ bal̲u̲t̲ 'egg with a partially developed embryo'.

Because of the influence of borrowed words from Spanish, there are a few word pairs in Tagalog where a change from e̲ to i̲, or o̲ to u̲ results in the change of meaning:

mésa	'table'	mísa	'mass'
óso	'bear'	úso	'fad'

Stress on different syllables can lead to a change in meaning in identical words.

áso	'dog'	asó	'smoke'
gábi	'yam'	gabí	'night'

A shift in stress too may lead to a change in part of speech.

bíhis (n)	bihís (adj)
'way of dressing'	'dressed up'
bútas (n)	butás (adj)
'hole'	'punctured'

4. Orthography

The ABAKADA or the Tagalog alphabet consists of
20 letters in the following sequence: a, b, k, d,
e, g, h, i, l, m, n, ng, o, p, r, s, t, u, w, and y.

Note that k follows b and ng follows n. ng is
the digraph representation of the velar nasal sound
as it appears in English 'sing'.

The glottal catch is not represented in the
alphabet. It is symbolized in the orthography by
an apostrophe (') only when it occurs in word final
position. Elsewhere, it is not indicated. Note the
following contrasts.

báta	'robe'	báta'	'child'
bága	'live coal'	bága'	'lung'

For borrowed words with letters not found in the
Tagalog alphabet, the following symbols and sounds
are substituted:

Eng.	(j)	janitor	→	(dy)	dyanitor
Eng.	(Ch)	chief	→	(ts)	tsip
Eng.	(z)	zipper	→	(s)	siper
Sp.	(ll)	silla	→	(ly)	silya
Sp.	(f)	frito	→	(p)	prito
Sp.	(n)	señora	→	(ny)	senyora
Eng.	(x)	taxi	→	(ks)	taksi
Sp.	(v)	verde	→	(b)	berde
Eng.	(q)	quota	→	(k)	kota
Sp.	(c)	corto	→	(k)	korto
Sp.	(j)	trabajo	→	(h)	trabaho
Sp.	(ue)	casquero	→	(e)	kaskero
Sp.	(rr)	carretela	→	(r)	karetela

For borrowed diphthongs ia, ie, io, ua, ue, ui,
and uo, the Tagalog substitutes are ya, ye, yo, wa,
we, wi and wo. Note the following.

Sp. (io)	descripcion	→	(yo) deskripsyon/-siyon
Sp. (ue)	cuento	→	(we) kwento/kuwento
Sp. (ia)	desgracia	→	(ya) desgrasya/-siya

The i and u are sometimes inserted to follow
the regular cannonical syllable pattern in Tagalog
which is consonant-vowel (CV) rather than vowel
clusters (VV) or consonant clusters (CC).

5. Parts of Speech

Root entries have been classified as nouns,
pronouns, adverbs, verbs, conjunctions, markers,
particles, interjections, numerals, quantifiers,
prepositions, pseudo verbs (or modals), interroga-
tives and demonstratives.

a. Nouns (n.)

Nouns may consist solely of roots, e.g.
báta' 'child', báhay 'house'; or a combination of a
noun forming affix and a root, e.g.

```
(taga-) + luto              taga-lúto 'cook'
upo + (-an)                 upuán 'seat'
(ka-) + ligaya + (-an)      kaligayáhan 'happiness'
```

A few common compounds like bahay-báta (house-
child) 'uterus', dahong-paláy (leaf of the rice plant)
'name of a poisonous rice snake' appear in the listings.

The nouns are the only entries that occur as
bases or as stems (except for borrowed words). All
the rest of the entries except for a few conjunctions
are listed as base words. This is due to the fact
that noun forming affixes are not as productive as
the verbal and adjectival forming affixes are.

When the nouns are entered as stems, each is
followed by its root word enclosed in parentheses:

[ha-]	habilin	n.	(rw. bilin)	...
[ka-]	kalahati'	n.	(rw. háti')	...
[ka- -an]	kaarawan	n.	(rw. áraw)	...
[pa-]	pahinga	n.	(rw. hingá)	...
[pa- -an]	paaralan	n.	(rw. áral)	...
[pag-]	pagbabago	n.	(rw. bágo)	...
[pag + ka-]	pagkatao	n.	(rw. táo)	...

Most of the noun stems can take the <u>ka-</u> or <u>ka- -an</u> affixes.

Where the spelling of the stem changes when an affix is attached to the root, the components of the stem, affix + root, are enclosed in parentheses following the entry:

pambutas n.   (fr. <u>pang</u> + <u>butas</u>) ...

b. Pronouns (pro.)

(1) Personal pronouns

Personal pronouns act as substitutes for noun phrases introduced by the noun markers <u>ang</u>, <u>ng</u> and <u>sa</u>. The following chart gives the three sets of personal pronouns and their characteristic particle identification.

Personal Pronouns	Ang- Pronouns		Ng- Pronouns	Sa- Pronouns
Singular				
First	ako		ko	akin
Second	ikaw.../ ka#		mo	iyo
Third	siya		niya	kaniya
Plural				
First (excl)		kami	namin	amin
(incl)		tayo	natin	atin
Second		kayo	ninyo	inyo
Third		sila	nila	kanila

(2) Indefinite pronouns

Indefinite pronouns such as <u>lahat</u> 'all', <u>kapwa</u> 'both', <u>iba</u> 'other' are labelled as pronoun (pro.) too in the dictionary.

c. Demonstratives (Dem.)

Another type of pronoun, the demonstrative, indicates the relative distances of objects from the speaker and the listener. Like the personal pronoun, these pronouns may be divided into <u>ang-</u> demonstratives,

ng- demonstratives and sa- demonstratives. A chart
of these pronouns follows.

Demonstrative Pronouns	Ang-Dem.	Ng-Dem.	Sa-Dem.
Near speaker	ito/ire 'this (one)'	nito/nire 'of this'	dito/dine 'here'
Near listener	iyan 'that (one)'	niyan 'of that'	diyan 'there'
Far from both	yon 'that (one), yonder'	niyon 'of that, yonder'	doon 'over there'

d. Adjectives (adj.)

Adjectives are words that modify nouns. They
are listed either as roots or as roots followed by
their adjective forming affixes. The most common of
the adjectival affixes is the prefix ma-.

Sometimes the only signal to indicate the change
from a noun to an adjective is the shifting of the
stress to a following syllable. If this change occurs,
the part of speech is followed by the base in parentheses with the corresponding shift in stress.

    bútas   n.   'hole'
             adj.   (butás) 'punctured'

e. Adverbs

Words modifying the verbs are classified as
adverbs. Most adverbs listed are roots, e.g. bigla'
'suddenly', naman 'also, too', noon 'then' etc.
Adverb forming affixes are very limited. A few are
listed in the dictionary:

    na- + sa- demonstratives   narito 'here'
    ga- + ng- demonstratives   ganito 'this way'

f. Markers

There are two types of markers: the relation markers (mkr.) and the non-relation markers (conj.).

(1) The relation markers (mkr.)

The relation markers are the noun marking particles that indicate the grammatical function (actor, goal, location, beneficiary, instrument) of the noun or noun phrase that they introduce and the marker <u>ang</u> that introduces the topic of the sentence. Note the following sentence.

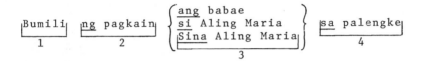

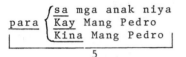

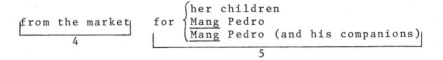

Ng marks the goal (<u>pagkain</u> 'food'), <u>sa</u> marks the location (<u>palengke</u> 'market'), and <u>para sa</u> marks the beneficiary ([<u>mga</u>] <u>anak</u> 'children'), <u>para kay</u>, the beneficiary (Mang

Pedro) <u>para kina</u>, the beneficiary (Mang Pedro and his companions). <u>Ang</u> marks the topic (<u>babae</u> 'woman'), <u>si</u>, the topic (<u>Aling</u> Maria) and <u>sina</u>, the topic (<u>Aling</u> Maria and her companions).

The markers of the instrument and the actor are illustrated in the following sentence.

Pinunasan 1 { ng bata / ni Maria / nina Maria } 2 ang mesa 3 ng basahan 4

The child / Maria / Maria (and her companions) 2 { wiped 1 the table 3 with a rag 4

<u>Ng</u> marks the actor (<u>bata</u> 'child') <u>ni</u>, the actor (Maria) and <u>nina</u> the actor (Maria and her companions). The second <u>ng</u> marks the instrument (<u>basahan</u> 'rag'). <u>Ang</u> again marks the topic (<u>mesa</u> 'table').

(2) <u>The non-relation markers (conj.)</u>

The non-relation markers are mostly conjunctions. They are particles that join words, phrases or sentences. Conjunctions are either coordinators (particles that link two items of equal rank) or subordinators (particles that join sentences of unequal rank). Some of the conjunctions listed are roots and others are stems:

<u>kasí</u>   conj.   'because'
<u>habang</u>   conj.   (rw. <u>hába'</u>)   'while...'

Some entries indicate the most common
words that occur with the conjunction followed
by the change in meaning:

<u>nang</u>   conj.   ...usually with <u>at</u>
              'so that' (in order that)

<u>at</u>   conj.   ...
                       (+ <u>baká</u>) lest
                       (+ <u>náng</u>) so that
                       (+ <u>baga</u> <u>man</u>) although

g. <u>Interjections (Intj.)</u>

Interjections are exclamatory words used to
express sudden or strong feeling. Examples of interjections included in the dictionary are as follows:

<u>Hoy</u>!   'Hey'
<u>Aba</u>!   (sudden reproach or emphatic denial)
<u>Aray</u>!   'ouch'

h. <u>Particles (Part.)</u>

There are some short words in the language
which are untranslatable. The meaning can only be
deduced when they are used in context. These words
are important for giving semantic nuances to the
sentence. Examples of these particles are <u>lang</u>, <u>man</u>,
<u>naman</u>, <u>nga</u>, <u>pa</u>, <u>pala</u>, and <u>na</u>.

i. <u>Quantifiers (Qnt.)</u>

Some common nouns act as modifiers to nouns.
These are nouns of quantity or quantifiers. Examples
of these are <u>tumpok</u> 'pile or heap', <u>yarda</u> 'yard',
<u>salop</u> 'ganta', <u>gatang</u> 'tin can', <u>sako</u> sack'.

They occur before the nouns they modify:

isang   <u>sakong</u>   bigas
'one   sack of   rice'

tatlong <u>yardang</u> tela
'three   yards of   cloth'

j. Interrogatives (Int.)

Interrogative words include entries like ano
'what', sino 'who', bakit 'why', etc. A few are
affixed such as pa-ano 'how', ga-ano 'how much' and
na-saan 'where'.

k. Numerals (Num.)

Numerals like adjectives modify nouns. In
the dictionary, however, they are classified separately
for easy reference. The listing of numerals is not
exhaustive because once the counting system is mastered
higher numbers are easy to generate. Entries include
terms for one to ten and units such as pu' 'ten(s)',
libo 'thousand(s)', daan 'hundred(s)' etc.

l. Pseudo Verbs (p.v.)

A special class of verbs is called 'pseudo
verbs' or modals. Unlike regular verbs, these verbs
are often used to precede another verb in the infinitive form and are not usually inflected for aspect.
Examples are gusto 'want, like', kailangan 'must,
need to', maari 'can'.

m. Verbs (v.)

Verbs, unlike the other parts of speech
mentioned here, can be inflected for aspect, kind of
action, and focus.

The verbs are entered as roots followed by their
actor-focus and goal-focus affixes (if permitted).

Only what may be called the infinitive forms of
the verbs are listed in the dictionary.

There are four aspectual forms of the verb:
neutral (infinitive), completed (past), incompleted
(progressive) and contemplated (future).

There are six kinds of action in Tagalog: indicative (mag-, -um-, ma-, i-, -in, -an and pag-an
verbs), distributive (mang- and pang--in verbs),
aptative (maka- and ma verbs), social (maki- and

paki- verbs), causative (<u>magpa</u>-, <u>pa</u>--<u>in</u>, <u>pa</u>--<u>an</u>, and <u>ipa</u>- verbs) and imperative (all neutral or infinitive forms of the different types of verbs except for the aptative verbs).

The indicative involves a single action directed toward a single object. The action is neutral.

The distributive indicates a habitual or professional action directed toward or distributed over several people, things or several ways.

The aptative indicates the ability or possibility of doing something.

The social indicates a polite or indirect way of requesting or describing an action.

The causative signifies that someone permits or causes an action to take place.

The imperative expresses a command or a request.

Only the first of these kinds of action and occasionally the third are indicated in the dictionary. Most of the sentences illustrating the verb forms are in the imperative because the verbs are in the infinitive form and therefore uncomplicated by reduplications.

The test sentence used in determining what affixes are permitted with a verb base is of the predicational type (i.e., a sentence starting with the comment followed by the topic). This sentence type has been chosen over the identificational type of sentence (i.e., topic before a marked comment), because the former is a more common type than the latter. The root <u>bawal</u> 'to prohibit' for example is limited to just the <u>mag</u>-affix because the -<u>um</u>- affix does not occur in a predicational sentence although it does occur in an identificational sentence.

For example:

Predicational: <u>Nagbawal</u> ang konduktor ng pagsi-sigarilyo sa sasakyan. 'The conductor prohibited smoking in the vehicle'.

Identificational: Ang konduktor ang <u>bumawal</u> ng
pagsisigarilyo sa sasakyan.
'It was the conductor who
prohibited smoking in the
vehicle'.

There are five types of focus: actor (<u>mag</u>-*,
<u>ma</u>-*, <u>mang</u>-*, <u>maka</u>-*, <u>maki</u>- and <u>magpa</u>- verbs), goal
(-<u>in</u>*, <u>i</u>-*, -<u>an</u>*, <u>pang</u>--<u>in</u>*, <u>ma</u>-, <u>paki</u>-, <u>ipa</u>-, <u>pa</u>--<u>an</u>
verbs), locative (-<u>an</u>*, <u>pag</u>--<u>an</u>*, <u>pang</u>--<u>an</u>, <u>ma</u>--<u>an</u>,
<u>mapag</u>--<u>an</u>, <u>paki</u>--<u>an</u>, and <u>pa</u>--<u>an</u> verbs), benefactive
(<u>ipag</u>-, <u>i</u>-, <u>ipang</u>-, <u>ma</u>-, <u>mai</u>-, <u>ipaki</u>-, <u>ipa</u>-, <u>ipagpa</u>-
verbs), and instrumental (<u>i</u>-, <u>ipang</u>-, <u>maipang</u>-,
<u>ipakipang</u>-, and <u>ipapang</u>- verbs).

Only the first two types of focus are indicated
in the dictionary. Of these two, only the affixes
marked with asterisks (*) are included. Occasionally
the locative focus is listed, especially after <u>in</u>-
transitive verb roots. The sentences illustrating
the use of the verbs are usually actor-focus sentences
except when the verb is used more often as a goal-
focused verb.

(1) <u>Aspect</u>

Aspect indicates, by means of verbal inflection, whether the action has started or not, and
if started, whether it has been completed or if
it is still continuing. Verbal inflection in-
cludes affixation and/or reduplication (i.e.
repetition of parts of the affix or base).

The three aspects of the verbs are 1) completed, for action started and terminated; 2) contemplated, for action not started; and 3) incompleted, for action started but not yet completed
or action still in progress. The form of the
verb that does not imply any aspect or is not
inflected for aspect is neutral or is in the
infinitive form.

The closest equivalent in English to the
completed aspect is the past tense, the contemplated aspect corresponds to the future tense,
and the incompleted aspect to the progressive.

The process or processes involved in the
verbal inflection to indicate aspect differ
according to the affix taken by the verb.

(a) The -um- verb

The neutral or infinitive form of the
-um- verb is constructed by placing -um-
before the first vowel of the verb root or
base. The completed form is identical to
the neutral form, e.g. um + langoy → l-um-
angoy 'to swim; swam', um + inom → um-inom
'to drink; drank'.

The contemplated aspect is formed by
reduplicating the first syllable (CV or V)
of the root, e.g. langoy → la-langoy, inom
→ i-inom.

The incompleted form affixes -um- to
the base in the same manner as in the neutral
form and also reduplicates the first syllable of the root, e.g. lalangoy → l-um-a-
langoy, iinom → um-i-inom.

(b) The mag- verb

The neutral form of this verb is constructed by prefixing mag- to the verb root,
e.g. mag + laba → maglaba 'to wash (clothes)'.

The completed form is constructed by
changing m- of the affix to n-, e.g. maglaba
→ naglaba 'washed (clothes)'.

The contemplated aspect is formed by
reduplicating the first syllable of the root
and prefixing mag-, e.g. lalaba → maglalaba
'will wash (clothes)'.

The incompleted aspect is formed by
prefixing nag- to the verb root and reduplicating its first syllable, e.g. naglalaba
'washing (clothes)'.

(c) The ma- verb

The ma- verb follows the same aspect
formation as does the mag- verb. N- replaces
the m- of the prefix for the started action
and the first CV- or V- of the root is reduplicated for action not terminated.

Base: tulog   'to sleep'
Neutral: matulog   'to sleep'
Completed: natulog   'slept'
Incompleted: natutulog   'sleeping'
Contemplated: matutulog   'will sleep'

(d) The mang- verb

The mang- affix undergoes the same m-
to n- replacement for started action and
reduplication for non-terminated action,
but there are some changes in the final
nasal sound of the affix as it gets influ-
enced by the following initial sound of the
root. This change is followed by also
dropping the first consonant of the root.
These changes are called morphophonemic
changes. The morphophonemic changes of
the mang- affix may be represented by the
following rule:

$$
\begin{bmatrix}
\text{mang} + \begin{Bmatrix} b\ldots \\ p\ldots \end{Bmatrix} \\[2ex]
\text{mang} + \begin{Bmatrix} t\ldots \\ d\ldots \\ s\ldots \end{Bmatrix} + \begin{matrix}\text{remainder}\\\text{of root}\end{matrix} \rightarrow \\[3ex]
\text{mang} + \begin{Bmatrix} k\ldots \\ i\ldots \end{Bmatrix}
\end{bmatrix}
\begin{bmatrix}
\text{mam}\ldots \\[2ex]
\text{man}\ldots \\[2ex]
\text{mang}\ldots
\end{bmatrix} + \begin{matrix}\text{remainder}\\\text{of root}\end{matrix}
$$

Examples:

        mang + bili'   → mamili'
                pili'   → mamili'

$$
\text{ma}\underline{ng} + \begin{cases} \underline{t}ahi' & \to \text{ma}\underline{n}ahí' \\ \underline{d}alangin & \to \text{ma}\underline{n}alángin \\ \underline{s}unog & \to \text{ma}\underline{n}únog \end{cases}
$$

$$
\text{ma}\underline{ng} + \begin{cases} kuha & \to \text{ma}\underline{ng}úha \\ \underline{i}sda & \to \text{ma}\underline{ng}isdá' \end{cases}
$$

H's and g's do not influence the final nasal of the prefix mang- to change; e.g.

$$
\text{ma}\underline{ng} + \begin{cases} gulo & \to \quad \text{ma}ngguló \\ huli & \to \quad \text{ma}nghúli \end{cases}
$$

After the affixed verb form has undergone morphophonemic changes, the second syllable is reduplicated to form the incompleted and contemplated forms.

Contemplated		Incompleted
mamimili	→	namimili
mananahi'	→	nananahi'
mangunguha	→	nangunguha

Where no morphophonemic changes occur, the first syllable of the root is reduplicated.

| manggugulo | → | nanggugulo |
| manghuhuli | → | nanghuhuli |

(e) The maka- verb

The maka- verb is inflected like the ma-/mag- verbs, except that the last syllable of the affix or the first syllable of the root may be reduplicated. Both are acceptable to native speakers:

Contemplated		Incompleted
makakasayaw	→	nakakasayaw
makasasayaw	→	nakasasayaw

(f)   The -in verb

The neutral form of the -in verb is formed by suffixing -in to the verb root.

alís + in   alisín
bása + hin   basahín

If the base ends in a vowel, -hin is suffixed to the root rather than -in. With the addition of the suffix -in, there is also a shift in stress to the next syllable toward the end of the word.

The completed aspect is formed by placing -in- before the first vowel of the root.

in-alis
b-in-asa

The incompleted aspect is affixed the same way plus the first syllable of the root is reduplicated.

in-a-alis
b-in-a-basa

The contemplated aspect is similar to the neutral form with the first syllable of the base reduplicated; e.g.

a alis in
ba-basa-hin

When roots begin with l or n, the affix in is inverted to ni only in the completed and incompleted forms.

linis + in- → nilinis → nililinis
nakaw + in- → ninakaw → ninanakaw

(g) The -an verb

The -an verb inflects the same way the -in verb does.

	Púnas + an	Puntá + han
Neutral:	punás-an	punta-hán
Completed:	p-in-unás-an	p-in-unta-hán
Incompleted:	p-in-upunás-an	p-in-u-punta-hán
Contemplated:	pu-punás-an	pu-punta-hán

-In follows a consonant sound and -hin a vowel sound. There is also an accompanying shift in stress to the next syllable with the addition of the suffix.

(h) The i- verb

The neutral aspect of the i- verb is formed by prefixing i- to the verb root, e.g. ihagis; the completed aspect by placing -in between the first CV of the root or by ni before h, y, n, l and the vowel initial sounds of the root; e.g. inihagis, itinapon. The non-terminated action of the incompleted and contemplated aspects are indicated by the reduplication of the first CV- or V- of the root.

Root	Completed	Incompleted	Contemplated
hagis	→ inihagis	→ inihahagis	→ ihahagis
yari'	→ iniyari'	→ iniyayari'	→ iyayari'
abot	→ iniabot	→ iniaabot	→ iaabot
tapon	→ itinapon	→ itinatapon	→ itatapon

(i) The ipag- verb

The ipag- verbs behave like the other prefixed verbs except that the -in- or the indicator of action started is infixed in the prefix rather than in the root.

```
Neutral:          ipag-luto
Completed:        ip-in-ag-luto
Incompleted:      ip-in-ag-lu-luto
Contemplated:     ipag-lu-luto
```

(j) The ipang- verb

The ipang- verb is inflected in the
same manner as the ipag- verb, except that
its final nasal sound undergoes the same
morphophonemic changes the mang- affix
undergoes e.g., ipang + tahi' → ipanahi'.
Other forms are as follows:

```
Completed:        ipinanahi'
Incompleted:      ipinananahi'
Contemplated:     ipananahi'
```

Note also the following:

```
ipang + bili      →    ipamili
ipang + kawit     →    ipangawit
ipang + butas     →    ipambutas
   Completed:           ipinambutas
   Incompleted:         ipinambubutas
   Contemplated:        ipambubutas
ipang + damo      →    ipandamo
ipang + linis     →    ipanlinis
```

(2) Focus

Focus refers to the grammatical relation-
ships that exist between the verb and one verbal
complement marked by the focus marker ang. The
verbal complement marked by ang or any of its
substitutes is referred to as the topic of the
sentence. The relationship of the topic to the
verb may be any one of the following. A glossary
for the Tagalog sentences appears at the end of
this section.

(a) The actor who does or originates the
action:

Aspect	-UM- Verb	Actor
Completed:	Bumili	ako
Incompleted:	Bumibili	si Nena
Contemplated:	Bibili	ang bata
		ito

Object	Location	Beneficiary
ng saging	sa kaniya	sa kanila
nito	sa dyanitor	sa guro'
	kay Maria	para kay Pablo
	sa tindahan	diyan
	dito	

(b) The <u>goal</u> which is the object of the action:

Aspect	-IN- Verb	Actor
Completed:	Binili	ko
Incompleted:	Binibili	ni Nena
Contemplated:	Bibilhin	ng bata
		nito

Object	Location	Beneficiary
ang saging	sa kaniya	sa kanila
ito	sa dyanitor	sa guro'
	kay Maria	para kay Pablo
	sa tindahan	diyan
	dito	

(c) The <u>locative</u> which is the place of the action:

Aspect	-AN Verb	Actor
Completed:	Binilhan	ko
Incompleted:	Binibilhan	ni Nena
Contemplated:	Bibilhan	ng bata
		nito

Object	Location	Beneficiary
ng saging nito	siya ang dyanitor si Maria ang tindahan ito	para	sa kanila sa guro' kay Pablo diyan

(d) The benefactive who or which is the beneficiary of the action.

Aspect	I- Verb	Actor
Completed:	Ibinili	ko
Incompleted:	Ibinibili	ni Nena
Contemplated:	Ibibili	ng bata nito

Beneficiary	Object	Location
sila ang guro si Pedro iyan	ng saging nito	sa kaniya sa dyanitor kay Maria sa tindahan dito

(e) The instrument which is the tool or means used to bring about the action.

Aspect	Ipang- Verb	Actor
Completed:	Ipinambili	ko
Incompleted:	Ipinambibili	ni Nena
Contemplated:	Ipambibili	ng bata nito

Object	Instrument
ng saging nito	ang pera niya ito

The instrument phrase is seldom used in ordinary Tagalog sentences. When in its non-focused form it is preceded by the non-focus marker ng or the phrase sa pamamagitan ng 'by means of'. The ng phrase can be substituted by the ng pronouns or demonstratives.

xxx

Gloss for above Tagalog sentences.

Actor	Verb	Object
I	bought	bananas
Nena	is buying	these (ones)
The child	will buy	
This (one)		

	Location		Beneficiary
from	her	for	them
	the janitor		the teacher
	Maria		Pablo
	the store		that (place)
	this (place)		

(Instrument)

by means of {his money / this}

(3) Verbal paradigms

The following verbal paradigms illustrate the use of different aspects and focuses in the indicative, distributive, and aptative kinds of action.

VERBAL CHART

	Indicative	
Affix Class + Base	-UM- + káin 'to eat'	MAG- + linis 'to clean'

Focus & Aspect:

A. Actor

	kumain	maglinis
Completed	kumain	naglinis
Incompleted	kumakain	naglilinis
Contemplated	kakain	maglilinis

B. Goal

Neutral	ka(i)nin	linisin
Completed	kinain	nilinis
Incompleted	kinakain	nililinis
Contemplated	kaka(i)nin	lilinisin

C. Locative

Neutral	ka(i)nan	linisan
Completed	kinainan	nilinisan
Incompleted	kinakainan	nililinisan
Contemplated	kaka(i)nan	lilinisan

D. Benefactive

Neutral	ikain	ipaglinis
Completed	ikinain	ipinaglinis
Incompleted	ikinakain	ipinaglilinis
Contemplated	ikakain	ipaglilinis

E. Instrumental

Neutral	ipangkain	ipanlinis
Completed	ipinangkain	ipinanlinis
Incompleted	ipinangkakain	ipinanlilinis
Contemplated	ipangkakain	ipanlilinis

VERBAL CHART (continued)

Indicative	Distributive	Aptative
MA- +	MANG- +	MAKA- +
túlog 'to sleep'	húli 'to catch'	súlat 'to write'
matulog	manghuli	makasulat
natulog	nanghuli	nakasulat
natutulog	nanghuhuli	nakakasulat
		nakasusulat
matutulog	manghuhuli	makakasulat
		makasusulat
	panghulihin	masulat
	pinanghuli	nasulat
	pinanghuhuli	nasusulat
	panghuhulihin	masusulat
tulugan	panghulihan	masulatan
tinulugan	pinanghulihan	nasulatan
tinutulugan	pinanghuhulihan	nasusulatan
tutulugan	panghuhulihan	masusulatan
itulog	ipanghuli	maisulat
itinulog	ipinanghuli	naisulat
itinutulog	ipinanghuhuli	naisusulat
itutulog	ipanghuhuli	maisusulat
ipantulog	ipanghuli	maipanulat
ipinantulog	ipinanghuli	naipanulat
ipinantutulog	ipinanghuhuli	naipapanulat
ipantutulog	ipanghuhuli	maipanunulat

VERBAL PARADIGM-PUTOL

A. Actor Focus

	Indicative		Distributive
Affix Class	-UM-	MAG-	MANG-
Neut.	pumutol	magputol	mamutol
Comp.	pumutol	nagputol	namutol
Inc.	pumuputol	nagpuputol	namumutol
Cont.	puputol	magpuputol	mamumutol

Aptative

	MAKA-	MAKAPAG-
Neut.	makaputol	makapagputol
Comp.	nakaputol	nakapagputol
Inc.	nakapuputol / nakakaputol	nakakapagputol
Cont.	makapuputol / makakaputol	makakapagputol

Social / Causative

	MAKI-	MAGPA-
Neut.	makiputol	magpaputol
Comp.	nakiputol	nagpaputol
Inc.	nakikiputol	nagpapaputol
Cont.	makikiputol	magpapaputol

VERBAL PARADIGM-<u>PUTOL</u>

B. Goal Focus

Affix Class	Indicative		Distributive
	-UM-	MAG-	MANG-
Neut.	put<u>úlin</u>	put<u>úlin</u>	pamut<u>úlin</u>
Comp.	p<u>in</u>útol	p<u>in</u>útol	p<u>in</u>amútol
Inc.	p<u>in</u>upútol	p<u>in</u>upútol	p<u>in</u>amumútol
Cont.	puput<u>úlin</u>	puput<u>úlin</u>	pamumut<u>úlin</u>

Aptative

	MAKA-	MAKAPAG-
Neut.	<u>ma</u>pútol	<u>ma</u>pagpútol
Comp.	<u>na</u>pútol	<u>na</u>pagpútol
Inc.	<u>na</u>pupútol	<u>na</u>pagpupútol
Cont.	<u>ma</u>pupútol	<u>ma</u>pagpupútol

Social / Causative

	Social	Causative
	MAKI-	MAGPA-
Neut.	<u>paki</u>pútol	<u>ipa</u>pútol
Comp.	<u>pinaki</u>pútol	<u>ipina</u>pútol
Inc.	<u>pinakiki</u>pútol	<u>ipina</u>pupútol
		<u>ipina</u>papútol
Cont.	<u>pakiki</u>pútol	<u>ipa</u>pupútol
		<u>ipapa</u>pútol

VERBAL PARADIGM—PUTOL

C. Locative Focus

	Indicative		Distributive
Affix Class	-UM-	MAG-	MANG-
Neut.	putúlan	pagputúlan	pamutúlan
Comp.	pinutúlan	pinagputúlan	pinamutúlan
Inc.	pinuputúlan	pinagpuputúlan	pinamumutúlan
Cont.	puputúlan	pagpuputúlan	pamumutúlan

Aptative

	MAKA-	MAKAPAG-
Neut.	maputúlan	mapagputúlan
Comp.	naputúlan	napagputúlan
Inc.	napuputúlan	napagpuputúlan
Cont.	mapuputúlan	mapagpuputúlan

	Social	Causative
	MAKI-	MAGPA-
Neut.	pakiputúlan	paputúlan
Comp.	pinakiputúlan	pinaputúlan
Inc.	pinakikiputúlan	pinapaputúlan
		pinapuputúlan
Cont.	pakikiputúlan	papaputúlan
		papuputúlan

VERBAL PARADIGM-<u>PUTOL</u>

D. Benefactive Focus

	Indicative		Distributive
Affix Class	-UM-	MAG-	MANG-
Neut.	i<u>pú</u>tol	i<u>pagpú</u>tol	i<u>pamú</u>tol
Comp.	i<u>pinú</u>tol	i<u>pinagpú</u>tol	i<u>pinamú</u>tol
Inc.	i<u>pinupú</u>tol	i<u>pinagpupú</u>tol	i<u>pinamumú</u>tol
Cont.	i<u>pupú</u>tol	i<u>pagpupú</u>tol	i<u>pamumú</u>tol

Aptative

	MAKA-	MAKAPAG-
Neut.	ma<u>ipú</u>tol	ma<u>ipagpú</u>tol
Comp.	na<u>ipú</u>tol	na<u>ipagpú</u>tol
Inc.	na<u>ipupú</u>tol	na<u>ipagpupú</u>tol
Cont.	ma<u>ipupú</u>tol	ma<u>ipagpupú</u>tol

	Social	Causative
	MAKI-	MAGPA-
Neut.	i<u>pakipú</u>tol	i<u>pagpapú</u>tol
Comp.	i<u>pinakipú</u>tol	i<u>pinagpapú</u>tol
Inc.	i<u>pinakikipú</u>tol	i<u>pinagpapapú</u>tol
Cont.	i<u>pakikipú</u>tol	i<u>pagpapapú</u>tol

VERBAL PARADIGM-PUTOL

E. Instrumental Focus

	Indicative		Distributive
Affix Class	-UM-	MAG-	MANG-
Neut.	ipamútol		
Comp.	ipinamútol		
Inc.	ipinamumútol		
Cont.	ipamumútol		

Aptative

	MAKA-	MAKAPAG-
Neut.	maipamútol	maipamútol
Comp.	naipamútol	naipamútol
Inc.	naipamumútol	naipapamútol
		naipamumútol
Cont.	maipamumútol	maipapamútol
		maipamumútol

	Social	Causative
	MAKI-	MAGPA-
Neut.	ipakipamútol	ipapampútol
Comp.	ipinakipamútol	ipinapamútol
Inc.	ipinakikipamútol	ipinapapamútol
Cont.	ipakikipamútol	ipapamumútol

SUMMARY OF AFFIXES

		Indicative		Distributive
Affix Class	-UM-	MAG-		MANG-
A. Actor				
Neut.	-um-	mag-		maN-
Comp.	-um-	nag-		naN-
Inc.	-um-	nag-		naN-
Cont.		mag-		maN-
B. Goal				
Neut.	-in	pag-, -in		paN-
Comp.	-in-	pinag-		pinaN-
Inc.	-in-	pinag-		pinaN-
Cont.	-in	pag-, -in		paN-
C. Locative				
Neut.	-an	pag-, -an		paN-, -an
Comp.	-in-, -an	pinag-, -an		pinaN-, -an
Inc.	-in-, -an	pinag-, -an		pinaN-, -an
Cont.	-an	pag-, -an		paN-, -an
D. Benefactive				
Neut.	i-	ipag-		ipaN-
Comp.	i, -in-	ipinag-		ipinaN-
Inc.	i, -in-	ipinag-		ipinaN-
Cont.	i-	ipag-		ipaN-
E. Instrumental				
Neut.	ipaN-	ipaN-		ipaN-
Comp.	ipinaN-	ipinaN-		ipinaN-
Inc.	ipinaN-	ipinaN-		ipinaN-
Cont.	ipaN-	ipaN-		ipaN-

SUMMARY OF AFFIXES
(continued)

Aptative

Affix Class	MAKA-	MAKAPAG-
A. Actor		
Neut.	maka-	makapag-
Comp.	naka-	nakapag-
Inc.	naka-	nakakapag-
	nakaka-	
Cont.	maka-	makakapag-
	makaka-	
B. Goal		
Neut.	ma-	mapag-
Comp.	na-	napag-
Inc.	na-	napag-
Cont.	ma-	mapag-
C. Locative		
Neut.	ma-, -an	mapag-, -an
Comp.	na-, -an	napag-, -an
Inc.	na-, -an	napag-, -an
Cont.	ma-, -an	mapag-, -an
D. Benefactive		
Neut.	mai-	maipag-
Comp.	nai-	naipag-
Inc.	nai-	naipag-
Cont.	mai-	maipag-
E. Instrumental		
Neut.	maipaN-	maipaN-
Comp.	naipaN-	naipaN-
Inc.	naipaN-	naipaN-
Cont.	maipaN-	maipaN-

SUMMARY OF AFFIXES
(continued)

Affix Class	Social MAKI-	Causative MAGPA-
A. Actor		
Neut.	maki-	magpa-
Comp.	naki-	nagpa-
Inc.	nalaki-	nagpapa-
Cont.	makiki-	magpapa-
B. Goal		
Neut.	paki-	ipa-
Comp.	pinaki-	ipina
Inc.	pinakiki-	ipina-
		ipinapa-
Cont.	pakiki-	ipa-
		ipapa-
C. Locative		
Neut.	paki-, -an	pa-, -an
Comp.	pinaki-, -an	pina-, -an
Inc.	pinakiki-, -an	pina-, -an
		pinapa-, -an
Cont.	pakiki-, -an	pa-, -an
		papa-, -an
D. Benefactive		
Neut.	ipaki-	ipagpa-
Comp.	ipinaki-	ipinagpa-
Inc.	ipinakiki-	ipinagpapa-
Cont.	ipakiki-	ipagpapa-
E. Instrumental		
Neut.	ipakipaN-	ipapaN-
Comp.	ipinakipaN-	ipinapaN-
Inc.	ipinakikipaN-	ipinapapaN-
Cont.	ipakikipaN-	ipapapaN-

Sentences Illustrating the Different
Types of Focus of the Base Putol
in the Imperative

Non-Causative Sentences

-UM- Verb:

Actor Focus: Pumutol ka ng sanga sa kahoy.
Goal Focus: Putulin mo ang sanga sa kahoy.
Locative Focus: Putulan mo ng sanga ang kahoy.
Benefactive Focus: Iputol mo ang Nanay ng sanga
sa kahoy.
Instrumental Focus: Ipamutol mo ang itak ng
sanga sa kahoy.

MAG- Verb:

Actor Focus: Magputol ka ng sanga sa kahoy.
Goal Focus: Pagpuputulin mo ang sanga sa kahoy.
Locative Focus: Pagpuputulan mo ng sanga ang kahoy.
Benefactive Focus: Ipagputol mo ang Nanay ng
sanga sa kahoy.
Instrumental Focus: Ipamutol mo ang itak ng
sanga sa kahoy.

MANG- Verb:

Actor Focus: Mamutol ka ng sanga sa kahoy.
Goal Focus: Pamutulin mo ang sanga sa kahoy.
Locative Focus: Pamutulan mo ng sanga ang kahoy.
Benefactive Focus: Ipamutol mo ang Nanay ng
sangasa kahoy.
Instrumental Focus: Ipamutol mo ang itak ng sanga
sa kahoy.

MAKI- Verb:

Actor Focus: Makiputol ka ng sanga sa kahoy.
Goal Focus: Pakiputol mo ang sanga sa kahoy.
Locative Focus: Pakiputolan mo ng sanga ang
kahoy.
Benefactive Focus: Ipakiputol mo ang Nanay ng
sanga sa kahoy.
Instrumental Focus: Ipakipamutol mo ang itak ng
sanga sa kahoy.

Causative Sentences

MAGPA- Verb:

Actor Focus: <u>Magpa</u>putol <u>ka</u> ng sanga sa kahoy sa kaniya.

Goal Focus: <u>Ipa</u>putol mo <u>ang sanga</u> sa kahoy sa kaniya.

Locative Focus: <u>Pa</u>putul<u>an</u> mo ng sanga <u>ang kahoy</u> sa kaniya.

Benefactive Focus: <u>Ipa</u>gpaputol mo <u>ang Nanay</u> ng sanga sa kahoy.

Instrumental Focus: <u>Ipapa</u>mutol mo <u>ang itak</u> ng sanga sa kahoy.

Non-Causative Actor Focus: <u>Pa</u>putul<u>in</u> mo <u>siya</u> ng sanga sa kahoy.

BIBLIOGRAPHY

1. Unpublished Material

Ramos, Teresita and Guzman, Videa de. Tagalog for
    Beginners. Pacific and Asian Linguistics Institute,
    University of Hawaii, 1969.

2. Published Material

McKaughan, Howard P. and Macaraya, Batua A., compilers.
    A Maranao Dictionary. Honolulu: University of
    Hawaii Press, 1967.

Panganiban, Jose Villa. Talahuluganang Pilipino-
    Ingles. Manila: Kawanihan ng Palimbagan, 1966.

Selected Vocabulary Lists. (Publications of the Insti-
    tute of National Language) Special Edition.
    Manila: Bureau of Printing, 1964.

Surian ng Wika. "The ABAKADA and the Pilipino Writing
    System", Diwa, 5: 33-45, 1968.

Tablan, Andrea A. and Mallari, Carmen B. Pilipino-
    English, English-Pilipino Dictionary. New York:
    Washington Square Press, Inc., 1961.

á!	intj.	an exclamation of sudden recollection.
abá!	intj.	an exclamation of surprise, wonder, or disgust; emphatic denial.
abaká	n.	Manila hemp, abaca.
abakáda	n.	alphabet.
abála	n.	delay; detention; disturbance.
	v.	/mag-/ (mag-abalá) to trouble oneself over something or somebody. Huwag kang mag-abalá. Don't trouble yourself (too much).
		/mang-:-in/ to disturb. Nang-abála na naman sila kagabi. They caused some disturbance again last night.
abalóryo	n.	glass beads; bead work.
abaníko	n.	folding fan. --syn. pamaypáy.
abánte	v.	/i-/ to move something forward. Iabante mo ang kotse nang kaunti. Move the car forward a little.
		/-um-/ to move forward. Umabante ka nang kaunti. You move forward a little.
abáng	v.	/mag-:-an/ to wait or watch for someone or some vehicle to come by. Mag-abang ka ng sasakyan. Wait for a vehicle. Wait for a ride. (abangán)

ábay	n.	companion, best man, bridesmaid.
	v.	/um-/ to escort; to act as best man, maid of honor, or bridesmaid at a wedding. Umabay si Pedro sa kasal. Pedro was best man at the wedding.
abíso	n.	notice, notification.
	v.-	/mag-:i-:-an/ to announce; to inform; to notify. Abisuhan mo si Juan ng aking pagdating. Notify John about my arrival.
abitsuwéla (Sp)	n.	snap bean. --var. bitsuélas.
abó	n.	ashes.
	adj.	grey (color).
abokádo (Sp)	n.	avocado.
abogádo/a (Sp)	n.	lawyer; attorney-at-law.
abót	adj.	overtaken; abreast with; within reach.
	v.	/mag-:i-:-an/ to hand over; to give; to pass. Mag-abot ka ng pagkain. Pass some food.
		/um-:-in:-an/ to reach out for; to overtake or reach; to be in time for. Umabót ka ng ulam. Reach for the food (viand/main dish). Inábot niya ang bus. He got there in time for the bus. Inabutan niya ang bus. He caught up with the bus.
abreláta	n.	can opener. --syn. pambukás.
abrígo (Sp)	n.	wrap; lady's coat.
Abríl	n.	April.

abúbot	n.	knickknacks carried around.

abúloy   n.   contribution, help-fund, relief; aid; subsidy.

          v.   /mag-:i-/ to contribute. <u>Mag-abuloy ka sa patay</u>. Contribute (some money) for the funeral.

               /um-:-an/ to aid. <u>Umabuloy ka sa kanya</u>. Help him.

aburído (Sp) adj.   anxious, confused.

abusádo (Sp) adj.   abusive.

abúso (Sp)   n.   abuse; maltreatment.

akála'   n.   idea; belief.

          p.v.   to think. <u>Akala ko'y kumain ka na</u>. I thought you had already eaten.

               /mag-:-in/ to believe, to presume. to think, to conceive, to imagine, to opinion. <u>Huwag kang mag-akalang ako ay taksil</u>. Don't get the idea that I'm unfaithful. <u>Baka akalain mong ako ay taksil</u>. You might think I'm unfaithful.

ákap   v.   /mang-:-in/ to embrace with a connotation of farce. <u>Nang-akap siya ng babae</u>. He embraced a woman. (akápin)

               /um-:-in/ to embrace. <u>Inakap niya ako</u>. He embraced me.

akásya   n.   acacia tree; monkeypod.

ákay   n.   person led by the hand.

          v.   /mag-:-in/ to lead by the hand. <u>Inakay niya ang bata</u>. He led the child by the hand. (akáyin)

/um-/ to hang on (for support).
<u>Umakay siya sa akin</u>. He hung on
to me (for support or guidance).

akbáy   v.   /um-:-an/ to put one arm on
another person's shoulder.
<u>Umakbay siya sa akin</u>. He put his
arm across my shoulder. (akbayán)

ákin   pro.   my; mine.

ákit   v.   /um-,mang-:-in/ to charm, to
attract, to lure, to entice.
<u>Akítin mo ang mga mamimili sa
pamamagitan ng iyong ganda</u>.
Attract the buyers over by means
of your beauty.

aklát   n.   book. --syn. <u>libró</u>.

aklátan   n.   library.

akó   pro.   first person singular number
pronoun meaning 'I', 'me'.

akmá'   v.   /mag-:-i/ to set something.
<u>Iakma mo ang baril</u>. Aim the gun.

/um-/ to get ready to do something; to be properly fitted.
<u>Umakma siya</u>. He got ready (to
do something).

aksayá   n.   wastage.

adj.   /ma-/ wasteful.

v.   /ma-/ to be wasted, to go to
waste. <u>Baka maaksaya ang tubig</u>.
The water might be wasted.

/mag-:-in:pag--an/ to squander,
to use something wastefully.
<u>Nag-aksaya siya ng panahon</u>. He
wasted time. <u>Huwag pag-aksayahan
ng panahon ang hindi importanting</u>

<u>bagay</u>. Don't waste time with unimportant things.

aksidénte (Sp) n. accident.

v. /ma-/ to meet with an accident. <u>Naaksidente siya kahapon</u>. He met with an accident yesterday.

ákto (Sp) v. /um-/ to act, to perform as in a play, to behave. <u>Umakto siyang baliw sa isang palabas</u>. He took the role of a crazy person in the play.

akyát v. /mag-:i-/ to carry something up a height. <u>Mag-akyat ka rito ng isang baldeng tubig</u>. Bring a pail of water up here.

/um-:-in/ to climb up, to go up something. <u>Akyatin mo ang punong iyon</u>. Climb that tree.

adóbo n. a favorite Filipino meat dish cooked in vinegar, salt, garlic, pepper and soy sauce.

adórno (Sp) n. adornment, decoration.

v. /mag-:-an/ to decorate. <u>Nagadorno siya ng kanyang bagong bahay</u>. He decorated his new house.

adyós (Sp) farewell, goodbye.

ága adv. /ma-/ early.

agáhan n. breakfast. --syn. <u>almusál</u>.

agád adv. at once, soon, immediately, right away, promptly. <u>Tumbakbo siya agad</u>. He ran at once.

ágap	n.	promptness, quickness.
	adj.	/ma-/ prompt, punctual, quick.

ágap v. /um-:-an/ to anticipate, to watch for something, to make sure that one gets it; to take advantage of something by, being early or prompt. Agápan mo ang mga sariwang gulay sa palengke. Get to market early to get the fresh vegetables.

ágaw n. sudden snatching away.

v. /mang-:-in:-an/ to snatch, to grab. Nang-agaw siya ng bag. He snatched (somebody's) bag!

/um-/ to participate in grabbing. Umagaw ka sa pabitin. (Get in there and) grab for the hanging object.

aghám n. science.

ágila n. eagle.

ágiw n. cobweb.

ágos n. current.

adj. /ma-/ having swift currents.

v. /-in/ to be carried away by the current. Inagos ang mga damit sa ilog. The clothes were carried away by the current in the river.

/um-/ to flow. Umagos ang tubig. The water flowed.

Agósto n. August.

aguhílya (Sp) n. hair pin.

áhas	n.	snake.
ahénsiya	n.	pawnshop; agency.
ahénte	n.	agent; salesman.
áhit	n.	the shaved part; a shaving service.
	v.	/mag-:in/ to shave. <u>Inahit ni Pedro ang kanyang balbas</u>. Pedro shaved off his beard.
áhon	v.	/mag-:-in, i-/ to take something out of the water. <u>Iahon mo ang bata sa tubig</u>. Pull the child out of the water.
		/um-/ to get out of the water. <u>Umahon na tayo</u>. Let's get out of the water.
alaála	n.	remembrance, souvenir.
álak	n.	wine, liquor.
alakdán	n.	scorpion.
alága'	n.	pet, ward; person, animal or thing being taken care of.
	v.	/mag-:-an/ to take care of; to raise, to bring up. <u>Alagaan mo ang iyong kapatid</u>. (You) take care of your brother (or sister).
alagád	n.	disciple;follower; apostle; helper.
aláhas	n.	jewelry, jewels.
alahéro	n.	jewel maker; repairer; merchant.
alála	n.	memory, recollection.
	v.	/-in/ (alalahánin) to worry, to be anxious about something.

/maka-:ma-/ to remember someone
with something. <u>Aba, nakaalala
ka</u>. Ah, you remembered (him...
with something).

/mag-/ to worry, to be anxious.
<u>Huwag kang mag-alala</u>. Don't
worry.

alalahánin		see <u>alala</u> + <u>-in</u>.
alálay	v.	/mag-:-an/ to take precaution, to practice moderation or to act moderately. <u>Alalayan mo ang pagkain</u>. Take it easy on the food or eat moderately.
		/um-:-an/ to give support. <u>Umalalay siya sa maysakit</u>. He gave support to the sick (person) (physical support). <u>Alalayan mo ang maysakit</u>. Support the sick (person).
alám	n.	knowledge.
	adj.	/ma-/ knowledgeable, well-versed.
	p.v.	/-in/ to know, to have a knowledge of, to find out. <u>Alamin mo kung ano ang nangyari</u>. Find out what happened.
alamáng	n.	tiny shrimps.
alamát	n.	folklore, tradition.
alámbre	n.	wire.
alampáy	n.	shoulder kerchief.
alangán	adj.	uncertain, doubtful, insufficient, not fitted, unfit.

	v.	/mag-/ to be uncertain, to be doubtful, to be inadequate. <u>Nag-alangan siya sa sasabihin niya</u>. He was uncertain about what he would say.
alapaáp	n.	clouds.
alás (Sp)	n.	ace (in playing cards).
álat	n.	saltiness.
	adj.	/ma-/ salty.
	v.	/um-/ to become salty. <u>Umalat ang niluto ko</u>. My cooking became salty.
álay	n.	dedication; offering.
	v.	/mag-:i-:-an/ to dedicate, to offer. <u>Mag-alay ka ng bulaklak sa Birhen</u>. Offer flowers to the Virgin.
alkálde (Sp) n.		mayor.
alkansía (Sp) n.		piggy bank.
alkilá (Sp) n.		rent; hire.
	v.	/um-:in/ to hire, to rent. <u>Umalkila ka ng bahay</u>. Rent a house.
alkitrán (Sp) n.		tar, pitch.
ále	n.	aunt, step mother; expression addressed to a woman; reference to a woman.
Alemán	n.	German.
alikabók	n.	dust.
	adj.	/ma-/ dusty.

aligí	n.	fat of crabs, shrimps.
aligíd	adj.	circling around.
	v.	/um-/ to circle around, to hang around. <u>Umaligid sa kaniya ang maraming tao.</u> Many people hovered around him.
alíla'	n.	slave, maid, helper, servant.
alimángo	n.	a species of crab, big crab.
alimásag	n.	a species of crab; a crab with spreckled shell.
alín	pron.	which; which (one).
alindóg	n.	personal charm; gorgeousness.
alinsángan	adj.	/ma-/ warm, hot.
áling	adj.	a title of familiar respect used with the first name of a woman; when the name is not appended, the noun form is <u>ale</u>.
alingásaw	n.	effusion or emanation of an offensive odor.
	v.	/-um-/ <u>Umaalingasaw ang bulok na isda.</u> An offensive odor is emanating from the rotten fish.
alípin	n.	slave.
alipungá	n.	athlete's foot.
alipustá	v.	/mang-:-in/ to maltreat; to ridicule; to deride; to insult. <u>Nangalipusta siya ng mahihirap.</u> He insulted the poor.
alís	n.	departure.
	v.	/mag-:-in/ to take away, to remove; to deduct. <u>Alisin mo</u>

ang mesa sa kuwarto. Remove the
table from the room.

/um-/ to leave, to depart, to
go away. Umalis siya kahapon.
He left yesterday.

alitaptáp	n.	firefly.
alíw	n.	consolation; comfort.
	v.	/mang-:-in/ to console, to comfort. Aliwin mo siya. Console her.
aliwálas	n.	clarity, spaciousness.
	adj.	/ma-/ clear, spacious, open, well-ventilated.
almá (Sp)	v.	/-um-/ to rise on the hind legs. Umalma ang mailap na kabayo. The untamed horse rose on his hind legs.
almirés	n.	a small stone mortar.
almirol (Sp)	n.	laundry starch. --var. amirol.
almuránas (Sp)	n.	piles (med.), hemorrhoids.
almusál	n.	breakfast. --syn. agahan.
	v.	/mag-/ to have breakfast. Magalmusal tayo ng maaga. Let's have breakfast early.
alók	n.	offer.
	v.	/mag-:i-:-in/ to offer, to advertise. Alukin mo siya ng pagkain. Offer him some food.
alóg	n.	shaking up.

	v.	/mag-:-in/ to shake the contents of. <u>Alugin mo ang kahon</u>. Shake the box.
		/um-/ to shake. <u>Umalóg ang sasakyan</u>. The vehicle shook.
álon	n.	waves.
	v.	/um-/ to move like that of waves. <u>Umalon nang malakas kahapon sa dugat</u>. The waves were big on the ocean yesterday.
alpás	v.	/um-:-an/ to become free, loose, untied (as animals).
		/maka-/ to be able to break loose. <u>Naka-alpas ang bilanggo</u>. The prisoner was able to break loose.
alpilér	n.	pin; brooch.
alsá (Sp)	n.	a rising, as of dough.
	v.	/um-/ to rise. <u>Umalsa ang puto</u>. The rice cake rose.
		/mag-/ to rebel, to revolt, to rise up against, to stage a strike. <u>Nag-alsa sila laban sa mga dayuhan</u>. They rose up against the foreigners.
		/mag-:-in, i-/ to lift something. <u>Alsahin mo ito</u>. Lift this up.
altár	n.	altar, shrine.
alulód	n.	rain pipe, rain gutter, downspout.
alumpihît	adj.	wriggling and twisting (due to discomfort or pain).

alupíhan   n.   centipede.

ám   n.   broth of rice.

amá   n.   father.

ámag   n.   mold, mildew.

amaín   n.   uncle.

amáng   n.   reference to a boy.

ambá'   v.   /um-:-an/ to gesture threateningly. Inambaan niya ako. He gestured to me threateningly.

ambág   n.   contribution; share in a collective affair.

    v.   /mag-:i-/ to contribute; to give a share of any kind. Mag-ambag tayo para sa mga mahihirap. Let's give something for the poor.

ambón   n.   drizzle, light rain, shower.

    v.   /um-/ to drizzle; to shower lightly. Umambon kahapon. It showered lightly yesterday.

ambulánsiya (Sp) n.   ambulance.

amerikána   n.   suit (for men); sports jacket.

Amerikáno/a n.   American (male/female).

ámin   pro.   first person plural number pronoun (exclusive) meaning 'our', 'ours', 'us'; shows possession or location when preceded by sa. Pumunta ka sa amin. Go to our place.

amiról   n.   starch. --var. almiról.

ámo (Sp)   n.   boss; master; employer; manager.

ámo'   adj.   /ma-/ tame, not wild.

             v.   /-in/ to placate. <u>Amúin mo</u> <u>siya</u>. Placate him.

                    /um-/ to become tame; to become domesticated, submissive. <u>Umamo</u> <u>ang mabangis na lion</u>. The fierce lion became tame.

ámot   v.   /um-:-an/ to obtain, procure, buy at cost price. <u>Umamot ka</u> <u>sa kanya ng isang salop na</u> <u>bigas</u>. He bought a ganta of rice at cost.

amóy   n.   smell, odor; aroma; body odor; intensive smell; offensive smell.

             v.   /-in/ to smell something. <u>Amuyín mo nga ito</u>. Smell this.

                    /mang/ to become smelly or odorous. <u>Nangamóy ang sirang</u> <u>pagkain</u>. The spoiled food smelled bad.

ampalayá   n.   bitter melon; balsam apple; amargoso.

ampán   n.   sugared popcorn.

ampáw   n.   puffed rice or corn; sugared popcorn.

ampón   n.   adopted child; protection in the form of adoption.

             v.   /mag:-in/ <u>Ampunín mo ang bata</u>. Adopt the child.

anák	n.	child, son/daughter, offspring.
	v.	/ipang-/ to be born. Ipinanganak na bulag ang bata. The child was born blind.
anáhaw	n.	palm tree.
ánay	n.	termite; white ants.
andadór (Sp)	n.	walking aid for babies.
andámyo (Sp)	n.	gangplank.
andár (Sp)	v.	/-um-/ to work, function, to start as in machinery. Umandar ang kotse. The car started.
áni	n.	harvest, product.
	v.	/mag-, um-:-in/ to harvest, to reap. Umani kami ng palay. We harvested rice.
ánib	v.	/um-/ to join an organization; to be a member of. Umanib siya sa isang samahan. He joined an organization.
anibersáryo	n.	anniversary.
ánim	num.	six.
anínag	adj.	visible, transparent, translucent.
aníno	n.	shadow, reflection.
anís	n.	nutmeg.
ánit	n.	scalp.
aníto	n.	deity, idol.
anó	int.	what; as a greeting, it means hello.

ánod	v.	/ma-/ to be carried away by the current.
		/-in/ <u>Inanod ng tubig ang bakya</u>. The water carried the wooden shoes away.
antá	adj.	/ma-/ rancid (food).
anténa (Sp)	n.	antenna.
antimáno	conj.	beforehand.
anting-antíng	n.	amulet.
antók	v.	/-mag-, -in/ to be sleepy. <u>Antok/ inantok ang bata</u>. The child got sleepy.
anu-anó	int.	plural form of the question word <u>ano</u> 'what'.
anumán	pron.	whatsoever; usually occurs with <u>walang</u> as in <u>walang anuman</u> to mean 'not at all or there is nothing to it'.
anyáya	n.	invitation.
	v.	/mag-:-an/ to invite. <u>Nag-anyaya ako ng maraming bisita</u>. I invited a lot of visitors.
anyó'	n.	figure, form, appearance.
áng	mkr.	definite article similar to 'the' that marks the topic of the sentence; focus marker; topic marker.
angát	v.	/mag-:-in, i-/ to lift, to raise something. <u>Angatin mo ang silya.</u> Raise this up.

/um-/ to rise; to progress; to get lifted. <u>Umangat siya sa kanyang kabuhayan</u>. He raised his status in life.

angkán   n.   family, lineage.

angkás   v.   /mag-:i-/ to take someone for a ride. <u>Iangkas mo ako sa iyong bisikleta</u>. You take me for a ride on your bicycle.

/um-:-an/ to hitch a ride, to ride with someone. <u>Umangkas ako sa kotse niya</u>. I got a ride in his car.

angkín   adj.   inborn, native, having or possessing.

             v.   /mag-/ to possess (usually used in the incompleted aspect meaning 'possessing or having'. <u>Nag-aangkin siya ng tanging kagandahan</u>. She has natural beauty.

/mang-:-in/ to claim ownership usually of something that legally belongs to someone else. <u>Nang-angkin na naman ito ng di kanya</u>. He's claiming possession again of things that aren't his.

angkóp   adj.   fit, proper, becoming.

angháng   adj.   /ma-/ spicy (food); peppery hot.

anghél   n.   angel.

ápa   n.   thin rolled wafer of rice, starch, and red sugar; ice cream cone.

aparadór   n.   cupboard; clothes closet or cabinet.

ápat	num.	four.
ápaw	v.	/um-/ to overflow, to inundate. <u>Umapaw ang tubig sa kanal</u>. The water overflowed from the canal.
apdó	n.	bile, gall.
apelyído	n.	surname; last name.
apí	v.	/mang-:-in/ to maltreat, to abuse, to oppress, to harm. <u>Huwag mong apihin ang bata</u>. Don't maltreat the child.
apláya	n.	beach.
apó	n.	grandchild (term of reference).
ápog	n.	lime.
apóy	n.	fire.
	adj.	/ma-/ fiery, flaming.
apúhap	v.	/mang-, mag-:-in/ to feel something by extending the hand. <u>Inapuhap niya ang pera niya sa dilim</u>. He groped for his money in the dark.
		/um-/ to feel out by extending the hand.
apúlid	n.	water chestnut.
áral	v.	/mag-:-in/ to study. <u>Mag-aral ka ng iyong leksiyon</u>. Study your lesson.
aráro	n.	plow.
	v.	/mag-:-in/ to plow. <u>Mag-araro tayo ng bukid</u>. Let's plow the field.

áraw	n.	day; sun.
	v.	/um-/ to shine brightly (the sun's coming out). <u>Umaraw kahapon</u>. The sun was out yesterday.
araw-áraw	adv.	every day.
albuláryo	n.	a quack doctor who usually uses herbs for treatment of any kind of ailment.
arkitékto	n.	architect.
ári'	n.	property.
armádo (Sp)	adj.	armed.
armás (Sp)	n.	weapon; arms.
artísta	n.	actor/actress (of the movie, stage, television, etc.).
arugá'	v.	/mag-:-in/ tender care; nurture. <u>Magaruga' ka ng mga anak mo</u>. Take care of your children.
ása	v.	/um-:-an/ to hope for. <u>Asahan mong di kita malilimutan</u>. Bear in mind that I won't forget you.
ásal	n.	custom, habit, behavior, manners.
asaról	n.	a large hoe.
	v.	/mag-:-in/ to use a hoe, say to till the soil. <u>Asarolín natin ang halamanán</u>. Let's hoe the garden.
asáwa	n.	wife/husband, espouse (term of reference).

asikáso	v.	/mag-:-in/ to mind, to take care of, to entertain. <u>Asikasuhin mo ang mga panauhin</u>. Entertain the visitors.
ásim	n.	sourness.
	adj.	/ma-/ sour (food).
asín	n.	salt.
asindéro	n.	land owner, plantation owner.
asistí	v.	/um-:-an/ to assist, to help, to aid. <u>Asistihán natin ang mga nangangailangan</u>. Let's help the needy.
áso	n.	dog.
asó	n.	smoke.
aspilé (Sp)	n.	pin, straight pin.
asúkal	n.	sugar.
asúl	adj.	blue (color).
asuséna	n.	tuberose.
aswáng	n.	ghost, evil spirit.
át	conj.	and; connects words, phrases, or entire sentences of equal syntactic rank. (+ <u>baká</u>) lest. (+ <u>náng</u>) so that. (+ <u>baga man</u>) although.
at iba pá		etcetera; and so forth.
atáke	v.	/-in/ to attack, to have an attack. <u>Aatakihin siya ng sakit sa puso</u>. He will have a heart attack.

ataúl   n.   coffin, bier.

atáy   n.   liver.

áte   n.   appellation for elder sister;
                    used with or without the given
                    name (term of address reference).

átin   pron.   first person plural number
                    pronoun (inclusive) meaning
                    'our', 'ours', 'us'; shows
                    possession or location when pre-
                    ceded by sa.
atíp   n.   roof, roofing.

átis   n.   sugar apple; custard apple.

átomo   n.   atom.

atrás   v.   /um-/ to retreat; to back up;
                    to move back. Umatras ang kotse.
                    The car backed up.

atrasádo (Sp) adj. late, slow.

atsára   n.   pickles (papaya).

atsuwéte (Sp) n.   shrub with burry fruits used
                    for food coloring.

áwa'   n.   grace; pity; charity; compassion.

            v.   /ma-/ to take pity. Maawa
                    ka sa akin. Pity me.

áwas   v.   /-um-/ Umawas ang tubig sa
                    banyo. The water overflowed
                    in the bathroom.

áwat   n.   pacification of quarreling
                    people.

            v.   /mang-, um-:-in/ to pacify a
                    quarrel, to stand between a
                    fight. Awatin mo sina Teria
                    at Violeta. Pacify Teria and
                    Violeta.

áway   n.   a quarrel; dispute.

           v.   /mag-/ to quarrel (with each other). <u>Nag-away ang matalik na magkaibigan</u>. The close friends had a quarrel.

                    /mang-:-in/ to quarrel with somebody. <u>Nang-away na naman si Minda</u>. Minda started another quarrel.

áwit   n.   song, chant, hymn.

           v.   /um-:-in/ to sing. <u>Umawit si Nenita sa klase</u>. Nenita sang in class.

áwto   n.   car; automobile. --syn. <u>kotse</u>.

áy   prt.   connects the topic of the sentence and the predicate when the sentence is given in the reverse order; sentence inversion marker. <u>Umalis siya</u>   <u>Siya ay umalis</u>. He left.

áy!   int.   an exclamation of surprise or pain.

áyaw   p.v.   /um-:-an/ to back out from; to reject, to dislike, to refuse (opposite of gusto). <u>Umayaw siya sa aking plano</u>. He didn't like my plan.

áyon   adj.   parallel to; in agreement.

           adv.   according to...; as alleged by. <u>Ayon sa sabi ng tao mabait ka raw</u>. According to what people say you are good.

           v.   /um-:-an/ to agree, to conform, to go along with. <u>Umayon si Ernesto sa balak ni Rosita</u>.

23

Ernesto went along with Rosita's plan.

áyos   n.   order, orderliness.

   adj.   /ma-/ orderly, arranged, (well) fixed, just right.

   v.   /mag-:-in/ to arrange, to put in order, to fix. <u>Ayusin mo ang buhok ni Linda</u>. Arrange Linda's hair.

aywán   be ignorant of. <u>Aywan</u> <u>ko</u>. I don't know. --var. <u>ewán</u>. --syn. <u>dî alám</u>.

bá	prt.	question marker; expressive of interrogation in yes/no questions. <u>Mayroon ba silang ginawa</u>? Have they done anything?
babá'	n.	descent.
	v.	/um-:-in/ to go down, to descend. <u>Bumaba siya sa hagdan</u>. He went down the stairs.
bába'	n.	chin.
	v.	/mag-:i-/ to reduce, to take down, to carry to a lower level. <u>Ibaba mo ang iyong timbang</u>. Reduce your weight.
bába'	adj.	short, low.
	v.	/um-/ to become shorter; to become cheaper. <u>Bumaba ang presyo ng mga bilihin</u>. The price of goods went down.
bábae	n.	woman.
	adj.	female.
bábad	v.	/mag-:in, i-/ to soak. <u>Ibabad mo ang damit sa sabon</u>. Soak the dress in soap.
babalá'	n.	notice, sign.
bábaw	adj.	shallow.
báboy	n.	pig, pork.
báboy-ramó	n.	wild pig.

24

báka	n.	cattle; cow; beef.
baká	adv.	possibly; perhaps; maybe; might.
	p.v.	maybe; perhaps. Expressive of undenied contingency negative of wishes and fears. <u>Baka ka maputulan ng daliri</u>. You might get your finger cut off.
bákal	n.	iron; steel.
bakaláw	n.	cod.
bakás	n.	print; mark; trace.
	v.	/um-/ to mark or leave a mark; to leave a trail or vestige. <u>Bumakas ang kanyang sampal</u>. His slap left a mark.
bakasyón	n.	vacation; rest.
	v.	/mag-/ to take a vacation; to leave for a vacation; to go on a vacation. <u>Magbabakasyon si Vida sa Texas</u>. Vida is vacationing in Texas.
bakbák	adj.	detached; decorticated.
	v.	/-an/ to remove the bark or thick skin of something; to chastise (someone).
bakbákan	n.	fight; altercation.
bákit	int.	why. <u>Bakit ka naparito</u>? Why have you come here?
baklá'	adj.	effeminate man; hermaphrodite. --syn. <u>binabae</u>.
baklî'	adj.	broken.

bákod	n.	fence.
bákol	n.	a big basket (flat); a four-cornered bamboo basket with round opening.
baku-bakó'	adj.	rugged.
bakúna	n.	vaccination.
bakúran	n.	yard.
bakyá'	n.	wooden shoes.
bága	n.	embers; glowing coal.
bága'	n.	lung.
bagá	adv.	emphatic marker; throws more stress on the interrogation. Ikaw baga, y nagasawa? Did you (ever) get married?
	conj.	(+ man) although.
bagáhe (Sp)	n.	baggage.
bágal	adj.	slow; sluggish.
bagáng	n.	molar (tooth).
bágay	n.	thing, object.
bágay	adj.	becoming; proper, fit.
	v.	/um-:-an/ to suit, to conform. Bagayan mo ang ugali niya. Make adjustments to suit his manners.
báging	n.	vine; climber; creeper.
bágo	n.	/pag-/ (pagbabágo) change.
	adj.	new, recent, modern.
bágo	adv./ conj	before; recently.

bagón	n.	freight car; wagon; van.
bagoóng	n.	salty small fish or shrimp relish; anchovies; wet-salted small fish or tiny shrimps (<u>alamáng</u>).
bagsák	v.	/um-/ to fall; to fail. <u>Bumagsák ang eroplanong sina-sakyan ng pangulo</u>. The airplane the president was riding on crashed.

/mag-:i-/ to drop. <u>Ibinagsák ni Totoy ang telepono</u>. Totoy slammed down the telephone.

bagsík	adj.	violent, fierce, merciless; strict, cruel, severe.
bagyó	n.	storm; typhoon.
	v.	(phenomenal verb) /-in/ to have a storm/typhoon. <u>Baka ka bagyuhín sa probinsya</u>. You might get hit by a storm in the province.

(phenomenal verb) /um-/ to rain violently as in a storm or typhoon. <u>Bumabagyó ng malakas</u>. The storm is raging strong.

bahá'	n.	flood.
	v.	(phenomenal verb) /-in/ to flood. <u>Binahá ang buong bayan</u>. The whole town was flooded.

/um-/ to flood. <u>Bumahá dahil sa lakas ng ulan</u>. It flooded because of the strong rain.

bahág	n.	G-string; loin cloth with a part pulled between the thighs.

bahaghári	n.	rainbow.
bahági'	n.	part; portion; piece.
bahagyá'	adj.	hardly, barely.
bahála'	n.	an expression of uncertainty or responsibility; e.g. bahala na kayo. The decision is yours; or it's up to you.
	adj.	be responsible; manage, take charge; take care of. Mabahála'. To feel concerned; worried; anxious.
báhay	n.	house.
baháy-batá'	n.	uterus.
bahín	n.	sneeze.
	v.	/um-/ to sneeze. Bumahin siya sa harap ko. He sneezed in front of me.
báho	adj.	foul odor, bad smell; stinking odor.
bahúra	n.	reef.
baí	n.	lagoon. --syn. lawa'.
bailarína (Sp)	n.	dancer (feminine); taxi-dancer.
baíle (Sp)	n.	ball, dance.
baít	n.	kindness.
	adj.	kind; good; gentle, virtuous.
baitáng	n.	steps of a staircase.
baiwáng	n.	waist.
bála	n.	bullet.

balábal	n.	mantilla; wrap; shawl (apparel).
	v.	/mag-:-in, i-/ to wrap oneself with a shawl, mantle, or kerchief. <u>Magbalábal ka at nang hindi ka ginawin</u>. Wrap yourself so you won't get cold.
bálak	n.	plan, intention.
	v.	/mag-:-in/ to plan; to intend to do. <u>Binálak kong dalawin ka</u>. I planned to visit you.
balakáng	n.	hips.
balákid	n.	obstacle.
balakúbak	n.	dandruff.
baláe	n.	parents and parents-in-law relationship (term of reference); a parent of one's son or daughter-in-law.
balahíbo	n.	fine body hair; feathery hair of fowls or woolly hair of animals.
balánse (Sp)	n.	balance, remainder.
bálang	n.	locust.
balangá'	n.	wide mouthed earthen cooking pot.
balangkás	n.	framework.
balaríla'	n.	grammar. --syn. <u>gramátika</u>.
balása	v.	/mag-:-in/ to shuffle playing cards. <u>Balasahin mo na ang baraha</u>. Shuffle the cards (now).
bálat	n.	birthmark (on skin).

balát   n.   bark of a tree; skin; peelings;
                           leather.

balatkayó   n.   costume; disguise.

baláto (Sp) n.   money given away by a winning
                           gambler as goodwill.

               v.   /mag-:-an/ Balatuhan mo sila.
                           Give them some of your winnings.

balátong   n.   soybean.

balbás (Sp) n.   beard.

balkón (Sp) n.   porch; balcony. --var. balkonáhe.

baldádo (Sp) adj.   overused; disabled; crippled.

baldé   n.   large can; pail.

baldósa (Sp) n.   tile.

bále (Sp)   value (used commonly as hindi
                           bale, it's all right, never mind;
                           bale wala, of no value).

bále (Sp)   n.   promissory note.

               v.   /um-/ to get a cash advance.
                           Bumále ako dahil sa kapos ako
                           ngayon. I got a cash advance
                           because I'm broke now.

bale-bále (Sp) adj. of quite some value.

balediktóryan (Eng) n./adj. valedictorian.

báli'   n.   fracture.

               adj.   (balí') fractured, broken.

               v.   /um-:-in/ to break (usually
                           with the hands). Bináli
                           ni Rogelio ang lapis sa kanyang
                           galit. Roger broke the pencil
                           in anger.

balibág	n.	heave of throwing something like a boomerang or a piece of wood or cane.
	v.	/um-/ to be thrown, hurled.

/mag-:i-/ to throw, hurl, cast an object. <u>Ibinalibág ng bata ang kanyang laruan</u>. The child threw down his toy.

/mang-:-in/ to throw, hurl, cast an object at someone or something. <u>Nangbalibág si Pedro ng kahoy sa kanyang mga kalaro</u>. Pedro threw the stick to his playmates.

balíbol	n.	awl; auger; bit. --syn. <u>baréna</u>.
balík	v.	/um-/ to come back; to return. <u>Bumalík si McArthur sa Pilipinas</u>. McArthur returned to the Philippines.

/mag-:i-/ to return something; to restore. <u>Ibalík mo agad ang libro</u>. Return the book early.

/ma-/ to be returned to former status. <u>Nabalik sa kanya ang dati niyang bahay</u>. He got back his former house.

balíkat	n.	shoulder.
balikwás	v.	/um-/ to turn suddenly to the opposite side; sudden rising from a lying position. <u>Bumalik-wás ako sa kama nang narinig ko ang putok ng baril</u>. I jumped out of bed when I heard the gunshot.

/mag-:-in/ to turn something suddenly to the opposite side.

baligtád	adj.	inside-out; up-side down. --var. baliktad.
	v.	/mag-:-in, i-/ to turn something over; to invert; to reverse; to turn inside-out. <u>Baligtarin mo ang kinula ko</u>. I turned over those things (cloth) I was sun bleaching.
		/um-/ to turn over. <u>Bumaligtad ang sasakyan</u>. The vehicle turned completely over.
balimbíng	n.	starfruit; a small tree whose edible fleshy fruit has five longitudinal, angular lobes.
balintawák	n.	woman's native costume with butterfly sleeves, informal; historical place north of Manila where the first cry of the Revolution against Spain was made by Andres Bonifacío.
balintuwád	adj.	bottom-up; upside-down. --syn. <u>baligtad</u>.
balísa	n.	anxiety.
	adj.	(<u>balisá</u>) anxious; restless.
balisóng	n.	fan knife made in Batangas.
balíta'	n.	news.
	adj.	well-known; famous; talked about.
	v.	/mag-:i-/ to tell; to report; to relay the news. <u>Ibalita mo naman sa amin ang nangyari</u>. Let us know what happened.
balíw	n.	crazy or demented person.
	adj.	crazy, demented.

bálo	n.	widow; widower. --var. báo. --syn. biyudo/biyuda.
balón	n.	a well (of water); a deep hole in the ground.
bálot	n.	covering; wrapping; take home food.
	adj.	(balót) covered, wrapped.
	v.	/mag-:-in, i-/ to wrap, to encase, to envelope. Magbálot ka ng makakain natin. (You) wrap the food we're going to eat.
balsá	n.	raft.
bálse (Sp)	n.	waltz.
balták	n.	sudden; strong pull.
	v.	/mang-:-in/ to pull suddenly. Baltakin mo siya at baka mahulog. Pull him or he might fall.
baltîk	n.	stubborness; head strongness.
baluktót	adj.	crooked; curved; bent.
balunbalúnan	n.	gizzard (of fowls).
balút	n.	boiled duck's egg with partially developed embryo (a native delicacy).
balútan	n.	(rw. bálot) bundle; package.
balyéna (Sp)	n.	whale; white wax candle.
bának	n.	mullet (adult).
banál	adj.	pious, virtuous.

banás	n.	sultriness and humidity. --syn. alinsangan.
	adj.	/ma-/ sultry and humid.
bánat	n.	a strike, sock, box or stroke to hit something; a pull to stretch.
	adj.	(banát) taut, stretched
	v.	/mag-:-in/ to pull; to stretch. Banátin mo ang iyong buto sa trabaho. Stretch your bones with some work.
banáyad	adj.	moderate, soft (in manner).
bandá	adj.	towards or about a certain place or time; in the direction of.
bánda	n.	band of musicians; an organized group of musicians.
bandána (Eng) n.		kerchief; scarf.
bandéha (Sp) n.		tray.
bandehádo (Sp) n.		platter; oblong china tray.
bandéra (Sp) n.		flag. --var. bandila'.
bandíla'	n.	flag.
bangáy	n.	cadaver, corpse.
bandído (Sp) n.		bandit.
banidóso/a (Sp) adj.		vain.
baníg	n.	mat.
bánil	n.	adhering dirt on neck.
banílya	n.	vanilla.

banláw	v.	/mag-:-an/ to rinse; to cleanse. <u>Banlawán mo ang mga kinula</u>. Rinse the things you have sun bleached.
banlí'	n.	scalding.
	v.	/mag-:-an/ to scald; to sterilize. <u>Banlián mo ang mga tinidor at kutsara</u>. Scald the forks and spoons.
bansá'	n.	country; nation.
bansót	adj.	stunted (in growth); arrested in development.
bantá'	n.	threat.
	v.	/mag-:-an/ to threaten. <u>Binantaán niya ako</u>. He threatened me.
bantád	adj.	sated; satiated. --syn. <u>sawá'</u>, <u>suyá'</u>.
bantáy	n.	guard; watcher.
	v.	/mag-:-an/ to watch closely; to be on guard. <u>Bantayán mo ang bahay</u>. Guard the house.
bantáyog	n.	monument.
bantóg	adj.	famous.
banyága'	n.	foreigner.
bányo (Sp)	n.	bathroom; shower room.
banyós (Sp)	n.	sponge bath.
bangá'	n.	jar, earthen jar; for drinking water.
bángaw	n.	big fly.

bangká'	n.	boat; banca.
bangkáy	n.	corpse, cadaver.
bangkéro	(Sp) n.	boatman; banker; dealer and/or payer in gambling (shortened to bangka, colloquially).
bangkéta	(Sp) n.	sidewalk.
bangkéte	(Sp) n.	banquet.
bángko	n.	bank.
bangkó'	n.	bench; stool.

banggá' v. /-um-/ to hit something; to collide with something. Bumanggá ang kotse sa pader. The car ran into a stone wall.

/ma-/ to hit; collide against accidentally; to bump into. Nábangga' ang kotse sa pader. The car ran against the stone wall.

/mag-:i-:-in/ to ram an object against something; to collide against something. Binangga ng kotse ang pader. The car ran into the stone wall.

/mang-:-in/ to hit or ram against. Binanggá niya ako. He bumped into me (intentionally).

banggéra (Sp) n. extension from windows where the chinaware is kept. --var. banggerahán.

banggít v. /-um-:-in/ to mention; to cite. Binanggít niya sa akin ang nangyari. He mentioned what happened to me.

bangín	n.	ravine; abyss; precipice.
bangís	n.	ferocity; wildness.
	adj.	cruel; fierce.
bangó	n.	aroma; fragrance.
	adj.	/ma-/ fragrant; sweet-smelling
bángon	n.	rising from a lying position.

bángon   v.   /-um-/ to rise from a lying position; to get up from bed. <u>Bumángon siya nang maaga kanina.</u> He got up early a while ago.

/mag-:i-/ to raise something; to set something in an upright position. <u>Ibangon mo ang maysakit.</u> Help the sick person get up.

bangús	n.	milk fish.
bá'o	n.	coconut shell without husk or meat; widow/ widower.
baól	n.	footlocker; chest; a rectangular trunk (for clothes).
báon	n.	provision or supply of food taken on a journey.

báon   v.   /mag-:-in, i-/ to carry provisions or supply usually food. <u>Magbáon ka nang di ka gutumin.</u> Take enough food to keep you from getting hungry.

baón   v.   /-um-/ to become buried; to sink. <u>Bumaón ang sapatos ko sa putik.</u> My shoes got covered with mud.

/mag-:i-/ to bury something.
<u>Ibaón mo ang patay na pusa</u>.
Bury the dead cat.

bapór	n.	ship, boat; steamship.
bará	v.	/-um-/ to cause an obstruction. <u>Bumará sa daan ang nabuwal na kahoy</u>. The uprooted tree blocked the road (path).

/mag-:i-/ to bar, to hinder; to obstruct with something. <u>Ibará mo ang mga bato sa daan.</u> Block the road (path) with stones.

baráha	n.	playing cards.
baráso	n.	arm.
barát	adj.	niggardly; stingy, miserly.
bárbel	n.	a weight (used in weight lifting).
barbero	n.	barber.
barberyá	n.	barbershop.
baréta	n.	bar.
baríl	n.	gun.
	v.	/-um-/ to shoot with a gun. <u>Bumaríl si Pedro</u>. Pedro shot the gun.

/mag-/ to shoot oneself. <u>Magbaril ka</u>. Shoot yourself.

/mang-:-in/ to shoot at something. <u>Barilin mo ang ibon</u>. Shoot the bird.

barnís	n.	varnish

báro'	n.	dress; upper garment. --syn. bestido, damit.
bárungbarong	n.	make-shift shack.
barong-Tagálog	n.	man's native shirt, formal.
barumbádo	adj.	temperamental.
baryá	n.	loose or small change; coins.
báryo (Sp)	n.	barrio; subdivision of a town.
bása	v.	/-um/ to read. Bumasa ka ng tula. Read a poem.
		/mag-:-in/ to read something. Basáhin mo ang diyaryo. Read the newspaper.
basá	adj.	wet.
	v.	/ma-/ to become wet, drenched.
básag	adj.	(baság) broken.
	v.	/maka-:ma-/ to break china, glassware or earthenware accidentally; to be able to break. Nabasag niya ang mga pinggan. He broke the plates.
		/mag-:-in/ to break glassware, china, earthenware; to crack; to break repeatedly. Baka baságin ng bata ang plorera. The children might break the flower vase.
basáhan	n.	cleaning rag.
básket (Eng)	n.	basket.
basketból (Eng)	v.	/mag-/ to play basketball.
bási'	n.	rice wine.
báso	n.	drinking glass; drinking cup.

bastá (Sp)	adv.	an interjection meaning enough; just; as long as.
bastón	n.	cane; walking cane.
bastós	adj.	uncouth; rude, impolite, impertinent.
basúra	n.	trash; garbage.
básura (-hán)	n.	garbage container; trash can; any place where garbage or trash is disposed.
basuréro	n.	(rw. basúra) garbageman, garbage collector.
báta	n.	nightgown; robe.
bata'	n.	child.
báta'	adj.	young; immature.
batá	v.	/mag-:-in/ to endure; to tolerate; to bear; to suffer. Nagbatá ng hirap ang aking ina para sa aking kinabukasan. My mother endured hardships for my future.
bátak	v.	/-um-:-in/ to pull; to stretch. Batakin mo ang lubid. Stretch/pull the rope.
batalán	n.	rear of barrio house for washing and for storage of water.
batás	n.	law.
bátaw	n.	hyacinth bean.
bátay	v.	/i-/ to base on something. Ibinatay sa tula ni Rizal ang drama. The drama was based on Rizal's poem.

batería (Sp)n.	storage battery; flashlight battery.
Bathala' n.	God.
báti' v.	/-um-:-in/ to greet; to welcome; to salute; to congratulate (batiin). Binati namin ang mga bagong dating. We welcomed the new arrivals.
bating sut n.	bathing suit.
bátis n.	stream; creek, spring.
bató n.	stone; kidney.
bátok n.	nape (of neck); back of neck.
batóg n.	shelled and boiled corn to which grated coconut and salt are added.
batsoy (Ch) n.	chopped and sautéed entrails of pig with soup.
batubaláni' n.	magnet.
batúgan adj.	lazy, indolent.
batúta (Sp) n.	police club; conductor's wand; baton.
batýa' n.	laundry tub.
baúl (Sp) n.	clothes chest.
báwal adj.	forbidden; prohibitive.
v.	/mag-:i-:-an/ to prohibit; to forbid. Ibáwal mo ang pagsisigarilyo sa loob ng klase. Prohibit smoking in the classroom.
báwang n.	garlic.

báwas	v.	/mag-:i-/ to lessen; to remove (something) from.
bawa't	pron.	each; every; as in bawa't isa; everyone; everybody.
báwi'	n.	recovery; retraction.
	v.	/-um-:-in/ to recover. Bumáwi ka na lang sa susunod. Just make up for it the next time. /mang-:-in/ to get back what was given away. Bináwi ni Jose ang singsing na ibinigay niya sa akin. Joe took back the ring he gave me.
báa'	v.	/-an/ to allow or tolerate (a situation); to let (someone) alone. Bayáan mo siya. Let him alone.
bayábas	n.	guava.
báyad	n.	payment; fare.
	adj.	(bayád) paid for.
	v.	/mag-:-an/ to pay for; to compensate. Magbayad tayo ng utang. Let's pay the debt. Bayaran mo ang kinain natin. Pay for what we have eaten.
bayág	n.	testicle.
báyan	n.	town; country; fatherland.
bayáni'	n.	hero.
bayáw	n.	brother-in-law (term of reference).

bayáwak	n.	large lizard.
baybáy	n.	seashore.
baybáyin	n.	coast.
baylarína	n.	ballerina; ballet dancer. --var. bailarina.
bayó	v.	/mag-:-in/ to pound; to crush. Bayuhin mo ang palay. Pound the unhusked rice.
bayóng	n.	large bag.
baytáng	n.	grade; level; step.
baywáng	n.	waist.
béking páwder	n.	baking powder.
békon	n.	bacon.
beísbol (Eng)	n.	baseball.
bélo (Sp velo)	n.	veil.
bénda (Sp venda)	n.	(surgical)bandage.
bendisyón (Sp)	n.	benediction.
bénta (Sp)	n.	sales; income from sales.
	v.	/mag-:i-/ to sell. Ibenta mo ang niluto kong pansit. Sell the pancit you cooked.
bentiladór (Sp)	n.	ventilating fan; electric fan.
benggánsa (Sp)	n.	vengeance.
bérde	adj.	green.
berdúgo (Sp)	n.	executioner of death sentence.

beribéri (Sp, Eng) n.   (med) beriberi.

bestído   n.   dress. --syn. <u>báro</u>.

beteráno (Sp) n.   veteran.

bétsin   n.   monosodium glutamate, food
                         seasoning.

béynte   num.   twenty.

béynte-síngko num.   twenty-five.

bibéro (Sp) n.   bib.

bíbi   n.   duck.

bibíg   n.   mouth.

bibíngka   n.   rice cake.

bíki'   n.   mumps. --var. <u>béke'</u>.

bikíg   n.   foreign matter (as fishbone)
                         stuck in the throat.

Bikoláno/a n.   a person from the Bikol region.

bída   v.   /mag-:i-/ to tell or relate
                         a story or happening. <u>Ibída</u>
                         <u>mo naman sa amin ang biyahe mo</u>.
                         Tell us about your trip.

bigás   n.   rice (husked); uncooked rice.

bigát   n.   weight; heaviness.

               adj.   /ma-/ heavy.

bigáy   v.   /mag-:i-:-an/ to give. <u>Ibigay</u>
                         <u>mo ang lapis sa kanya</u>. Give
                         the pencil to him.

bigkás   n.   pronunciation.

bigháni'	n.	charm; seduction.
biglá'	adv.	suddenly; immediately.
bigó'	adj.	frustrated; disappointed.
bigóte	n.	moustache.
bigti	v.	/mag-:-in/ to hang or strangle oneself. <u>Nagbigti siya sa sama ng loob</u>. He strangled himself because of sadness.
bíhag	n.	prisoner of war; captive.
bihása (Sk)	adj.	accustomed; used to.
bihílya (Sp)	n.	fasting.
bihíra'	adv.	seldom; rarely.
bíhis	n.	the dress one wears.
	adj.	(bihís) well-dressed; dressed up.
	v.	/mag-:i-:-an/ to change clothes. <u>Bihísan mo ang bata</u>. Dress the child.
bíhon	n.	rice noodle.
biík	n.	young of a pig.
bilád	v.	/mag-:i-/ to put under the sun; to dry; to expose to the sun. <u>Ibilad mo ang palay</u>. Spread the palay (under the sun).
bílang	n.	number; numeral.
	v.	/-um-/ to count. <u>Bumilang ka hanggang sampu</u>. Count up to ten.
		/mag-:-in/ to count something. <u>Bilángin mo ang mga sisiw</u>. Count the chickens.

bilanggó'	n.	prisoner.
	v.	/ma-/ to be imprisoned; to be put in jail. <u>Ibinilanggo siya</u>. He was imprisoned.
		/mag-:i-/ to imprison; to captivate. <u>Ibinilanggó ang nakapatay</u>. The murderer was imprisoned.
bilanggúan	n.	(rw. <u>bilanggó</u>') prison. --syn. <u>bilíbid</u>.
biláo	n.	winnowing basket (for removing rice chaff).
bilás	n.	brother-in-law's wife or sister-in-law's husband (term of reference).
bilasá'	adj.	stale; not fresh.
bilí	v.	/-um-:-in/ to buy; to purchase. <u>Bumili ng bahay si Gng. Cruz</u>. Mrs. Cruz bought a house.
		/mag-:ipag-/ to sell. <u>Ipinagbili nila ang kanilang lupa at bahay</u>. They sold their house and lot.
bilíbid	n.	prison. --syn. <u>bilanggúan</u>.
	v.	/i-/ to tie around a twine or card several times. <u>Ibilibid mo ang lubid sa poste</u>. Tie the rope around the post.
bilin	v.	/mag-:i-/ to make a request or order for something. <u>Magbilin ka na ng gusto mo habang narito pa ako</u>. Order what you want while I'm still here.
biling	adj.	turned over; bent; inclined.
	v.	/-um-/ to turn aside. <u>Bumiling ka</u>. Turn over.

/ma-/ to be turned aside.
Nabiling ang mukha niya sa
lakas ng sampal. His head
was turned aside by the force
of the slap. His face was swung
aside by the force of the blow.

/mag:-in,i-/ to turn over; to
turn around. Ibiling mo ang
ulo ng bata sa unan. Turn the
head of the child on the pillow.

bílog	n.	circle; roundness.
	adj.	/ma-/ round; circular.
bínat	n.	relapse.

v.   /ma-/ to have a relapse.
Nabinat siya sa katratrabaho.
He had a relapse because of
overwork.

/-in/ to cause a relapse.
Huwag mo siyang binatin. Don't
strain him (or he might have a
relapse).

bilís   n.   speed.

adj.   /ma-/ speedy; rapid; fast;
swift.

v.   /-an/ (bilisán) to make fast;
speed up. Bilisán mo ang takbo
ng kotse. Drive the car faster.

biloy	n.	dimples.
bilyár (Sp)	n.	billiards.
bímpo (Ch)	n.	small face towel.
binabáe	adj.	hermaphrodite; effeminate.
		--syn. baklá'.

bináta'	n.	unmarried man; bachelor.
binatóg	n.	steamed or boiled grains of corn mixed with coconut gratings and salt.
bindisyón (Sp)	n.	benediction.
bindíta (Sp)	n.	holy water.
binditádo (Sp)	adj.	blessed; holy.
binhî'	n.	seed (chosen for the nursery).
binibíni	n.	miss; unmarried young woman.
binlíd	n.	rice particles.
bínta (Sp)	n.	small swift sailboat.
bintána'	n.	window.
bintáng	v.	/mag:i-/ to lay the blame on somebody; to impute; to accuse somebody. Ibintáng mo ang lahat kay Rosita. Blame everything on Rosita.
bintî'	n.	leg; calf of a leg.
binyág	n.	baptism.
	v.	/mag-:-an/ to baptize someone. Nagbinyág ng mga bata ang pare kahapon. The priest baptized the children yesterday.
bingî (Ch)	adj.	deaf.
bíngit	n.	edge; rim. --syn. gilid.
bingwît	n.	pole; hook; line and sinker for fishing. --var. binwit.

v.   /mang-:-in/ to fish with a
hook, line and sinker. <u>Mam-
ingwit tayo ng isda bukas</u>.
Let's go fishing (with hook,
line and sinker) tomorrow.

bíro'   n.   a joke.

v.   /mag-:-in/ to tease; to make
fun of. <u>Huwag magbiro sa lasing</u>.
Don't make fun of drunks.

bísa'   adj.   /ma-/ forceful; effective.

biskwít   n.   cookies; crackers, and the like.

bíse   adj.   vice. e.g. <u>bise-presidente</u>.
Vice-president.

bisikléta   n.   bicycle.

bísig   n.   arm, forearm.

bisíta   n.   guest; visitor.

v.   /-um-:-in/ to pay a visit.
<u>Bumisita kami sa ospital</u>. We
visited (someone) in the hospital.

bisték (Eng) n.   beefsteak.

bísto (Sp) adj.   obvious; discovered.

bísyo (Sp) n.   vice.

bítag   n.   snare for birds, based on a
looped twine.

bitáw   n.   release of hold.

v.   /-um-/ to release one's hold.
<u>Huwag kang bumitaw</u> sa renda
<u>ng kabayo</u>. Don't release the
reins of the horse.

bitay		/mag-/ to hang oneself by the neck. **Magbitay ka**. Hang yourself.
	v.	/-in, i-/ to hang (by the neck). **Ibitay mo ang kriminal**. (You) hang the criminal.
bitbit	v.	/mag-:-in/ to carry or hold dangling from the fingers or the hand. **Bitbitin mo nga ang mga daeng**. Carry the dried fish.
bitin	n.	dangling prizes and favors.
	adj.	(**bitin**) hanging; suspend.
	v.	/-um-/ to hang. **Bumitin si Rogelio sa punong kahoy**. Rogelio/Roger dangled from the tree.
		/mag-:i-/ to hang something. **Ibitin mo ang mga daeng**. Hang the dried fish.
bitiw	v.	/-um-/ to release one's hold or grip. **Bumitiw siya sa aking pagkakahawak**. He released himself from my grip.
		/mag-:-an/ to resign; to let go. **Nagbitiw ang kalihim sa kanyang katungkulan**. The secretary resigned from his job.
bits	n.	beets.
bitsin (Ch)	n.	flavoring powder; seasoning. --var. **betsin**.
bituka	n.	intestine.
bituin	n.	star.
biyak	v.	/mag-:-in/ to cleave; to split; to break into two. **Biyakin mo nga ang niyog**. (You) cleave the coconut open.

biyáhe	n.	trip; journey.
biyahéro (Sp)	n.	voyager; traveller.
biyás	n.	flank; internode.
biyáya'	n.	favor; grace; mercy.
biyenán	n.	mother-in-law or father-in-law (term of reference for parents-in-law). --var. biyanán.
Biyérnes	n.	Friday.
Biyernes Sánto	n.	Good Friday.
biyolín	n.	violin.
biyolinísta	n.	violinist.
biyúdo/a (Sp)	n.	widow/widower.
blángko (Sp)	adj.	nothing; blank.
blúsa	n.	blouse.
bóbo	adj.	dumb; stupid; dull.
bokabuláryo (Sp)	n.	vocabulary.
bóksing	n.	boxing.
boksingéro	n.	boxer.
bódabil	n.	vaudeville.
bodéga	n.	storeroom; warehouse.
bóla	n.	ball.
	v.	/mang-:-in/ to flatter; to jest; to put someone on. Nambóla siya ng husto. He flattered (someone) a lot.

bóling	v.	/mag-/ to bowl.
bólpen	n.	ball point.
boluntáryo	n.	volunteer; peace corps volunteer.
bómba	n.	pump.
Bombáy	n.	Indian (native of India).
bombéro	n.	fireman.
bombílya (Sp)		electric light bulb.
bóses	n.	voice. --syn. tínig.
bóta	n.	boots; rainboots.
bóte	n.	bottle. --syn. botelya.
botíka	n.	drugstore; pharmacy. --syn. parmásya.
bóto	n.	vote.
	v.	/-um-/ to vote. Bumoto tayo sa darating na halalan. Let's vote in the coming elections.
		/i-/ to vote for someone. Ibóto natin ang mabuting kandidato. Let's vote for the good candidate.
brá	n.	bra. --var. brasiyér.
brás	n.	brush. Bras sa buhok. Hairbrush.
brasiyér	n.	bra.
bráso	n.	arm.
brilyánte	n.	diamond.
brótsa (Sp)	n.	painter's brush (large).

brúha	n.	witch; old hag.
bubóng	n.	roof.
bubót	adj.	unripe, immature.
bubúyog	n.	bumble-bee.
buká	adj.	open.
	v.	/-um-/ <u>Bumuka na ang buko</u>. The bud opened.
		/i-/ <u>Ibuka mo ang bibig mo</u>. Open your mouth.
bukáka'	adj.	/naka-/ wide apart (as legs when standing with feet wide apart). --syn. <u>bikaká'</u>.
bukána	n.	front; threshold.
bukáng-bibíg	n.	favorite expression. --var. <u>bukámbibig</u>.
bukáng-liwaywáy	n.	break of dawn; dawn. --syn. <u>madaling-araw</u>.
búkas	adv.	tomorrow.
bukás	v.	/-um-/ to be opened. <u>Bumukas ang pinto sa lakas ng hangin</u>. The door was opened because of the strong wind.
		/mag-:i-, -an/ to open something. <u>Buksan mo ang bintana</u>. Open the window.
bukáyo'	n.	grated coconut cooked with sugar.
bukbók (Ch)	n.	bol weevil; wood borer; wood tick; decay (teeth).
búkid	n.	field; farm; rice field.

buklát   v.   /mag-:-in, i-/ to open a book or a magazine; to turn the pages of a reading material. <u>Buklatin ninyo ang aklat</u>. Open the book.

búko   n.   bud; young coconut.

bukód   v.   /-um-/ to separate from; to segregate. <u>Bumukod na siya sa amin</u>. He separated himself from us.

/mag-:i-/ to set apart; to exclude; to set aside. <u>Ibukód mo ang para kay Dadong</u>. Set aside what is for Dadong.

bukód   conj.   besides; in addition to. <u>Bukod sa asawa</u> (besides his wife...).

búkol   n.   tumor; swelling.

bukungbúkong n.   ankle.

budbód   v.   /mag-:i-/ to sprinkle; to scatter; to sow. <u>Magbudbod ka ng palay sa man</u>ok. Scatter palay for the chickens.

budhî'   n.   conscience.

buena máno (Sp) n.   first customer of the day who is believed to bring good luck in business; (lit.: good hand, borrowed from Spanish).

buéno (Sp)   part.   if that is so; in that case; well then.

bugá   v.   /-um-:-in/ to spit or blow some liquid from the mouth. <u>Binuga niya ang mainit na kanin</u>. He threw up the hot rice.

/mag-:i-/ to force out of the mouth by a sudden blow. <u>Ibuga mo ang tubig</u>. Spit out the water.

bugambílya	n.	bougainvilla.
bugbóg	adj.	bruised; squashed (of fruits, vegetables).
	v.	/mang-:-in/ to club or pound. <u>Binugbog siya ng kanyang kaaway</u>. He was beaten up by his enemies.
bugháw	adj.	blue.
bugnót	n.	exasperation.
bugók	adj.	putrid; rotten.
bugtóng	n.	riddle.
bugtóng	adj.	one and only (child).
buhaghág	adj.	spongy; loose (not adhesive).
buhángin	n.	sand.
búhat	v.	/-um-:-in/ to lift; to carry.
búhay	n.	life.
	adj.	(<u>buháy</u>) alive.
búhay-mayáman	n.	rich life; an easy-going, affluent life.
buháwi'	n.	cyclone; tornado.
buhók	n.	hair.
buhól	v.	/mag-:i-/ to make a knot; to tie securely. <u>Ibuhol mo ang lubid</u>. Make a knot with the rope.

búhos	v.	/-um-/ to pour. <u>Bumuhos ang malakas na ulan</u>. The heavy rain poured.
		/mag-:i-/ to pour something. <u>Ibuhos mo ang tubig sa ulo ni</u>. Pour the water on his head.
bulá'	n.	foam; bubbles.
búlak	n.	cotton.
bulakból	adj.	truant; vagabond; jobless.
bulaklák	n.	flower.
	v.	/mang-/ to bloom. (<u>mamulaklák</u>) <u>Namulaklak ang mga halaman sa hardin</u>. The plants bloomed in the garden.
bulalákaw	n.	shooting star; meteor.
bulág	adj.	blind.
bulastóg	adj.	(sl) mean; rudeness; boastful; rash; bluffing.
buláti	n.	earthworm.
bulból	n.	pubic hair.
bulkán	n.	volcano.
bulgár (Sp)	adj.	vulgar; coarse.
búlik	adj.	white and black (feather of roosters).
bulíd	v.	/ma-/ to fall off or down.
bulíg	n.	medium-sized mudfish.
bulílit	adj.	dwarfish; small.
bulók	adj.	decayed; spoiled; rotten.

bulóng	v.	/-um-/ to whisper; to mumble. **Bumulong siya sa akin.** He whispered to me.
		/mag-:i-/ to whisper something. **Ibulong mo sa kanya ang sinabi ko.** Whisper what I said to him.
bulsá	n.	pocket.
búlto	n.	volume.
buluntáryo (Sp) n.		volunteer. --var. boluntáryo.
bulútong	n.	smallpox.
bulyáw	n.	loud or shouted rebuke or reproach; angry and sudden shout to drive away fowls and animals.
	v.	/-an/ to shout at; to rebuke or reproach. **Bulyawán mo ang mga maingay na bata'.** Shout at the noisy children.
bumbúnan	n.	crown or top of head, specially of babies when still soft.
bundát	adj.	glutted; full (so well-fed that the abdomen is distended).
bundók	n.	mountain.
búni	n.	ringworm.
bunó'	v.	/mag-/ to wrestle with each other. **Nagbuno sila.** They wrestled with each other.
		/mang-:-in/ to wrestle. (bunuín) **Bunuín mo nga siya.** Wrestle with him.
bunót	n.	coconut husk.

búnot	v.	/-um-:-in/ to pull out; to uproot; to extract. (bunútin) Bunútin mo ang damo. Pull out the grass.
		/mag:-in/ to pull out something (a gun). Nagbúnot siya ng baril. He pulled out a gun.
bunsó'	n.	youngest in the family (term of reference).
buntál	v.	/mang-:-in/ to give a blow; to knock with fists. Binuntal ng butangero ang matanda. The gangster gave the old (man) a blow.
buntís	adj.	pregnant.
buntót	n.	tail.
buntón	n.	heap; pile.
	v.	/-um-/ to pile up; to crowd in. Bumunton ang basura sa bangketa. The garbage piled up on the side-walk. /mag-:i-/ to put into a pile; to put in a heap or mound. Ibunton mo ang maruming damit sa batya'. Pile the dirty clothes on the wash basin.
búnga	n.	fruit; betel nut palm.
búngad	n.	front. --syn. harapan, bukana.
bungang-áraw	n.	prickly heat.
bungánga' ng bulkán	n.	(volcano) crater.
bungkál	v.	/mag-:-in/ to till the soil; to dig out.
bungkos	n.	bundle; package.

buó'   adj.   entire; complete.

bunggó'   n.   impact.

               v.   /-um-/ to hit; to bump with something. <u>Bumunggo ang ulo niya sa pader</u>. His head hit the wall.

/má-/ to hit or bump against accidentally; to make an impact. <u>Nábunggo ang kotse sa pader</u>. The car hit the wall.

/mag-:i-/ to ram an object against something; to bump against something. <u>Ibunggo mo ang ulo niya sa pader</u>. Ram his head against the wall.

/mang-:-in/ to hit or bump against. (<u>bungguín</u>) <u>Bungguín mo ang pader</u>. (You) ram against the wall.

búngi'   n.   jag; dent; notch; nick.

               adj.   (<u>bungí'</u>) toothless, missing tooth.

               v.   /ma-/ <u>Nabúngi siya</u>. He lost his tooth.

bungisngís adj.   giggling.

bungó'   n.   skull.

burá   v.   /mag-:-in/ to erase; to remove traces of. (<u>burahín</u>) <u>Burahín mo ang maling sagot</u>. Erase the wrong answers.

burdá   n.   embroidery.

               v.   /mag-:-an/ to embroider. (burdahán) <u>Burdahán mo ang punda ng unan</u>. Embroider the pillow-case.

burdádo	adj.	embroidered.
burí	n.	a kind of palm tree.
búro	n.	pickles (usually green mangoes). e.g. búrung mangga.
	adj.	preserved in salt; pickled or salted.
	v.	/mag-:-in, i-/ to pickle; to salt. Binúro niya ang manggang hilaw. He pickled the green/ unripe mangoes.
buról	n.	hill.
bús	n.	bus.
busábos	n.	lowly slave.
búsal	n.	corncob.
busál	n.	muzzle.
buslú'	n.	a kind of basket.
busóg	v.	/ma-/ to be full; satisfied; satiated (from eating).
butangéro/a	n.	gangster; ruffian.
bútas	n.	hole.
butéte	n.	tadpole.
búti	n.	goodness.
	adj.	/ma-/ fine; good.
butikí'	n.	lizard.
bútil	n.	grain; cereal; kernel.
butlíg	n.	little cyst-like growth on the skin.

butó	n.	seed; bone.
butónes	n.	buttons.
butsé	n.	crop of a chicken.

buwál   v.   /-um-/ to fall down; to drop down. Bumuwal siya sa gitna ng mga tao. He fell at the midst of the people.

/ma-/ to fall flat on the ground; to pass out. Nabuwal ang puno'. The tree fell.
/mag-:i-/ to cut down; to push down. Ibinuwal niya ang puno. He felled the tree.

buwán	n.	month; moon.
buwáya	n.	crocodile.

buwélta   v.   /-um-/ to turn around; to go back; to return. Bumuelta siya pagdating sa kanto. He turned back when he reached the corner.

/i-/ to turn a vehicle around; to go back. Ibuwelta mo na ang kotse. Turn the car around.

buwíg	n.	bunch or cluster of bananas (fruits).
buwís	n.	tax, as on land.
buwísit (Ch)	adj.	jinx; ill-omened. --syn. málas. annoying; vexing.

buyó   v.   /mang-, mag-:i-/ to incite; to induce; to stimulate. Huag mo siyang ibuyo sa away. Don't incite him to quarrel.

<u>K</u>

ká		you (sing).
ka-	af.	(+ reduplication of the first consonant and vowel of the verb root) means a recently completed action.
Ká	adj.	appellation for elders and distant uncles or aunts, as <u>Ka Pedro</u>, <u>Ka Juana</u>.
kaánib	n.	(rw. <u>ánib</u>) partner.
káarawan	n.	(rw. <u>áraw</u>) birthday.
kaáway	n.	(rw. <u>áway</u>) enemy; opponent.
kababáan	n.	(rw. <u>bába'</u>) lowland.
kababáyan	n.	(rw. <u>báyan</u>) townmate.
kábag	n.	gas pain.
kabán	n.	measure of palay; a sack; a cavan.
kabáong	n.	coffin.
kábaret (Eng) n.		cabaret; dance hall.
kabáyo	n.	horse.
kabeséra (Sp) n.		the head of a table (at meal). --var. <u>kabisera</u>.
kabíbi	n.	empty clam shell.
kábig	v.	/-um-:-in/ to draw or pull towards one's self; to collect the winnings in gambling. <u>Kumabig siya ng malaki</u>. He gathered in a big share.

62

/mang-:-in/ (kabígin) Kabígin
mo ang pinanalunan mo. Get your
winnings.

kabihasnán	n.	(rw. bihása) culture.
kabilá'	adv.	otherside.
kábinet	n.	cabinet; dresser.
kabísa	v.	/mang-:-in/ to memorize. Kabisáhin mo ang tula. Memorize the poem.
kabisádo (Sp)	adj.	memorized; learned by rote.
kabisóte (Sp)	adj.	dull-headed.
kabutíhan	n.	(rw. búti) goodness.
kabit	v.	/-um-/ to fasten, attach, connect; to cling to. Kumabit sa kaniya ang linta'. The leech clung onto him.
		/mag-:i-/ to fasten, link, join; connect something to something. Ikabit mo ang kandado sa pinto'. Put the padlock on the door.
kabulastugán	n.	(rw. bulastóg) (sl) bluff, boastfulness.
kabutí	n.	mushroom.
kakanín	n.	(rw. káin) tidbits, dainties, sweetmeats.
kakáw	n.	cocoa.
káki (Sp)	n./adj.	khaki (a kind of brown cloth specially used for military uniforms).
kakilála'	n.	(rw. kilála) acquaintance.

kaeskuwéla n. (rw. eskuwéla) classmate.

kadalásan adv. (rw. dalás) /ka:-an/ often, usually. ...kadalasay nagaanyong parang ulol. ...usually acts as if crazy ...

kadéna (Sp) chain. --syn. tanikalá'.

kadéna de amor n. chain of love; Mexican creeper.

kadéte (Sp) n. cadet.

kagabí adv. (rw. gabí) last night.

kagalít n. (rw. galít) one with whom a person has quarreled; an enemy.

kagampán adj. (rw. ganáp) in the last month of pregnancy; maturity of pregnancy.

kagát (Mal) n. bite.

v. /-um-:-in/ to bite. Kumagat siya sa aking bayabas. She took a bite off my guava.

/mang-:-in/ to bite. Nangangagat ang aso nila. Their dog bites.

kágaw n. germs, bacteria.

kagitná' n. (rw. gitná') half-pint.

káha n./qnt. a pack, usually of cigarettes; a case.

kahalíli n. (rw. halíli) successor, substitute.

kahápon adv. (rw. hápon) yesterday.

kaháti' n. (rw. háti') shareholder; share.

kahawíg adj. (rw. hawíg) similar, resemble

kahél	n.	a citrus tree of the sweet orange variety, producing fruit that is usually sweet but occasionally sour. --syn. dalandán.
kahéra/o	n.	cashier.
káhig	n.	scratching off a loose surface, as soil scratched off by chickens.
	v.	/-um-/ Kumahig ng lupa ang manok. The chicken scratched the ground. /-in/ Kahigin mo ang mga dahong nahulog sa lupa. Rake the leaves off the ground.
káhit	conj.	(+ na) although; even if; in spite of.
kahól	n.	bark of a dog.
kahón	n./qnt.	box, crate; drawer of a table.
káhoy	n.	wood; lumber; tree.
kahulugán	n.	meaning, significance.
kaibígan	n.	(rw. íbig) friend.
kailá'	v.	/mag-:i-/ to deny, to profess ignorance of. Ikinaila niya ang nangyari. He professed ignorance of what happened.
kailan	int.	when. --var. káylan, kélan. Kaylan pa kaya... (when will) Kaylan man... (at any time)
kailángan	p.v.	need; ought; must; necessary; indispensable.
káin	n.	/pag-/ food, act of eating.

	v.	/-um-:-in/ to eat. <u>Kumain</u> <u>siya nang marami</u>. She ate a lot.
		/mang-:-in/ to eat. <u>Nangáin</u> <u>ng tao ang leon</u>. The lion ate the people.
kaingín	n.	slash and burn agriculture.
kalabása	n.	pumpkin; squash.
kalabáw	n.	carabao.
kalabít	n.	touching with the tip of the finger.
	v.	/mang-:-in/ (<u>mangalabít</u>) <u>Huwag kang mangalabit ng tao</u>. Don't touch the person.
kalabóg	n.	crashing sound of a fallen body.
kalabós (Sp)	n.	prisoner.
	v.	/i-/ <u>Ikinalabos siya ng pulis</u>. The police imprisoned him.
kalákal	n.	merchandise; goods.
kalág	adj.	untied, loosened.
kalagúyo'	n.	(rw. <u>lagúyo'</u>) intimate friend, paramour, concubine.
kalaháti'	adj.	(rw. <u>háti'</u>) half.
kaláhi'	adj.	(rw. <u>láhi'</u>) of the same race.
kalamansí'	n.	small citrus fruit.
kalámbre (Sp)	n.	cramp.
kalán	n.	stove.
kalansáy	n.	skeleton.

kálang (Sp) n. wedge.

kalapáti n. dove; pigeon.

kalás v. /-um-/ to break away from;
to untie; to unstitch. <u>Kumalás
siya sa kaniyang barkada.</u> He
broke away from his clique.

/mag-:-in/ to rip apart.
<u>Kalasín mo ang tinahi.</u> Rip
apart what I sewed. (Rip apart
what has been sewed.)

kalát adj. /mag-/ widespread.

kalatsútsi n. plumeria (frangipani).

kálaw n. hornbill (bird).

kaláwang n. rust.

kaláwit n. hook.

kalaykáy n. rake.

kalbó n. bald, hairless.

kaldéro n. kettle.

kalésa n. horse-drawn rig or chaise; a
two-wheeled vehicle drawn by a
horse.

kalíkot n. a slender tube with a poking
rod with which to crush and mix
<u>buyo'</u>.

v. /-in/ to poke and stir, or
poke and scrape into a hole.
<u>Huag mong kalikútin ang ilong
mo.</u> Don't poke your finger in
your nose.

kaligíran n. (rw. <u>lígid</u>) environment.

kalíhim   n.   (rw. líhim) secretary. --syn.
                       sekretarya.

kalindáryo n.   calendar.

kalingkíngan n.   little finger.

kaliskís   n.   scales (fish).

kaliwá'   adj.   left hand; left; left side.

kaliwéte (Sp) adj.   left-handed.

kálma   adj.   calm, quiet.

kalóg   v.   /-um-/ to rattle, to shake.
                       Kumalog ang bola sa kahon.
                       The ball rattled around in the
                       box. (The ball rattled freely
                       in the box.)

                       /mag-:-in, i-/ to shake or
                       rattle the contents of a box or
                       bottle. Huwag mong kalugín ang
                       itlog sa kahon. Don't shake
                       the eggs around in the box.

kálong   v.   /-um-/ to sit on one's lap.
                       Kumalong ang bata sa kandungan
                       ng nanay niya. The child sat
                       on his mother's lap.

                       /mag-:-in, i-/ to hold on one's
                       lap; to take someone, something
                       on your lap. Kalúngin mo ang
                       bata. Take the child in your
                       lap.

kalsonsílyo n.   briefs; undershorts. --var.
                       karsonsílyo.

káluluwa   n.   spirit, soul.

kálye   n.   road; street. --syn. daán.

kályo   n.   corn (feet).

káma	n.	bed.
kamakalawa	adv.	(rw. <u>dalawá</u>) day before yesterday.
kamag-ának	n.	relative (term of reference).
kamagóng	n.	mahogany.
kamálig	n.	warehouse; granary.
kamandág	n.	poison.
kamatáyan	n.	(rw. <u>patay</u>) death.
kamátis	n.	tomatoes.
kamatsile	n.	guamachile.
kamáy	n.	hand.
kambál	n.	twin (term of reference).
kambíng	n.	goat.
kamí	pron.	we (exclusive, I and others).
kaminéro	n.	street cleaner.
kamisadéntro	n.	long-sleeved shirt.
kamisatsína (Sp)	n.	outside shirt that is closed-necked, and without collar and lapel.
kamiseta	n.	undershirt.
kamisóla (Sp)	n.	lady's shirt dress. --syn. <u>bestído</u>.
kamisón	n.	chemise.
kamít	v.	/mag-:-in/ to obtain; to gain; to get an award. <u>Nagkamit siya ng malaking gantímpala</u>. He obtained a large award. /um-/

kámot	v.	/-um-:-in/ to scratch (one's self). <u>Kumámot na lang siya ng ulo</u>. He just scratched his head. <u>Kinamot na lang niya ang ulo niya</u>. (He was so exasperated that) all he could do was scratch his head.
		/mag-/ to scratch (repeatedly). <u>Nagkamót siya ng ulo</u>. He scratched his head.
		/mang-:-in/ to scratch somebody. <u>Nangamot ang pusa ng tao</u>. The cat scratched people. (The cat scratched the people.)
kamóte	n.	sweet potato; yam.
kamoteng-kahoy	n.	cassava or tapioca plant.
kampána'	n.	bell.
kampánya (Sp)		campaign.
kampeón	n.	champion.
kampí	v.	/-um-:-an/ to take sides. <u>Kumampi siya sa akin</u>. She took sides with me. [She took my side (pertaining to an argument).]
kámpo	n.	camp; field.
kampón	n.	disciple; follower.
kámya	n.	white/yellow ginger or ginger lily.
kanál	n.	canal.
kánan	adj.	right (side).
kandóng	adj.	held on the lap of a skirt.
kandúngan	n.	(rw. <u>kandóng</u>) lap of a woman.

kanáryo	n.	canary.
kandádo	n.	padlock, lock.
kandidáto	n.	candidate.
kandíla'	n.	candle.
kandúli'	n	salt water catfish.
kandúngan	n.	lap.
kanéla	n.	cinnamon.
kanilá	pron.	(sa-pronoun) their; theirs.
kánin	n.	(rw. káin) cooked rice (boiled); steamed rice.
kanina	adv.	a little while ago; earlier. Sinabi ko na po sa inyo kanina na... I just told you a little while ago that...
kaníno	int.	whose.
kanitá	pron.	(sa-pronoun) yours and mine; of the two of us; poss. of kata; for the two of us.
kaniyá	pron.	(sa-pronoun) his; her; hers; poss. of siya; for him/her.
kaniyá'	conj.	therefore, as a result, consequently. --var. kanya'. Kaniya siya umalis... (the reason he left...)
kanlóng	v.	/-um-/ to hide from view, to take shelter or cover. Kumanlong siya sa ilalim ng puno. He took shelter under the tree. /mag-:i-/ to hide something from view. Ikinanlong niya ang binilad sa silong. He brought in from under the house the clothes that he had been hanging to dry.

kanlúran	n.	western; west; occidental.
kantá	n.	song. --syn. áwit.
	v.	/-um-, mag-:-in/ to sing. Kantahín mo ang bagong awit. Sing the new song.
kantéro	n.	mason.
kantína (Sp)	n.	snack bar; metal flask for carrying liquids.
kánto	n.	street corner; cornerstone.
kanyón	n.	cannon.
kangkóng	n.	swamp cabbage; watercress.
káong	n.	palm (cabo negro).
kapá'	v.	/-um-/ to grope; to feel about.
		/mang-:-in/ to grope for something; to feel about for something. Nangapá siya sa dilim. He groped in the dark.
kapág	conj./ adv.	if, when, in case, whenever. (single events viewed as completed in the future) --var. pag, pagka, kapagka. Kapag ipinang putol mo iyan... If you use that for cutting...
kapál	n.	thickness.
	adj.	/ma-/ thick.
kapaláran	n.	(rw. pálad) luck, fortune, fate.
kapanganákan	n.	(rw. anák) birthday.
kapangyaríhan	n.	(rw. yári) power; authority.
kapatás	n.	foreman.

kapatíd	n.	brother or sister, sibling (term of reference).
kapkáp	adj.	feeling or frisking (the pockets).
kapé	n.	coffee.
	adj.	brown (color).
kapetírya	n.	cafeteria.

kápit   v.   /-um-:-an/ to hold, to grasp. <u>Kumapit siya sa akin</u>. He held onto me.

/i-/ to attach to; to connect to. <u>Ikápit mo ang kamay mo sa balikat ng bata</u>. Put your hand on the child's shoulder.

/mag-/ to hold onto each other; to join hands. <u>Magkápit kayo at baka kayo mahulog</u>. Hold onto each other's hands because you might fall.

kapitán/a	n.	captain.
kapitan/a del báryo	n.	captain, head of the barrio.
kapitalísta	n.	capitalist.
kápit-báhay	n.	neighbor; next-door neighbor.
kapitéra	n.	coffee pot.
kápok	n.	kapok; cotton tree.
kapón (Sp)	adj.	castrated; gelded.
kapós	adj.	insufficient; lacking; wanting.
kapóte	n.	raincoat.
kaprítso (Sp)	n.	caprice, whim, fancy.

kápwa	pron.	kindred, both; fellow-being, equally (applied to one of a pair). Kapwa sila magnanakaw. They are fellow thieves. Kapwa sila malakas. They are equally strong.
karamdáman	n.	(rw. damdám) ailment, sickness. --syn. sakít.
karaníwan	adj.	ordinary, common, usual.
karangálan	n.	(rw. dangál) honor. --syn. púri.
karapatán	n.	rights and privileges.
karayóm	n.	needle.
karbón	n.	coal.
karbúro (Sp)	n.	carbide.
karéra (Sp)	n.	race, racing; career, profession.
karetéla	n.	two-wheeled cartlike horse-drawn passenger-and-freight vehicle.
kárdinal	n.	cardinal.
kargá (Sp)	n.	load, burden; freight.
	adj.	carried, loaded.
kargadór	n.	porter, baggage carrier, stevedor.
karíhan	n.	local restaurant.
karindería	n.	small store where food is served.
kárit	n.	sickle, scythe.
karitón	n.	cart.
karnabál	n.	carnival; fair.
kárne	n.	meat.

karne nórte	n.	corned beef (usually canned).
károt	n.	carrots.
karpentéro	n.	carpenter.
kartamunéda	n.	purse. --var. portamoneda.
kartéro	n.	mailman; postman.
kartolína	n.	cardboard; bristol board.
kartón (Sp)	n.	pasteboard; binder's board.
kasabáy	adv.	(rw. sabáy) together; at the same time; simultaneously.
kasál	n.	wedding.
kasalánan	n.	(rw. sála) fault; sin.
kasalukúyan	adv.	at the present time.
kasáma	n.	(rw. sáma) a companion; tenant; farm help.
	adj.	/mag-/ being together.
	adv.	in company with, along with.
kasangkápan	n.	(rw. sángkap) household belongings, tools, furniture, equipment.
kasápi'	n.	(rw. sápi') member.
kaskó (Sp)	n.	long river boat with sheltering roofings at either end, navigated by pushing with long poles.
kaséra	n.	landlord, landlady.
kaseróla	n.	casserole; pan.
kasí	conj.	because.

kasílyas	n.	toilet; restroom or comfort room.
kasintáhan	n.	sweetheart; fiance/fiancee.
kásiya	adj.	sufficient, enough, adequate, fit.
káso (Sp)	n.	case in court; disagreement.
kastányas	n.	chestnuts.
kasúy	n.	cashew nuts.
katá	pro.	the two of us.
kátad	n.	animal skin, leather.
katám	n.	carpenter's planer.
katangían	n.	(rw. tángi') characteristic.
katapusan	n.	(rw. tápus) end, conclusion.
katarúngan	n.	(rw. taróng) justice, equity.
katás	n.	sap, juice.
katawán	n.	body.
kátay	v.	/-um, mag-:-in/ to butcher; to cut into slices, especially meat; to slaughter. Kinatay ng matadero ang baka. The butcher butchered the cow.
káti'	n.	lowtide.
katí	adj.	/ma-/ itchy; scratchy.
katók	n.	sharp knock or rap. --syn. tuktók.
katóliko	n.	Roman Catholic.
katotohánan	n.	(rw. totoó) truth.

kátre	n.	bed.

katúlong n. (rw. túlong) helper, maid, houseboy.

katungkúlan n. (rw. tungkól) occupation, office, official designation.

katuwíran n. (rw. tuwíd) reason.

káunti adj. little, few.

kaúsap n. (rw. úsap) person with whom one is conversing.

　　　　v. /-in/ to talk with.

káwa n. big kettle.

kawág n. movement of hands and/or feet, specially when swimming or drowning; also movement of wings.

káwal n. soldier.

kawáli n. frying pan.

kawáwa adj. pitiful.

kawáy v. /-um-:-an/ to wave with the hand. Kumaway siya sa akin bago umalis. He waved at me before he left.

kawáyan n. bamboo.

káwit n. hook.

　　　　v. /-um-/ to get hooked. Kumawit ang pantalon niya sa pako'. He caught his trousers on the nail.

78

/ma-/ to get hooked accidentally. Nakáwit ang bagong pantalon niya ng pako'. His new pair of pants was caught by a nail.

/mag-:-in, i-/ to hook something. Ikawit mo ang alambre sa pako. Hook the wire on the nail.

kay *part.* singular sa proper noun marker; also marks possession; the plural form is kina, to, from, for.

kaysa *conj.* than, more than. Kaysa asukal. Sweeter than sugar.

káya *adj.* competence, ability.

kayá' *conj.* perhaps; maybe; so; that's why; therefore. Kaya ako naparito... I have come here so that... ...kaya siya... That is why he...

mod. perchance; perhaps; might (expresses doubt or possibility of choice). Ano kaya ang iniútos mo sa kanya? What perchance did you order him to do? Baka kaya nawala siya. He might have gotten lost.

káyag *v.* /mang-:-in/ to invite; to induce. --var. yakag. Kayagin mo ang ibig sumama. Induce the ones that want to come along.

kayamánan *n.* wealth; richness.

kayimíto *n.* star-apple. --var. kaymíto.

kayo *pron.* you (plural).

káyod	v.	/-um-:-in/ to scrape; to grate. <u>Kumáyod kami ng niyog.</u> We scraped the coconut.
		/mag-:-in/ <u>Kayurin mo ang niyog.</u> Grate the coconut.
kayumanggi	adj.	brown (race, complexion, color).
kayurán	n.	grater.
kéndi	n.	candy.
kerída (Sp)	n.	paramour; mistress. --syn. <u>babái</u>.
kérot	n.	carrot.
késo	n.	cheese.
kétong (Ch)	n.	leprosy.
kétsap	n.	ketchup.
kibó'	v.	/-um-/ to talk; to move; to stir. <u>Kumibo ka naman diyan.</u> Say something.
		/-in/ to break the silence with someone by talking.
kibót	n.	throb; pulsation.
kíkel	n.	carpenter's file.
kidlát	n.	lightning.
	v.	/-um-/ to flash as of lightning. <u>Kumidlat kagabi.</u> There was lightning last night.
kilábot	n.	goose-pimples; gooseflesh.
kilalá	adj.	famous, well-known; acquainted with one another. (<u>magkakilála</u>)
	v.	/magka-:ma-/ to happen to know; to happen to meet; to become acquainted.

kílay	n.	eyebrow.
kílik	v.	/-um-, mag-:-in/ to carry against the hips. <u>Kilíkin mo ang bata</u>. Carry the child on your hip.
kilikíli	n.	armpit.
kilíg	v.	/mang-:-in/ to shudder; to shiver; to chill. <u>Kinilig siya sa ginaw</u>. She shivered with cold.
kíling	n.	inclination towards a side.
	adj.	inclined towards a side.
kilití'	n.	ticklish feeling; tickle.
kílo	n.	kilogram.
kímiko	n.	chemical.
kina	part.	plural <u>sa</u>-proper noun marker, for.
kinakapatíd	n.	godbrother or sister.
kináng	adj.	/ma-/ glittering.
kindát	n.	wink (of the eye).
kiníg	v.	/ma-/ to listen.
kinína (Sp)	n.	quinine.
kínis	adj.	/ma-/ smooth, fine.
kintáb	adj.	/ma-/ shiny.
kintsáy	n.	Chinese celery (kinchay).
kínse	num.	fifteen.

kipkíp	v.	/mag-:-in/ to carry under the armpit; to carry with the arm pressed against the body. <u>Kipkipin mong mabuti ang bag mo</u>. Hold the bag tightly under your arm.
kípot	adj.	/ma-/ narrow, tight.
	v.	/mag-:-an/ to make tighter.
kirí (Ch)	adj.	coquettish; flirtatious.
kiród	n.	stinging pain.
kísame	n.	ceiling.
kiskís	v.	/-um-/ to rub against a surface. <u>Kumiskis ang magaspang na tela sa balat niya</u>. The rough cloth rubbed on his skin.
		/mag-:i-/ to rub something against a surface. <u>Ikiskis mo ang kutsilyo sa bato</u>. Sharpen the knife on the whetstone.
kísig	adj.	/ma-/ handsome/dashing; elegant; well-dressed (man).
kisláp	n.	sparkle.
kíta	n.	earnings; salary; wage.
	v.	/-um-:-in/ to earn. <u>Kumita siya ng malaki sa kompanya</u>. He earned a lot at the company.
kíta	v.	/mag-/ to meet;to see each other; to find. <u>Nagkita sila sa sine</u>. They saw each other at the movie.
kitíkití	n.	mosquito larva.
kítid	adj.	/ma-/ narrow.

kliénte (Sp) n.   client.

kláse   n.   class, kind.

klérk   n.   clerk.

klíma   n.   climate; weather.   --syn. panahon.

klínika   n.   clinic.

ko   pro.   I; my; mine.

kobradór   n.   bill collector.

kódigo (Sp) n.   code of laws of rules; (sl) notes hidden by students during examination.

kolektá   v.   /mang-:-in/ to collect something; to gather. Nangolekta siya ng abuloy para sa patay. He collected contributions for the dead.

kolehiyo   n.   college.

koloréte (Sp) n.   rouge.

kolyár (Sp) n.   collar, especially for animals.

komádre (Sp) n.   lady sponsor in baptism, confirmation or matrimony of one's child.   --var. kumádre.

komadróna (Sp) n.   midwife.   --syn. hílot.

kombénto   n.   convent; rectory.

kométa   n.   comet.

kómika   adj.   comical.

kómiks   n.   comics.

kompádre (Sp) n.	male sponsor in baptism, confirmation or matrimony of one's child. --syn. <u>kumpádre</u>.	
kompiyánsa (Sp) n.	confidence, reliance; courage, firmness of opinion.	
kompléto (Sp) adj.	complete.	
kondoktór/a n.	conductor of a public vehicle.	
kondól n.	wax gourd.	
konsehál/a n.	councilor.	
kontribusyón n.	contribution.	
kongkréto adj.	concrete, made of cement.	
kópya n.	a copy.	
v.	/in-/ to copy.	
Koreano/a n.	Korean.	
kóro (Sp) n.	chorus; choir.	
koróna n.	crown.	
koronasyón n.	a program or ball where a beauty queen is crowned.	
kórse n.	girdle, corset.	
kórte (Sp) n.	shape. --syn. <u>húgis</u>. Court (royal or justice).	
kórto n.	short pants.	
kostúmbre.(Sp) n.	custom, habit, tradition. --syn. <u>ugalí'</u>.	
kótse n.	car; automobile. --syn. <u>awto</u>.	
kótso (Sp) n.	thick-soled lady's slippers.	
krayóla n.	crayons.	

kréma   n.   cream.

krim   n.   cream.

krímen (Sp) n.   crime.

kriminál (Sp) n.   criminal.

krúdo   n.   oil.

krús (Sp)   n.   cross. --var. kurús.

kúba'   n.   hunchback.

kubábaw   n.   astride over the top.

kubéta (Sp) n.   pail (to receive refuse); toilet.
                      --syn. kasílyas.

kublí   adj.   hidden; away from prying eyes.

kúbo   n.   hut.

kubradór (Sp) n.   bill collector.

kubrekáma (Sp) n.   bedspread.

kubyértos (Sp) n.   table-silver (spoon, fork, knife);
                      a meal, as a unit or order in a
                      restaurant, different from short
                      orders.

kukó   n.   fingernail.

kudkód   n.   (kudkúran) /-an/ grater.

             adj.   (kinudkód) grated.

             v.   /mag-:-in/ Kudkurin mo ang niyog.
                      Grate the coconut.

kudkúran   n.   (rw. kudkúd) grater; shredder.

kudrádo (Sp) adj.   square.

kugón   n.   cogon grass.

kúha	v.	/-um-:-in/ to get; to obtain.
kuhól	n.	snail.
kulambó'	n.	mosquito net.
kuláni' (Sp)	adj.	swelling of the lymphatic gland, especially in the grain.
kúlang	adj.	/mag-/ short, incomplete, lacking, insufficient, inadequate.
kúlay	n.	color.
	adj.	/ma-/ colorful.
kulíg	n.	suckling pig. --syn. biík.
kulisap	n.	insects.
kulíti'	n.	stye (in the eye).
kulítis	n.	native spinach.
kuló'	v.	/magpa-:pa-in/ to boil water.
kulóg	n.	thunder.
	v.	/-um-/ to thunder. Kumulóg ng malakas. It thundered loudly.
kulóng	n.	(kulugan) canal, pen; prison; cage. --syn. haula.
	adj.	surrounded, encircled; imprisoned, jailed.
	v.	/i-/ to cage, imprison. Ikulong mo ang ibon. Cage the bird.
kulungán	n.	(rw. kulóng) cage; prison.
kulót	adj.	curly, wavy.
	v.	/mag-:-in/ to give a permanent; to make curly or wavy.

kulubóng   n.   protecting mantle over something,
                          or a person, especially the
                          latter's head.

kulubót   adj.   wrinkle.

kulugó   n.   wart.

kumadre (Sp) n.   lady sponsor in a baptism, con-
                          firmation or wedding. Kumpadre
                          (masculine form).

kumáre (Sp) n.   derived from the Spanish word
                          comadre, a reciprocal appellation
                          for the godmother or for the child's
                          mother. Kumpare (masculine form).

kumbidádo (Sp) n.   invited guest.

kumedór (Sp) n.   dining room.

kúmot   n.   blanket, bed sheet.

kumpás (Sp) v.   /-um-/ to beat, as a conductor
                          of a band or orchestra; to gesture
                          with the hands. Kumumpas siya
                          sa harap ng banda. He conducted
                          in front of the band.

kumpíl (Sp) n.   Sacrament of Confirmation.

kumpisál (Sp) v.   /mang-, mag-:i-/ to confess.
                          Nangumpisal siya sa pare'.
                          She confessed to the priest.

kumpól   n.   bunch, cluster.

kumpórme (Sp) adj.   agreeable, confirming, resigned,
                          satisfied.

kumpuní (Sp) v.   /mag, -um-:-in/ to repair, alter
                          (as in clothes); to mend.
                          Nagkukumpune siya ng sirang
                          kasangkappan. He fixes broken
                          appliances.

Kumunísta (Sp) n.   Communist.

kumunóy   n.   quicksand.

kumustá (Sp) n.   regards, greeting form. <u>Kumusta</u> <u>ka</u>? How are you?

v.   /mang-:-in/ to inquire about the condition of the health of a person. <u>Kumustahin mo ang</u> <u>maysakit</u>. Say hello to the sick.

kúnat   n.   ductility; resiliency.

adj.   /ma-/ stingy; resilient.

kundí'   conj.   but, on the contrary. <u>Kung</u> <u>hindi</u>. If not for; nothing but.

kudkúran   n.   shredder.

kundíman   n.   native song.

kunduktór (Sp) n.   conductor (in buses or trains).

kuného (Sp) n.   rabbit.

kunsentidór (Sp) n.   person allowing or approving acts that are not supposed to be done.

kunsumisyón (Sp)   vexation; exasperation. --syn. <u>yamót</u>.

kunsúmo (Sp) n.   consumption (of provisions, fuel, merchandise, etc.).

kunwá'/kunwári' adv.   simulatedly.

kúng   conj.   when, whenever, if during (conjunction used to indicate non-actual occurrences viewed as unreal, hypothetical or repeated).

(+ <u>di</u>) if not.
(+ <u>maári'</u>) whether possible.
(+ <u>minsan</u>) sometimes.
(+ <u>paano</u>) how done.
(+ <u>saan</u>) where.

kúpad	n.	sluggishness, slowness in working.
kupás	adj.	/um-/ faded, out of date, out of use.
kupkóp	adj.	kept and protected under one's care; held against one's chest, as a mother holding a child.
kúpit	n.	pilfering, filching.
kurál (Sp)	n.	corral; pen. --syn. <u>kulungán</u>.
kuráles (Sp)	n.	coral stone.
kúrba (Sp)	n.	curve.
kurbádo (Sp)	adj.	curved.
kurbáta (Sp)	n.	tie, necktie.
kurdón (Sp)	n.	round cord.
kurípot	adj.	stingy.
Kurismá (Sp)	n.	Lent.
kúro'	n.	opinion, estimate.
kurót	v.	/-um-/ to take a piece.
		/mang-:-in/ to pinch. <u>Nangungurot siya kapag natutuwa'</u>. She pinches people when she's happy.
kursé (Sp)	n.	corset.

kursó   n.   diarrhea.

          v.   /mag-:-in/ to suffer from diarrhea, to be sick of diarrhea. <u>Baka ka kursohin kapag kain ka nang kain.</u> If you keep on eating you might get diarrhea.

kursunáda (Sp)   impulse of the heart; liking.

kurtína   n.   curtains.

kurús   n.   cross. --var. <u>krús</u>.

kuryénte   n.   electric current.

kúsa'   adj.   spontaneous; initiative.

kúsang-loob   voluntary.

kuskós   v.   /mag-:-in/ to scrub. <u>Kuskusin mo ang sahig.</u> Scrub the floor.

                 /mag-:i-/ to scrub with. <u>Ikuskós mo ang basahan sa sahig.</u> Scrub the floor with the rag.

kuskus-balúngos n.   superfluity of statements, requisitions or details.

kusína (Sp) n.   kitchen.

kusinéro/a (Sp) n.   cook.

kusinílya (Sp) n.   gas stove.

kusíng   n.   a coin worth half a centavo.

kusót   adj.   rumpled; crumpled. --syn. <u>gusót</u>.

          v.   /ma-/ to get wrinkled. <u>Nakusot ang damit ko sa kauupo.</u> My dress got wrinkled in sitting down.

/mag-:-in/ to crumple; to wash clothes by rubbing vigorously. Kusutin mo ang damit sa batya. Wash the dress (by rubbing vigorously) with your hands in the basin.

kustílyas (Sp) n.   ribs; chops.

kusturéra (Sp) n.   female cutter (in a milliner's shop).

kúta   n.   fort.

kutíng   n.   kitten.

kútis (Sp) n.   skin surface.

kúto   n.   lice.

kutós   v.   /mang-:-an/ to give a knuckle blow on the head. Nangungutos siya kapag maingay ka. She raps people's heads with knuckles when you're noisy.

kutsára (Sp) n.   spoon.

kutsaríta (Sp) n.   teaspoon.

kutséro (Sp) n.   rig driver.

kutsílyo (Sp) n.   knife.

kutsón (Sp) n.   cushion.

kutyá'   v.   /mang-:-in/ to mock; to scorn; to ridicule; to deride. Kinutya niya ang mga kaaway niya. He ridiculed his enemies.

kuwadérno (Sp) n.   notebook.

kuwádro (Sp) n.   picture frame.

kuwágo (Sp) n.   owl.

kuwáko	n.	pipe (for smoking).
kuwádra (Sp)	n.	stable for horses.
kuwán	pro.	whatchamacallit (used in place of an idea not immediately expressible).
kuwarésma	n.	holy week, season.
kuwárta	n.	money. --var. kuwálta.
kuwárto	n.	bedroom.
kuwárto	num.	one quarter; one-fourth; fifteen minutes.
kuwátro	num.	four.
kuwéba	n.	cave.
kuwélyo	n.	collar.
kuwénta (Sp)	n.	account; debt.
kuwénto	n.	story; narration; short story. --syn. istórya.
	v.	/mag-:i-/ to tell or relate a story. Ikuwento mo ang nangyari. Tell what happened.
kuwintás	n.	necklace.
kuwítis	n.	sky-rocket; fireworks.
kúya	n.	older brother (term of address, reference).

D

daán	num.	a unit of hundred.
daán	n.	road, street, way. --syn. kálye.
	v.	/-um-/ to pass by.
		/mag-:i-/ to drop something by.
dábog	v.	/-um-/ to stamp the feet in irritation or vexation.
dakíla'	adj.	great, eminent, majestic, noble.
dáko'	n.	spot, place.
dakót	v.	/-um-:-in/ to grasp a handful.
		/maŋ-/ to grasp somebody.
dagá'	n.	rat, mouse.
dagán	v.	/-um-, mang-/ to put one's weight on something.
		/mag-:i-/ to put a weight; to press; to put something over something.
dágat	n.	ocean; sea.
dagdág	v.	/mag-:i-:-an/ to add; to supplement; to increase.
dágok	v.	/mang-:-an/ to give a blow on the nape of the neck or with the flat of the hand.
dagsá'	n.	sudden tumultuous and confusing flow, jumble, or bustle of people or things.
dagtá'	n.	sap, juice.
dáhan	adj.	/ma-/ slow.
dahan-dáhan	adv.	slowly.

dahás	n.	force, violence of action. --syn. puwersa, lakás. Intrepidity. --syn. tapang. Ruthlessness. --syn. lupít, bangis, bagsik.
dáhil	conj.	because; reason; cause; in account of; through this...
dahilán	n.	reason; cause.
dáhon	n.	leaf of a plant or book.
daíg	adj.	surpassed; excelled; beaten. --syn. talo.
daigdíg	n.	world; universe.
dáing	n.	dried fish.
daíng	n.	complaint.
	v.	/-um-/ to moan; to complain. /mag-:i-/ to express one's suffering, lamentation or distress.
dalá	n.	load.
	v.	/mag-:-in/ to carry; to bring or take away.
dalág	n.	mud fish.
dalága	n.	unmarried woman.
dalahíra'	adj.	(applied to women) gossipy. --syn. satsát, daldál, daldaléra, tsismósa. Provocative; free and easy. --syn. landí'.
dalamháti'	n.	extreme sorrow; grief.
dalámpasigan	n.	beach.
dalandán	n.	orange (fruit).
dálang	adj.	/ma-/ few; not frequent.

dalángin   n.   prayer.

                 v.   /-um-, mang-:i-/ to pray fervently.

dalás   adj.   /ma-/ often; frequent; regular. **Madalas magkumpisal.** A regular confessor.

dálaw   v.   /-um-:-in/ to visit; to make a call.

dalawá   num.   two.

               adj.   /maka-/ twice.

               adv.   /maka-/ (with <u>sa</u>) the day before yesterday.

daldál   adj.   talkative.

dalí'   adj.   /ma-/ easy; quick; prompt; not difficult.

dalíri'   n.   finger; toe.

dalísay   adj.   clean; pure; clear; chaste.

dalitá'   adj.   /ma-/ indigent; poor.

daló   v.   /-um-:-an/ to attend to; to succor. **Dinaluhan niya ang aking kaarawan.** He attended my birthday (party).

dalubhása adj./n. expert; specialist. --syn. <u>esperto</u>.

dalúyong   n.   tidal wave.

dálya   n.   dahlia.

dáma   n.   a native game of chess.

Dáma de Nótse n. (Lady of the Night); brunfelsia.

damág	n.	/mag-/ (<u>magdamág</u>) the whole night.
dámay	v.	/-um-/ to help; to condole; to sympathize.
		/mang-:i-/ to involve others (without notice) in a sort of unpleasant situation.
dambá	v.	/-um-/ to rise on the hind legs; to stamp the feet.
dambána'	n.	shrine; altar. --syn. <u>simbáhan</u>, <u>altár</u>.
damdámin	n.	feeling.
damdám	adj.	/ma-in/ overly sensitive.
	v.	/maka-/ to be able to feel; to be sensitive.
		/mag-:-in/ to feel bad about.
dami	adj.	/ma-/ (<u>marami</u>) plenty; many.
damit	n.	clothing; dress. --syn. <u>baró</u>, <u>bestido</u>.
damó	n.	grass; weeds.
dámot	adj.	/ma-/ selfish.
dampá'	n.	hut; hovel (poor and small). --syn. <u>barung-bárong</u>.
dampi' (Mal) n.		light and gentle touch (as by the soft breeze on one's skin); light, gentle application of medicament (as on wounds).
dampót	v.	/-um-:-in/ to pick up with the hand from the floor.
		/mang-/ to handle.

damúlag	n.	land monster; carabao. --syn. <u>kalabáw</u>, <u>tamaraw</u>.
dánas	n.	/ka-, -an/ (<u>karanasán</u>) experience.
dangál	n.	honor; reputation.
dangkál	n.	span from tip of thumb to tip of middle finger.
dapá'	v.	/-um-/ to lie flat on one's chest.
		/ma-/ to fall unexpectedly; to stumble.
		/mag-:i-/ to lay someone flat on his stomach or chest.
dapa'	n.	rough scaled brill sole.
dápat	adj.	worthy; deserving; fit; apt; adequate; proper; necessary.
	p.v.	must; ought to; should. <u>Dapat gawin</u>... This ought to be done.
daplís	adj.	barely missing.
dapó'	v.	/-um-:-an/ to alight (as a bird, butterfly, etc.) on something.
dápo'	n.	orchid.
darák	n.	rice bran.
dasál	n.	prayer.
	v.	/mag-:-in, i-/ to say a prayer.
datapwa't	conj.	but; however. --syn. <u>ngunít</u>, <u>subalít</u> (usually with <u>t</u>) (coordinating particle used to express contrasts).

dáti	adj.	former; previous.
	adv.	for a long time already; formerly; it is sometimes closely joined.
datíng	n.	arrival; coming.
	v.	/-um-:-an/ to arrive. <u>Dinatnan niyang patay na ang tatay niya.</u> On his arrival, he found his father dead.
dátu	n.	ruling head of a clan or tribe.
daúngan	n.	port; wharf.
daw	prt.	it is said; so (somebody) said (expresses that the sentence represents the saying of someone other than the speaker. The person so quoted may be the agent of the sentence itself). --var. <u>raw</u> (after vowels). <u>Aalis ka raw.</u> You're leaving, (I'm told).
dáya'	v.	/mang-, mag-:-in/ to trick; to cheat; to deceive; to delude.
dayámi	n.	hay.
dáyap	n.	lime (native); lemon.
dayukdók	adj.	extremely hungry.
debáte (Sp)	n.	debate; dispute. --syn. <u>pagtatálo</u>.
dedál (Sp)	n.	thimble. --var. <u>didál</u>.
deláta (Sp)	n.	canned goods.
delegádo (Sp)	n.	delegate.
delegasyón (Sp)	n.	delegation.
delikádo (Sp)	adj.	fragile; delicate; weak.

delíryo (Sp) n.   delirium. --var. <u>diliryo</u>.

demánda (Sp) v.   /mag-:i-/ to bring a case to court; to accuse.

demokrásya (Sp) n. democracy.

demokrátiko (Sp) adj. democratic.

demónyo (Sp) n.   demon; devil. --syn. <u>diyáblo</u>.

            intj.   the deuce. --var. <u>dimónyo</u>.

dentísta (Sp) n.   dentist.

departaménto (Sp) n. department. --syn. <u>kágawarán</u>.

depósitó (Sp) n.   money deposited in a bank.

            v.   /mag-:i-/ to make a deposit in the bank; to store up.

deretso (Sp) n.   rights. --syn. <u>karapatán</u>.

            adj.   straight; direct. --syn. <u>tuwíd</u>, <u>direkto</u>.

despálko (Sp) v.   /-um-, mang-:-in/ to embezzle; to swindle.

desperádo/a (Sp) adj. desperate.

desgrásya (Sp) n.   misfortune. --syn. <u>sakuná'</u>, <u>aksidente</u>. Disgrace. --syn. <u>kahihiyán</u>, <u>kasiraáng-puri</u>. --var. <u>disgrasya</u>.

desmáyo (Sp) n.   swooning, fainting fit.

despalkadór (Sp) n. embezzler.

despatsádo (Sp) adj. dispatched; dismissed.

despatsadór (Sp) n. seller at the store counter; dispatcher.

despedída (Sp) n. farewell, leave-taking; party given for people leaving.

dí' adv. no, not (short for hindí').

diamante (Sp) n. diamond. --var. diyamante.

diarea (Sp) n. diarrhea (med). --syn. pagtataé. --var. diyarea.

diaryo (Sp) n. newspaper. --syn. peryodikó, páhayagán. --var. diyáryo.

dibdíb n. chest; breast.

dibersiyón (Sp) n. diversion; amusement. --syn. líbangan.

dibórsiyo (Sp) n. divorce.

dikdík v. /mag-:-in/ to pulverize.

dikín n. ring stand for pot.

dikít adj. /ma-/ dainty; pretty.

dikít v. /-um-/ to stick; to adhere; to get stuck.

  /mag-:i-/ to paste; to stick; to glue something.

díko (Ch) n. appellation to the second eldest brother by younger brothers, sisters, and cousins.

diksiyonáryo n. dictionary.

diktá v. /mag-:i-/ to dictate.

diktadór (Sp) n. dictator.

didál n. thimble. --var. dedal.

diés (Sp)   n.   ten. --syn. <u>sampú'</u>. Ten centavos. --var. <u>diyés</u>.

díga   v.   /-um-, mang-:-an/ to court by using idle talk. <u>Digáhan mo siya</u>. Court her.

digmá'   n.   war.

diín   adj.   /ma-/ heavily pressed.

    v.   /-um-:i-/ to press hard; to press downward.

diít   n.   slight pressure on something.

díla'   n.   tongue.

dilág   n.   gorgeousness, splendor; lustrous beauty. --syn. <u>gandá</u>.

dilát   n.   act of opening of the eyelids. --syn. <u>múlat</u>.

    adj.   (<u>dilát</u>) wide-open eyes; wide-eyed.

    v.   /-um-/ to open (as of the eyes). <u>Dumílat ka</u>. You open (your eyes).

        /i-/ to open one's eyes; to raise one's eyelids. <u>Idílat mo ang mga mata mo</u>. You open your eyes.

        /mang-:pang-, -an/ <u>Pinangdilátan niya ako</u>. She glared at me.

diláw   adj.   yellow. <u>Manilaw nilaro</u>. Yellowish.

dilíg   v.   /mag-:-in, -an/ to sprinkle water on; to water (plants).

dilihénsiya   v.   /mag-:-in/ to resort to borrowing; to obtain what one needs.

dilím   adj.   /ma-/ dark.

dilíryo (Sp)   var. of <u>deliryo</u>.

dílis	n.	long-jawed anchovy.
din	prt.	too, also (expresses that the expression modified which may be the whole sentence or an element within the sentence is like a corresponding earlier idea). --var. rin (after vowels). Ako rin ang nagpaligo sa bata'. It was I, too, that bathed the child.
dinamíta (Sp)	n.	dynamite.
díni	adv.	here. --syn. dito, rito.
diníg	adj.	heard; loud enough to be heard.
	v.	/-in/ (dinggín) to listen to. Dinggín mo ang aking pakiusap. Listen to my plea.
		/ma-/ to hear.
díngas	v.	/mag-/ to flare out; to set aflame.
dingdíng	n.	wall.
Dios (Sp)	n.	God. --syn. Bathalá', Maykapál. --var. Diyós.
dipá	n.	span of two extended arms.
diperénsiya (Sp) n.		difference. --syn. kaibahán, kaibhán. Indisposition, illness. --syn. sakít. Disagreement.
direksíyón (Sp) n.		address. --syn. tinítirhan, táhanan. Direction (towards), course. --syn. bandá, gawí. Order, command. --syn. utos. Instruction. --syn. túro.
direktór	n.	director.

dirétso	v.	/-in/ to proceed on in a straight direction.
díri	n.	/pang-/ (pandidíri) feeling of loathing for what is foul or filthy. --syn. pagkarimarim, pagkasuklám.
	adj.	/naka/ (nakapandídiri) loathsome.
diskubrí	v.	/naka-:ma-/ to discover.
diskurso (Sp)	n.	speech. --syn. talumpáti.
diskusyón (Sp)	n.	discussion.
disinteria (Sp)	n.	dysentery. --syn. íti.
disiplína (Sp)	n.	discipline.
disisyón (Sp)	n.	decision.
	v.	/mag-:-an/ to decide; to make a decision.
distrunká (Sp)	v.	/mag-:-in/ to break off; destroy; locks.
disturnilyadór	n.	screwdriver.
Disyémbre	n.	December.
díto	dem.	here. --var. dine.
	adv.	/na-/ (nárito) it's here. --var. nándito.
	v.	/pa-/ (paríto) come here. --var. paríne.
ditsé (Ch)	n./adj.	appellation for second eldest sister.
disyérto	n.	desert.

díto	dem.	here; in this place.
díwa'	n.	spirit; thought.
diwáta'	n.	goddess.
diyabétes (Sp)	n.	var. of diabetes.
diyáket	n.	jacket.
diyán	dem.	there.
	adv.	/na-/ (nárito) it's there. --var. nándiyan.
	v.	/pa-/ (pariyán) go there.
diyánitor (Eng)	n.	janitor.
diyés (Sp)	num.	ten.
diyéta (Sp)	n.	prescribed or regulated meal; diet.
Diyós	n.	God. --var. Diós.
dóble (Sp)	adj.	double.
doktór/a	n.	doctor; physician. --syn. manggagamot.
dominánte	adj.	dominant, domineering.
Domínggo (Sp)	n.	Sunday. --var. Dumínggo, Linggó.
dónya (Sp)	n.	madam. --syn. ginang.
doón	dem.	there, yonder; over there; that place over there.
	adv.	/na-/ (nároon) it's there, yonder. --var. nándoon.
	v.	/pa-/ (paroón) go there, yonder.

dormitóryo   n.   dormitory.

dormitoryána/o (Sp) n. female/male resident of a
                      dormitory.

dos (Sp)   num.   two.

dose   num.   twelve.

doséna   n./qnt   dozen.

dúke (Sp)   n.   duke.

dukésa (Sp)   n.   duchess.

dukhá'   adj.   poor; destitute.

dúkot   v.   /-um-:-in/ to draw out from a
                        pocket, a bag or a container
                        with the hand.

                        /mang-:-an/ to pickpocket.

dúda (Sp)   n.   doubt. --syn. alinlángan.

              v.   /mag-/ to doubt. Huag kang
                        magduda sa akin. Don't doubt me.

dugó'   n.   blood.

              v.   /-in/ to bleed profusely, as in
                        a hemorrhage.

                        /-um-, mag-/ to bleed, as a
                        wound.

dugtóng   v.   /-um-:-an/ to add.

                        /mag-:i-/ to append; to annex.

dúhat   n.   plum (Java); blackberries.

dulá'   n.   drama; stage play. --syn. dráma.

dúlang   n.   low dining table.

dulás	adj.	/ma-/ slippery.
duldól	v.	/i-/ to shove or thrust (something) with force into another, as pen into ink bottle, food into mouth, or like relation.
dulíng	adj.	cross-eyed.
dúlo	n.	end; terminal extremity.
dulós	n.	trowel.
dúlot	n.	offering. --syn. álay, handóg.
dumalága	n.	pullet; female carabao at the age of puberty.
dumí	adj.	/ma-/ (marumí) dirty; unclean; filthy.
dúnong	n.	knowledge; wisdom.
	adj.	/ma-/ intelligent; sage; erudite; bright; talented; wise. Marunong gumupit. Knows how to cut hair.
dúngaw	v.	/-um-/ to look out of the window.
		/-in/ to look out at somebody from the window.
dúngis	n.	dirt on face.
	adj.	/ma-/ dirty.
dungó'	adj.	shy; timid.
dúplo (Sp)	n.	poetical game or contest dramatically strung to a short narrative sequence.

dupók	adj.	/ma-/ weak (not durable); frail; fragile; brittle; delicate. --var. rupók.
durá'	n.	saliva; spit. --var. lura'.
	v.	/-um-/ to spit.
		/mang-:-an/ to spit at something.
duriyán	n.	durian.
dúro'	v.	/-um-:-in/ to pierce or to penetrate sharply as with a pointed instrument.
		/mag-:i-/ to pierce, prick, penetrate something with a pointed instrument.
		/mang-/ to pierce, prick somebody.
dúsa (Sk)	n.	/pa-/ punishment; castigation; suffering; grief. --syn. hirap, pagtitiis.
	v.	/mag-/ to suffer.
duséna (Sp)	n.	dozen. --var. doséna.
duwág	adj.	coward.
duwénde (Sp)	n.	elf; dwarf. --syn. tiának.
duwéto (Sp)	n.	duet.
dúyan	n.	cradle; hammock.
dyáryo (Sp)	n.	newspaper. --var. diáryo.
dyíp (Eng)	n.	jeep; jeepney.

E

ebaporasyón (Sp) n. evaporation.

eklípse (Sp) n.   eclipse.

ekonomiyá (Sp) n.   economy. --syn. pagtitipíd.

eksákto (Sp) adj.   exact.

eksámen/   n.   examination; test.
  iksámen (Sp)

eksibisiyón (Sp) n. exhibition.

eksperiménto (Sp) n. experiment. --var. esperiménto.

ékstra (Sp) adj.   extra. --syn. dagdág. --var.
                     estra.

ekwadór (Sp) n.   equator.

edád (Sp)   n.   age. --syn. gúlang.

edukádo (Sp) adj.   educated; trained; well-bred.

edukasyón (Sp) n.   education.

eh   part. hesitation pause (something more
                     coming); used to close a sentence
                     to reinforce disagreement, contra-
                     diction or protestation.

elebétor (Eng) n.   elevator.

eleksiyón (Sp) n.   election; voting. --syn. hálalan.

elektrisidád (Sp) n. electricity.

elektrisísta (Sp) n. electrician.

elegánte (Sp) adj.   elegant; stylish.

eleménto (Sp) n.   element.

elepánte (Sp) n.   elephant.

empáke (Sp) n.   packing; wrapping.   --var. impáke.

        v.   /mag-:in/ to pack. Empakihin
                        mo na ang dadalin mo. (Start)
                        packing what you will take with
                        you.

empanáda (Sp) n.   meat pie.

empátso (Sp) n.   indigestion.

emperdíble (Sp) n.   safety pin.

empleyádo/a (Sp) n.   employee.

Enéro (Sp) n.   January.   --var. Inéro.

ensaláda (Sp) n.   salad.

entabládo (Sp) n.   stage.

entráda (Sp) n.   entrance.   --syn. pasukán.

entréga (Sp) v.   /mag-:i-/   to deliver; to hand in.

eropláno (Sp) n.   airplane.

eskiníta (Sp) n.   street corner turning into an
                        alley. --var. iskinita.

eskóba (Sp) n.   large hand brush; whisk broom.
                        --var. iskoba.

eskólar (Sp) n.   scholar.

eskrîma (Sp) n.   the art of fencing.

eskuéla (Sp) n.   school.

eskuwelahán (Sp) n.   school. --syn páaralan.

eskulptor (Sp) n.   sculptor.

esmerálda (Sp) n.   emerald.

espáda (Sp) n.   sword; spade in playing cards.

Espanyól (Sp) n./adj. Spanish.

espesyál (Sp) adj.   special.

espíritu (Sp) n.   spirit; soul. --syn. káluluwá.

ęspiyá (Sp) v.   / mag-, mang-/ to spy on.

estasyón (Sp) n.   station; e.g. estasyón ng bus
                        (bus station). --var. istasyon.

estórbo (Sp) v.   /mang-:-in/ to disturb; to cause
                        trouble; to bother.

estrélya (Sp) n.   star. --syn. bituín.

estudyante (Sp) n.   student.

éto   dem.   here it is; a variant form of
                        héto.

Európa (Sp) n.   Europe.

éwan   p.v.   don't know; a variant of aywan;
                        ewan ko means 'I don't know.'

G

gaán	adj.	/ma-/ light (of weight); easy.
gaáno	int.	how much; what quantity.
gabáy	n.	hand rail; support.
gábi	n.	taro; sticky edible tuber.
gabí	n.	night; evening.
	adv.	/ka-/ last night.
gabí-gabí	adv.	every night; every evening.
gagambá	n.	spider.
gágo/a	adj.	stupid; foolish (collog); stuttering, stammering; pronouncing badly. --var. hangál, tangá.
gahása'	v.	/-in/ to rape. Ginahasa ng mga sanggano ang babai. The woman was raped by the gangsters.
gahól	adj.	lacking in time. --syn. hulí.
gála'	v.	/-um-/ to wander about; to go about idly; to travel aimlessly.
galák	v.	/ika-/ to be pleased; to be happy.
galante (Sp)	adj.	gallant; chivalrous. --syn. máginoó.
gálang	adj.	/ma-/ polite; courteous; refined in manner; respectful.
	v.	/-um-/ to respect; to treat with reverence.

110

galáw	v.	/-um-/ to move.
		/mang-:-in, i-/ to touch; to move.
galíng	adj.	/ma-/ good; well-already; fine; skillful; clever; polite. ...<u>magaling gumamit ng</u>... Juan was clever at using the...
gáling	v.	/mang-/ to come from; to originate from.
galís	n.	itch.
gálit	n.	anger; resentment; indignation.
	v.	/ma-/ to get angry; to become angry.
gambála'	n.	delaying disturbance.
	v.	/-um-/ to cause disturbance.
		/mang-:-in/ to disturb; to bother.
gámit	n.	personal things; anything usable.
	v.	/-in/ to wear; to use.
gamót	n.	medicine.
	v.	/-um-:-in/ to treat, especially with medicine.
		/mag-/ to treat one's self.
		/mang-:-in/ to treat others (outside of self).
gamu-gamó	n.	moth.
gána	n.	appetite.
gána	n.	profit.

ganáp	adj.	complete. --syn. buó'. Fulfilled. Completed, finished. --syn. yarí', tapós. Exact. --syn. eksakto, hustó.
ganáp	v.	/-um-/ to perform; act. Gumanap siyang pare sa pelikula. He performed the role of a priest in the film.
ganda	adj.	/ma-/ beautiful; pretty; nice.
ganirí	adv.	(fr. ga + nirí or gaya nirí) like this (referring to something close to the body of the speaker). --syn. ganitó.
ganít	n.	toughness for mastication; relative tightness or firmness (making it hard to disengage).
ganitó	adv.	(fr. ga + nitó or gaya nitó) like this one; in this way or manner. --syn. ganirí.
ganiyán	adv.	(fr. ga + niyán or gaya niyán) like that one (referring to something near the person spoken to); in the same way or manner as that (referring to procedure being observed). --var. ganyán.
ganoón	adv.	(fr. ga + noon) like that yonder; in that manner or way.
gansá'	n.	goose.
gantí (Mal)	n.	recompense; repayment.
	v.	/-um-:-an/ to repay.
gantimpála'	n.	reward; prize.
gápang	v.	/-um-/ to crawl; to creep.
		/mang-:-in/ to get or obtain something.

gápas	v.	/mag-:-in/ to cut or mow (grass, rice stalk, or the like) with a scythe.
gápos	n.	manacle; rope tied around arms or hands.
	adj.	manacled.
	v.	/mag-:i-/ to tie up securely, usually by the arms.
		/mang-/ to tie up.
gára'	adj.	/ma-/ nicely dressed.
garáhe	n.	garage.
garapinyéra (Sp)	n.	ice cream freezer.
garapón (Sp)	n.	large wide-mouthed bottle or decanter.
garbánsos	n.	chickpeas.
gasgás	adj.	worn out (by friction); worn out (by use). --syn. gastádo.
gasláw	adj.	/ma-/ gauche; crude flirtatiousness.
gaspáng	adj.	/ma-/ rough, coarse.
gasolína (Sp)	n.	gasoline.
gastádo (Sp)	adj.	worn-out by much use. --syn. gasgás, gamít.
gástos	n.	expenses.
gastadór	n.	spend thrift.
gastá	v.	/-um-, mag-:-in/ to spend; to expend.

gatá'	n.	coconut milk, cream.
gátang	n.	chupa: a unit of measure for rice or other grains; dry measure.
gátas	n.	milk.
gáto	n.	jack.
gátong	n.	firewood; fuel.
	v.	/mag-:i-/ to feed with fuel; to put into the fire as fuel.
gawá'	v.	/-um-, mag-:-in/ to do; to make; to work; to build.
gáwad	n.	award; bestowal; grant; prize. --syn. gantimpála', prémyo.
gawgáw	n.	starch; cornstarch.
gawí'	n.	side; direction.
	v.	/-um-/ to go or move in a certain direction; to be inclined to or accustomed to.
gáya	n.	imitation.
	adv.	like; resembling; in the manner of. Hindi gaya ng bola (unlike the ball). Ay gaya ng (is like...).
	v.	/-um-:-in/ to imitate; to emulate.
		/mang-:-in/
gayák	v.	/mag-:-an, i-/ to decorate; to festoon.
gayón	pro.	(fr. ga + yaón) something like that.
	adv.	in that way or manner. --var. ganoón.

gayón		also; furthermore (always followed by <u>din</u>). <u>Siya' y isang taong may kaunting talino at gayon din may kaunting tapang</u>. He is a man of some cleverness and also of some courage.
gayúma	n.	love charm.
gibá'	v.	/mag-:-in/ to destroy; to demolish; to ruin.
gígi'	adj.	/ma-/ slow; fussy; meticulous.
géra (Sp)	n.	war. --syn. <u>digmá'</u>,<u>digmáan</u>.
gerílya (Sp)	n.	guerilla (man).
giít	v.	/-um-/ to intrude; to push one's way through.
		/mag-:i-/ to insist.
gilágid	n.	gums.
gílid	n.	border; edge; margin.
	adj.	edge; margin; border.
	adv.	<u>sa gilid</u> at the edge.
gilingán	n.	mill; grinder.
gíling	v.	/-um-/ to grind.
		/mag-:-in/ to grind something.
gilít	n.	incision; cut; incision or slice marks (on fish or wood); sliced piece.
gíliw	n.	love; affection.
	adj.	/ma-/ beloved; dear; esteemed.
ginang	n./adj.	Mrs.; matron; madam; abbr. <u>Gng</u>.

gináw	n.	cold; coldness; freezing temperature.
	adj.	/ma-/ cold; chilly; freezing.
	v.	/-in/ to become cold.
		/ma-/ to feel cold.
ginháwa	adj.	/ma-/ comfortable; easy.
ginóo	n.	mister.
	adj.	/ma-/ gentlemanly; well-bred man.
gintó'	n.	gold.
gipît	adj.	wanting or lacking in space. --syn. makípot. In straits; bankrupt.
gisá	v.	/mag-:-in, i-/ to sauté; to cook in oil, garlic, onions and or tomatoes.
gisantes	n.	peas.
gisîng	adj.	awake.
	v.	/-um-/ to wake up; to awaken.
		/mang-:-in/ to rouse someone.
gitára	n.	guitar.
gîting	adj.	courageous; heroic.
gitlîng	n.	hyphen.
gitná'	n.	middle.
	adv.	middle; center.
gobernadór	n.	governor.
gobiyérno	n.	government.

góma	n.	rubber. --var. ráber.
góra (Sp)	n.	cap.
góto	n.	tripe.
grádo	n.	degree.
grípo	n.	faucet.
grábe (Sp)	adj.	grave; weighty. --syn. malubha', mabigát.
grátis (Sp)	adj.	free; gratis; for nothing. --syn. waláng-bayad.
guántes (Sp)	n.	gloves. --syn guwantes.
gúbat	n.	forest; jungle.
gugó'	n.	native shampoo.
gúgol	v.	/-um-:-in/ to spend; to appro- priate.
		/mag-:i-, -in/ to spend; to appropriate (something).
gúhit	n.	line.
guhit	n.	a measure of weight equal to 100 grams.
guhó'	n.	/pag-/ collapse; cave-in; crumbling.
gulaman	n.	gelatin (native, made from sea- weed).
gulanît	adj.	ragged; worn-out.
gúlang	n.	age.
	adj.	/ma-/ shrewd; mature.
	v.	/-an/ to take advantage of some- one who has not had much experience yet.

gúlat	n.	shock.
	v.	/mang-:-in/ to frighten; to surprise; to shock someone.
gúlay	n.	vegetables.
guló	n.	riot; trouble; disorder; confusion.
	adj.	/ma-/ unruly; rowdy; disorderly.
	v.	/mang-:-in/ to create disorder, tumult or confusion.
gúlok	n.	bolo; large knife; machete.
gulód	n.	hill top.
gulóng	n.	wheel.
	v.	/-um-/ to roll.
		/mag-:i-/ to roll something.
gumaméla	n.	hibiscus.
gúnaw	n.	end of the world; destruction of all things; deluge.
guníguní	n.	imagination; apprehension; presentiment.
guntíng	n.	scissors.
gung góng	adj.	stupid; ignorant.
gupít	n.	haircut.
	v.	/-um-, mag-:-in/ to cut with a pair of scissors or shears; to trim.
guro'	n.	teacher; tutor. --syn. mestro/a, titser.
gusáli'	n.	building.

gusgós   adj.   /-in/ untidy; in rags; in tatters.

gusót   adj.   crumpled; entangled; confused.

gustó   p.v.   want; like. --syn. ibig.

            v.   /-um-:-in/ to like; to want; to
                    desire.

gutáy   adj.   torn into pieces.

gútom   v.   /ma-/ to (get) hungry.

guwápo/a   adj.   handsome; beautiful; good-looking;
                    pretty; dashing.

guwárdiya (Sp) n.   guard. --syn. bantáy, tánod.

guyabáno   n.   (guayabano) soursop.

ha?   interrogative particle meaning:
       What is it? or What do you mean?
       --syn. anó?, ano kamó? Ha?
       What's that again? Interrogative
       particle meaning: Do you under-
       stand? --syn. náiintindihán mo
       ba? Náuunawaan mo ba? Alam
       mo na ba, ha? Do you understand?
       Exclamatory interrogative particle
       with the element of surprise or
       reproach: Is that so? --syn.
       Ganoón ba? Siyangá ba? Ganoon
       pala, ha? So that's what it is,
       huh?

há!   intj.   (deprecatingly) So!; (reproaching-
               ly) So, that's it!; particle re-
               producing laughter (in series)
               Ha! Ha! Ha!

hába' n.   a length.

       adj.   /ma-/ long; elongated.

habág adj.   /ma-:-in/ kind-hearted; charitable.

habágat n.   a west or southwest wind; monsoon.

habang conj   (rw. hába) throughout; during;
               while. --syn. samantálang.
               Habang siya'y natutulog... While
               he was sleeping...

habang-búhay adv. for a lifetime; eternal.

habílin n.   (rw. bílin) something (as money,
               property, etc.) given in trust
               or for safekeeping.

hábol v.   /-um:-in/ to catch up with; to
               appeal; to run after.

               /mang-:-in/ to run after some-
               body.

120

habonéra (Sp)	n.	soap box or tray. --syn. sabunan. --var. <u>habunera</u>.
hakáb	adj.	tight-fitting.
hakbáng	n.	step; space of stepping; pace in walking or running.
hákot (Mal)	n.	load; loading (in quantity). --syn. <u>dalá</u>, <u>kargá</u>.
	v.	/-um-:-in/ <u>Hakutin mo ang mada dala mo</u>. Take what you can carry.
hadláng	v.	/-um-/ to stand on the way; to obstruct. <u>Humadlang si Pedro sa aking daan.</u> Pedro obstructed/ blocked my way.
		/mag-:i-/ to place an impediment; to obstruct; to bar.
hagdán	n.	stairs; stairway; steps; ladder. --var. <u>hagdánan</u>.
hagibís	n.	rapidity; velocity. --syn. <u>bilís</u>, <u>túlin</u>.
hagílap	v.	/-um-/ to search; to gather.
		/mag-:-in/ to try to get hold of something at the time of need around one's environment. <u>Mag-hagilap ka ng panggatong</u>. Gather firewood.
		/mang-:-in/ <u>Manghagilap ka ng makatutulong sa atin.</u> Look for someone who can help us.
háging	n.	buzzing sound as of something speeding by.

hagíp	v.	/maka-:-ma/ hit or caught by a moving body. <u>Nahagip siya ng kotse.</u> The car hit him.
hágis	v.	to hurl at; to cast something at.
		/-um-/ to be thrown off. <u>Humagis ang bata sa kotse.</u> The child was thrown off the car.
		/mag-:i-/ to throw; to cast. <u>Ihagis mo ang bola kay Pepe.</u> Throw the ball to Pepe.
hágod	n.	rubbing; massaging.
hagulhól	n.	sudden; loud weeping.
hagupít	n.	stroke of whip or lash.
háin	v.	/mag-:i-/ to set the table; to serve; to offer. <u>Iháin mo na adobong manok.</u> Serve the children adobo.
halá!	intj.	a warning: if you do that, there will be consequences!
halaán	n.	clam.
halabós	n.	scalding or half cooking in salted water.
halakhák	n.	loud laughter.
halagá	n.	price; value; importance.
	adj.	/ma-/ important; valuable.
halaghág	adj.	careless; neglectful. --syn. <u>pabayá'</u>, <u>bulagsák</u>.

| halál | v. | /mag-:i-/ to nominate; to elect. Ihalál natin ang mabuting kandidato. Let's elect the good candidate. |

| hálalan | n. | election; voting. --syn. eleksiyon. |

| haláman | n. | plant; garden; vegetation. |

| halamanan | n. | garden. --syn. hardin. |

| haláng | adj. | /pa-/ horizontal; traverse; lying across. |

| hálang | v. | /-um-/ to barricade; to use one's self as an obstruction. Humalang si Elsa sa aking balak. Elsa obstructed my plans. |

/mag-:i-/ to lay across; to put crosswise as an impediment. Inihálang niya ang mga bato sa kalye. They obstructed the road with stones.

| halatá' | adj. | noticeable; conspicuous. |

| hálay | adj. | /ma-/ depraved; lewd, sensual. |

| halík | n. | kiss. |

| | v. | /-um-/ to kiss. Humalik ang bata sa ina. The child kissed his mother. |

/mang-:-an/ to kiss somebody, something. Halikan mo ang kamay ng lola mo. Kiss the hand of your grandmother.

| halíka | v. | (You) come here. |

| halígi | n. | post. --var. poste. |

halíli	v.	/-um-/ to substitute; to replace. Humalíli ako sa kanya. I took his place.

/mag-:-an/ to change something. Hahalinhan mo ang kuya mo sa pagbabantay ng bahay. You will take turns with your older brother in watching the house. |
halimáw	n.	beast; monster.
halimbáwa'	n.	example; model; for example; for instance.
halimúyak	n.	fragrance; scent. --syn. bangó.
halîna	n.	fascination. --syn. gayúma.
	v.	come along. Halina (kayo). Let's go. Come here. Halika. (You) come here.
haliparót	adj.	vulgar; coquette; coarse.
hálo'	v.	/-um-/ to mix. Humálo siya sa aming biruan. He joined in our kidding around.

/mag-:-in, i-/ to stir; to add as another ingredient. Halúin mo ang aking niluluto. Stir what I am cooking. |
halo-halo	n.	a kind of dessert made of sweetened fruits and crushed ice.
hálos	adv.	almost. Halos lahat ng tao. Almost all people.
hálu	v.	/-in/ (halúin) to stir.
halúkay	v.	/mag-:-in/ to dig; to turn over and back either in search of something or to mix well. Hinalúkay

ni Maria ang aking mga kagamitan.
Maria rummaged through my things.

halukipkíp   adj.   /naka-/ with forearms crossed close to body below the chest.

halughóg   v.   /mag-:-in/ to search or examine minutely; to search every corner of a place thoroughly. Hinalughóg ng mga pulis ang bahay ni Berto. The policemen searched Berto's house.

halumigmíg   n.   moisture; humidity; condensation.

           adj.   humid.

halungkát   v.   /mag-:-in/ to turn over a pile of things in search for something; to search carefully among a number of things. Hinalungkát niya ang aking mga damit. He went through my clothes.

hámak   adj.   abject, lowly, contemptible; of small account, vile; insignificant.

hambálos   n.   flogging with a cudgel or club.

hambíng   v.   /mag-:i-/ to compare; to place side by side in companion. Ihambíng mo ang iyong ginawa sa gawa ni Jose. Compare your work with Jose's.

hambóg   adj.   /mag-/ proud; overbearing; boastful; arrogant.

hámo   (short form of Hayáan mo) don't mind it or don't worry about it.

hamóg   n.   dew.

hamón   n.   ham.

hámon	v.	/mang-:-in/ to challenge; to look for a competitor. <u>Hinámon niya sa boksing si Rene.</u> He challenged Rene to a bout (boxing).
hampás	v.	/-um-/ to slam against something. <u>Humampas ang ulo niya sa dingding.</u> His head hit the wall.
		/mang-:-in/ to strike something; to scourge.
hampaslúpa'	n.	vagabond; bum; tramp; good for nothing.
hánap	v.	/-um-:-in/ to look for; to search for (something).
hanapbúhay	n.	occupation, livelihood; means of earning a living.
hánay	n.	row; file.
	v.	/-um-/ to stay in line or in a row.
		/mag-:i-/ to place or put in line or in a successive order.
handá	adj.	ready; prepared.
	v.	/-um-/ to get ready; to be prepared.
		/mag-:i-/ to get something ready or to set something; to prepare something.
handóg	n.	offering; gift; present.
	v.	/mag-:i-:-an/ to offer; to dedicate.
handusáy	adj.	prostrate; fallen flat.
hánip	n.	chicken flea.

hantád	adj.	exposed. --syn. <u>lantád</u>.
hantóng	v.	/-um-/ to end up in; to stop; to terminate.
hánga'	n.	/pag-/ (<u>paghangá</u>) admiration; amazement; astonishment.
hangád	n.	desire; interest; intent.
hangál	adj.	stupid; idiotic; fool. --syn. <u>tangá</u>, <u>gunggóng</u>, <u>mangmáng</u>.
hanggá	n.	/-an/ (<u>hanggáhan</u>) result. --syn. <u>búnga</u>, <u>dúlo</u>, <u>resultádo</u>.
hangganan	n.	boundary; limit.
hanggáng	conj.	till; until; as far as.
	prep.	up to.
hángin	n.	air; wind.
	adj.	/ma-/ windy.
hángo'	v.	/-um-/ to appropriate a certain amount of goods.
		/mag-:-in/ to remove something being cooked from the fire; to adapt from literary material; to save someone from something. <u>Hanguin mo siya sa hirap</u>. Help him out (of his difficulties).
hángos	v.	/-um-/ breathless.
hapág	n.	(<u>kainán</u>) dining table. --var. <u>mesa</u>.
hapdí'	adj.	/ma-/ smarting.
hápis	adj.	sad; gloomy; grievous.
hapó'	adj.	tired; exhausted; fatigued.

hápon	n.	afternoon.
	adv.	/ka-/ yesterday.
Hapón	n.	Japanese.
hap-slip	n.	half-slip.
hapúnan	n.	dinner; supper; evening meal.
	v.	/mag-/ to have dinner.
harána	n.	serenade.
	v.	/mag-, mang-:-in/ to serenade.
hárang	v.	/-um-/ to block; to bar; to stand in the way. Humarang siya sa kalye. He blocked the road.
		/mag-:i-/ to put a block or a hindrance; to bar with something. Magharang ka ng kahoy sa pinto. Bar the door with a piece of wood.
		/mang-:-in/ to rob; to stop; to block. Nanghaharang siya ng mga tao. He robs people.
haráp	n.	front.
	adv.	sa harap. In front of, before (the class).
	v.	/mag-:-um/ to face.
hardín	n.	garden. --syn. hálamanán.
hardinero	n.	gardener.
hári'	n.	king.
harîna	n.	flour.
harót	adj.	/ma-/ unladylike; coarse; unrefined; boisterous.

hása' v. /mag-:i-, -in/ to sharpen.
Ihása mo ang kutsilyo. Sharpen
the knife.

hasmín n. jasmine.

hátak n. /pag-/ towing. --syn. batak, hila.

v. /-um-:-in/ to pull. Humatak ka
sa lubid. Pull the rope.

/mang-:-in/ Manghatak ka ng
kahit sino. Pull anyone.

háti' v. /-um-/ to share; to take a part
of.

/mag-:-in/ to apportion into
two; to divide.

hatíd v. /mag-:i-/ to conduct; to escort;
to accompany.

hátinggabi adv. late; midnight.

hátol v. /mag-:i-/ to judge; to give a
sentence or decision.

/mang-:-an/ to judge.

háula n. cage. --var. hawla.

háwa n. infection.

adj. (nakahahawa) contagious.

v. /mang-:-in/ to infect; to conta-
minate another; to stain.

háwak v. /-um-:-an/ to hold in hand; to
grasp.

/mag-/ to hold each other by the
hand.

hawás	adj.	well-proportioned (figure); oval (face).
háwig	adj.	similar; resembled.
hayán!	intj.	(fr. ha + iyan) there! There it is!
háyop	n.	animal.
hayún!	intj.	(fr. ha + iyón) Look there! There it is, yonder.
héko (Ch)	n.	dark sauce from salted shrimps.
helikópter	n.	helicopter.
henéral/a	n.	general.
hépe	n.	boss; chief; head.
héto	intj.	(fr. ha + ito) here it is. --var. eto.
híbi	n.	dried shrimp.
hibík	n.	pleading; supplication.
híka'	n.	asthma.
hikáb	v.	/-um-, mag-/ to yawn. --var. higáb.
hikahós	adj.	needy; broke; bankrupt.
híkaw	n.	earrings.
hikáyat	n.	persuasion.
hikbí'	n.	sob.
higá'	v.	/-um-/ to lie down.
		/mag-:i-/ to lay down something.
hígad	n.	caterpillar.

higánte (Sp) n.   giant.

higít   adv.   more; excessive; over.

hígop   v.   /-um-:-in/ to sigh.

higpít   adj.   /ma-/ tight; strict.

             v.   /-um-/ to become tight.

                       /mag-:-an/ to tighten.

híhip   n.   blowing (as of wind from mouth).

             v.   /-um-/ to blow (as of the wind
                       or from the mouth). --var. íhip.
                       Humihip ang hangin. The wind
                       blew.

                       /-an/ (hípan) to blow on some-
                       thing. Hipan mo ang apoy.
                       Blow at the fire.

híla   v.   /-um-/ to pull.

                       /mang-:-in/ to pull something.

hilága'   n.   north.

hilámos   v.   /mag-:-an/ to wash one's face.

hilát   adj.   stretched; pulled.

hilatsá (Sp) n.   thread unravelled from cloth.

hiláw   adj.   /-an/ raw (food); green; unripe;
                       uncooked; undercooked.

hilbána (Sp) n.   basting (sewing).

hiléra   n.   row; file.

hilík   v.   /-um-/ to snore. Humihilik siya
                       pag tulog. He snores while sleep-
                       ing.

hílig (Mal)	n.	inclination; leaning position; propensity; tendency.
	adj.	/ma-/ having the inclination or tendency to.
hilíng	v.	/-um-:-in/ to request.
hiló	adj.	dizzy.
	v.	/ma-/ to become dizzy; to become confused.
hílod	v.	/mag-:-in/ to scrub the skin to remove dirt.
hílot	n.	midwife.
himágas	n.	dessert.
himagsík	v.	/mag-/ to rebel; to revolt.
himalá'	n.	miracle.
	v.	/mag-/ to perform a miracle. <u>Naghimalá' ang Virhen</u>. The Virgin performed a miracle.
hímas	n.	gentle rubbing on skin by the palm of the hand; caressful rubbing; petting by rubbing the back of fighting roosters.
himások	n.	interference; meddling.
	v.	/mang-/ to meddle in (something one is not concerned about). <u>Huwag kang manghimasok sa buhay ng may buhay</u>. Don't meddle with the lives of others.
himatay	v.	/-in/ to faint; to pass out; to become unconscious.
himaymáy	n.	fiber.

himbíng (Ch)	n.	deep slumber.
himpapawíd	n.	atmospheric space.
himpíl	n.	stopping to rest or stay; station; headquarters.
himulmól	n.	plucking of feathers from fowls or birds, or of hair from animals.
humutók	n.	outcry of disappointment or distress; whimper.
hína'	adj.	/ma-/ weak; lack of strength.
	v.	/-um-/ to become weak.
		/mang-/ to feel weak.
hinagpís	n.	doleful sigh; plaint.
hínang	v.	/mag-:-in/ to solder; to weld.
hináhon	adj.	/ma-/ self-controlled; calm.
	v.	/-um-/ to be calm.
hinála'	n.	suspicion.
	v.	/mag-:-in/ to suspect; to presume.
hinanakit	n.	grudge; ill feeling.
hináyang	n.	(rw. sáyang) feeling of regret for not having utilized something or not having taken advantage of a situation.
		/pang-/ (panghihináyang) regret.
hindi'	adv.	no; not; negative particle.
		(+ ba) tag question roughly equivalent to 'isn't it', 'aren't they', 'did he' etc.

hinéte (Sp) n.   jockey; horseman.

hinhîn   adj.   /ma-/ modest; refined.

hiningá   n.   breath.

hinlalakî   n.   thumb.

hinlaláto   n.   middle finger or toe.

hinóg   adj.   ripe (particularly of fruits); mature.

             v.   /ma-/ to be ripe.

hintay   v.   /mag-:-in/ to wait; to wait for.

hintó   v.   /-um-/ to stop; to come to a halt.

                   /mag-:i-/ to stop something.

hintutúro'   n.   index finger.

hingá   v.   /-um-/ to breathe; to exhale. <u>Hu'minga siya ng malalim</u>. He took a deep breath.

                   /mag-:i-/ to expose; to bring out. <u>Maghinga ka ng sama ng loob mo</u>. Let off (a little) steam/pour out your ill feelings.

                   /magpa-/ to rest; to take a rest.

hîngal   v.   /-um-/ to pant; to gasp.

hingaló'   v.   /mag-/ to be in a state of dying.

hingî'   v.   /-um-:-in/ to ask for.

                   /mang-:-in/ to ask for (repetitively).

hípag	n.	sister-in-law (term of reference).
hípo'	n.	touch.
hípon	n.	shrimp.
hirám	v.	/-um-:-in/ to borrow; to ask for a loan.
		/mang-:-in/ to borrow; to ask for a loan (repetitively).
hírang	n.	choice, selection; the chosen one (usually a lover or sweetheart), darling. --syn. irog, mahál.
	v.	/-in/ to appoint to a position. Hinirang siyang bise-presidente. He was appointed vice-president.
hírap	adj.	/ma-/ poor; difficult; hard; destitute.
	v.	/-um-/ to become difficult. Umirap ang buhay. Life became (more) difficult.
		/ma-/ to be hard, difficult. Mahirap migiwi ng bata. It's hard to take care of children.
hírin	n.	choking (by a lump in the throat).
híta'	n.	thigh.
hitá'.	n.	contrary and unsatisfactory consequence obtained from a goodwill act but uncalled for or uninvited.
	v.	/ma-/ to obtain an unsatisfactory or frustrating reward for a voluntary effort done in good-will.

hitít	n.	smoking of cigars or cigarettes.
	v.	/-um-/ to smoke. <u>Humihitit siya ng tabako.</u> He smokes cigars.
híto'	n.	fresh water catfish.
hitsó	n.	betel nut leaf with lime and betel nut for chewing.
hitsúra	n.	form; aspect.
híwa'	n.	a slice.
	v.	/-um-, mag-:-in/ to cut with a blade or knife; to slice.
		/mang-:-in/ to cut deliberately with a blade or knife.
hiwága'	n.	mystery.
	adj.	/ma-/ wonderful; mysterious.
hiwaláy	v.	/-um-/ to separate from. <u>Humiwalay ka sa kaniya.</u> Leave him (go your own way).
		/mag-:i-/ to sort out; to set apart. <u>Maghiwalay ka ng pagkain para sa tatay.</u> Set aside some food for your father.
hiwás	adj.	slant; oblique; diagonal.
híya	adj.	/ma-in/ shy; bashful.
hiyáng	adj.	suited; compatible; agreeing (as medicine, food, company, etc.).
hiyás	n.	jewels; gems.
hiyáw	v.	/-um-/ to yell; to shout.
ho'	part.	colloquial form of <u>po'</u>.

hoy   intj. hey! an exclamation of warning
             or calling attention.

hubád   adj. naked; undressed from the waist
             up; not in possession of.

       v.   /mag-:-in/ to undress; to have
             nothing on from the waist up.
             Naghubad siya dahil sa init.
             He undressed because of the heat.
             Hubarin mo ang kamiseta mo.
             Take off your undershirt.

hubó'   adj. nude; undressed from the waist
             down.

       v.   /mag-:-in/ to take off the pants;
             to undress from the waist down.

húbog   adj. curves (figure).

húkay   v.   /-um-, mag-:-in/ to dig, excavate.
             Humukay siya ng butas. He dug a
             hole.

hukbó'   n.   army.

hukóm   n.   judge.

hukót   adj. bent; stoop-shouldered.

húdas (Sp) adj. traitor. --syn. taksil.

hudyát   n.   sign; password.

Hudyó (Sp) n./adj. Jew; Jewish; wily.

húgas   v.   /mag-:-an/ to wash. Maghugas
             ka ng plato. Wash the plate.

hugasán n.   sink.

húgis   n.   shape.

húgot   v.   /-um-/ to pull out; to draw.
Humugot siya ng damit sa aparador.
She pulled out a dress from the
cabinet.

/mang-:-in/ to pull out. Huwag
kang manghugot ng di mo ari.
Don't pull out what's not yours.

húla'   v.   /mang-:-an/ to predict; to guess;
to tell one's fortune. Nanghuhula
siya sa baraha. He tells fortunes
from cards.

hulí   adj.   late; tardy; last.

    v.   /ma-/ to be late or tardy.

húli   v.   /-um-/ to catch; to arrest; to
apprehend.

/mang-:-in/ to catch someone; to
chase after someone. Nanghuli
siya ng masasamang tao. He
caught bad people.

huling habílin   n.   last will of a dying person.

húlog   v.   /ma-/ to fall; to drop. Nahulog
siya sa kama. He fell from the
bed.

/mag-:i-/ to drop; to fail, as
in an examination; to pay in
installment; to deposit (money).
Maghulog ka ng pera sa bangko.
Deposit money in the bank.

Húlyo   n.   July.

humingí'   v.   to ask for; to request.

humpák   adj.   hollow; sunken; depressed.

húni   n.   chirping or hooting of birds or
fowls.

Húnyo	n.	June.
hurnó	n.	oven.
húsay	adj.	/ma-/ able; skillful; in good shape; orderly; well-arranged.
husgádo (Sp) n.		court of justice. --syn. hukúman.
hustó	adj.	sufficient; enough; fit; adequate. --syn. sapát.
huwád	adj.	counterfeit; forged; fake; false.
huwág	adv.	don't; negative command. --var. hwág.
Huwébes	n.	Thursday.
huwés	n.	judge.
huwéteng (Ch) n.		a number pairing game.

I

ibá	pro.	other; others; another.
	adj.	another; other; different; unlike.
	v.	/-um-, mag-:-in/ to switch; to change.
ibabá'	n.	lower part of the house, the basement.
ibábaw	n.	upper crust or surface; top; tip.
	adv.	(sa ibabaw) over; above; on top.
ibáyo	n.	opposite.
ibáyo	adj.	/mag-/ double; excessive; too much.
íbig	p.v.	want; like; wish; desire. --syn. gusto. Ibig niyang kumain ng suha. It is desired by him that be eaten (by him) the grapefruit. (He wants to eat the grapefruit).
	v.	/-um-, mang-:-in/ to want; to like; to desire; to wish; to love.
íbon	n.	bird.
ika-		a prefix used to show sequence, order; ika-apat (fourth).
ikatlo	num.	third; derived from ika-tatlo.
ikáw	pro.	you (singular); usually occurs initially in sentences.
íkit	v.	/-um-/ to turn around; to turn inward; to rotate.
		/mag-:-in, i/ to wind.

140

iklí   adj.   /ma-/   short.

ikmó   betel leaf.

íkot   v.   /-um-/ to turn around; to turn outward; to revolve. <u>Umikot siya sa buong bahay.</u> She went around the house.

                   /mag-:-i/ to turn around or to take around. <u>Iikot mo siya sa buong bayan.</u> Take him all around town.

iksámin (Sp) v.   /-um-/ to take an examination or a test. <u>Umiksamin siya kahapon.</u> He took a test yesterday.

                   /mag-:-in/ to examine. <u>Nagiksamin ako ng kanyang mga binili.</u> I examined the things he bought.

iksí'   adj.   /ma-/ short.

idlíp   n.   nap.

ígat   n.   eel.

igkás   v.   /-um-/ to spring suddenly; to be discharged; to let loose suddenly.

ígi   adj.   /ma-/ well; all right.

igíb   v.   /-um-, mag-:-in/ to fetch water; to carry water to a place.

igláp   n.   very brief moment. --syn. <u>saglít</u>, <u>sandalí'</u>.

ignoránte (Sp) adj. ignorant. --syn. <u>mangmáng</u>, <u>hangál</u>, <u>maáng</u>, <u>tangá</u>.

Igoróte (Sp) n./adj. Igorot. --var. <u>Igurót</u>.

íhaw	v.	/mag-:-in, i/ to broil; to roast.
íhi'	n.	urine.
	v.	/-um-/ to urinate.
ihít	n.	fit; convulsion (of laughter, anger or weeping).
ílag	v.	/-um-/ to avoid; to dodge; to keep off; to shun. Umilag ako sa bola. I dodged the ball.
		/mang-/ to be cautious; to be wary; to keep away from. Mangilag ka sa mga masamang tao. Avoid the undesirable people (avoid undesirable people).
ilálim	n.	bottom; space below or underneath.
	adv.	used with sa.
ilán	pron.	some; several; a few.
ilan	int.	how many?
iláp	adj.	/ma-/ not tame; wild.
ílaw	n.	light; lamp.
ilíng	n.	shaking of the head in denial or disapproval.
Ilokano/a	n.	a person from the Ilocos region.
ílog	n.	river.
ilóng	n.	nose.
imbák	v.	/mag-:-in, i-/ to hoard; to store away; to conserve.
imbénto	v.	/mag-:-in, um-/ to invent; to create.

imbestigasyón (Sp) n. investigation.

imbî   adj.   despicable; adject; mean.

imbitá   v.   /mag-:-in/ to invite (someone).

imbitasyón (Sp) n. invitation. --syn. anyáya, kumbidá.

imík   v.   /-um-/ to break the silence;
                        to talk; to answer or reply.

imigrasyón (Sp) n.   immigration.

imitasyón (Sp) n.   imitation.

impake   v.   /mag-:-in/ to pack.

impeksiyón (Sp) n.   infection.

impît   adj.   /mag-/ repressed; curbed.

impluénsa (Sp) n.   influenza. --syn. trangkáso.

impó (Ch)   n.   grandmother. --syn. lóla.

            adj.   /-ng/ a title for an old woman
                        used with a given name.

impók   v.   /mag-:-in/ to save, usually
                        money.

impormál (Sp) adj. informal.

imposíble   adj.   impossible.

iná   n.   mother. --syn. ináy, ináng,
                        nanáng.

inaanák   n.   godchild (term of reference).

inákay   n.   young of fowls.

inahîn   n.   egg-laying hen.

ínam	adj.	/ma-/ pleasant; tasty; good; exquisite; delicate.
ináng	n.	appellation for iná, mother, mamma. --syn. ináy, nánang.
inát	v.	/mag-/ to stretch (oneself).
ináy	n.	mama; mother.
indák	v.	/-um-/ to dance in time with the music.

indulhénsiya (Sp) n. indulgence (religion).

inhinyéro n. engineer.

iníp	v.	/ma-/ to be bored; to be impatient.
inís	v.	/ma-/ to be annoyed; to be disgusted; to be exasperated. Nainis siya sa akin. She's annoyed with me.
		/mang-:-in/ to vex; to annoy; to provoke; to exasperate. Huwag kang manginis ng kapwa. Don't annoy your fellowmen.
ínit	n.	heat; warmth; humidity.
	adj.	/ma-/ hot; warm; humid.
	v.	/mag-:-in/ to heat (something).

ínit (ang úlo) adj. /ma-/ short-tempered.

inóm	n.	drinks; beverage.
	v.	/-um-:-in/ to drink (something); to take as of medicine.
		/mag-:-an/ to have a drinking spree.

insúlto	v.	/ma-/ to be insulted.
		/mang-:-in/ to insult; to embarrass.
intindí	v.	/-um-/ to understand; to comprehend. <u>Hindi siya marunong umintindi</u>. He cannot comprehend.
		/mag-:-in/ to take care of; to look after; to attend to. <u>Intindihin mo ang mga kapatid mo</u>. Attend to your brothers (or sisters).
Intsik	n.	Chinese.
inútil	adj.	useless; worthless.
inyon	pron.	you; yours (plural).
îngat	adj.	/ma-/ cautious; careful.
	v.	/mag-:-in/ to take care of; to safeguard; to exercise care.
îngay	n.	noise; sound.
	adj.	/ma-/ noisy.
	v.	/-um-/ to become noisy. <u>Umingay ang kuwarto</u>. The room became noisy.
		/mag-/ to create noise. <u>Nagingay sila sa kalye</u>. They made a lot of noise in the street.
ingkantádo	adj.	enchanted.
ingkong	n./adj.	a title for an old man used with or without a given name; a reference to an old man; grandfather.

inggít   v.   /ma-/   to become envious; to begrudge. <u>Nainggit siya sa akin.</u> She was envious of me.

                   /mang-:-in/   to make others envious. <u>Nangiinggit lang sila.</u> They're just making (me) envious.

Ingglés   n./adj.   English; English man.

            v.   /mag-:-in/   to speak in English to (someone) <u>Ingglisín mo siya.</u> Speak to him in English.

                   /-in/   to translate (a passage or text into English). <u>Ingglisin mo itong tulang ito.</u> Translate this poem into English.

inín   adj.   food fully cooked (as rice) after having been kept over hot coals for some time.

inodóro (Sp) n.   water closet.

insó (Ch)   n.   appellation for the wife of an elder brother or male cousin.

inspirádo (Sp) adj. inspired.

intelihénte (Sp) adj. intelligent.   --syn. <u>matalíno</u>, <u>marúnong</u>.

interés (Sp) n.   percentage of profit or gain on a sum of money. --syn. <u>túbo'</u>, <u>patúbo'</u>. Participation in an enterprise. Sympathetic feeling. Desire to obtain or possess.

íngat (Mal) n.   /pag-/ (pag-iingat) carefulness.

            adj.   /ma-/ careful.

ingít   n.   whimper.

ipá   n.   chaff or husk of palay.

ipanganák	v.	to be born.

ipil n. hardwood tree used in house construction.

ipis n. cockroach.

ipit v. /-in/ to crush. <u>Huwag mong ipitin ang kamay mo</u>. Don't crush your hand (e.g. on the car door).

/ma-/ to get caught in between; to be clipped. <u>Naipit siya sa pinto</u>. She got pinched in the door [She (her hand, foot, etc.) got caught in the door].

/mag-/ to clip, pin (hair). <u>Magipit ka ng buhok</u>. Pin your hair in place.

/mang-:-in/ to clip; to clasp; to press; to catch in between.

ipókrita (Sp) n. hypocrite.

ipon v. /mag-/ to save; to collect; an abbreviated form of <u>magtipon</u>.

/-in/ to save; to collect; to put together; to hoard. <u>Ipunin mo ang sahod mo</u>. Save your salary.

ipot n. droppings of fowls and small animals.

ipu-ipo n. cyclone; tornado; whirlwind.

irap v. /-um-/ to give a sullen glance. <u>Umirap siya nang utusan ko</u>. She just closed her eyes and turned away when I made my request. (She made a face and turned away when I asked her to do something for me.)

/mang-/ <u>Nangirap na naman ang supladang babae</u>. That snobbish girl just closed her eyes and turned away again. (That snobbish girl did it again -- she made a face at me and turned away.)

irí	pron.	this (that which is attached or close to the person speaking). --var. <u>iré</u>.
	adv.	in this way or manner.
irí	n.	the act of muscular force in moving the bowels.
írog	n.	beloved; darling. --syn. <u>sintá</u>, <u>giliw</u>, <u>darling</u>.
isá	num.	one.
isá	n./adv.	next, as in <u>sa isang linggo</u>, next week.
ísaw	n.	large intestine.
iskíper	n.	T-shirt.
iskultór	n.	sculptor.
isdá	n.	fish.
ísip	v.	/-in/ to think it over. <u>Isipin mong mabuti bago ka magdesisyon</u>. You think it over carefully before you make your decision. (Think it over carefully before you make up your mind.)
ísla	n.	island.
istadyum	n.	stadium.
istórya	n.	story. --syn. <u>kuwento</u>.
istrayk	v.	/mag-/ to strike against (an employer).

iták	n.	bolo; large knife; cutlass; kitchen knife.
Itálya (Sp)	n.	Italy.
itáy	n.	father (term of address and reference).
íti	n.	dysentery.
ítik (Mal)	n.	species of duck that produces eggs made into balót.
itím	adj.	dark; black.
itlóg	n.	egg.
itó	dem.	this; this one here. --var. iré. /d-/ (díto) here. --var. díne. /ha/ here it is. --var. éto. /n-/ (nitó) of this. --var. niré.
íwan	v.	/mag-:-an/ to leave something behind; to be left behind. Iwanan mo ang mga nahuli. Leave the latecomers behind.
		/mang-/ Nangiwan siya ng kanyang mga kasama. He left his companions behind.
íwas	v.	/-um:-an/ to avoid. Umiwas ka sa sakuna'. Avoid accidents...
íwi	n.	/pag-/ (pag-iiwi) taking care of an animal (as pig, goat, cattle, etc.) for someone else who is the real owner.
	v.	/mag-/ to take care of children. Magíwi ka ng anak niya. Take care of her child.

iyák   v.   /-um-/ to cry. <u>Umiyak siya sa</u>
                      <u>pagalis ng nanay niya</u>. She
                      cried when her mother left.

iyán   dem.   that; that one there.
                      /d-/ (<u>diyán</u>) there.
                      /ha-/ (<u>hayán</u>) there it is.
                      /n-/ (<u>niyán</u>) of that.

iyó   pron.   your; yours (singular).

iyón   dem.   that (yonder); that one there.
                      /d-/ (<u>doón</u>) there; yonder.
                      /ha-/ (<u>hayún</u>) there; yonder;
                      it is.
                      /n-/ (<u>niyon</u>) of that; yonder.
                      --var. <u>noón</u>.

L

laán	adj.	/naka-/ reserved for; intended for; headed for.
labá	v.	/-an/ to wash (clothes). <u>Labhan mo ang mga damit</u>. Wash the dresses.
		/mag-/ to wash clothes; to launder.
labábo	n.	sink.
labág	v.	/-um-/ to violate. <u>Lumabag siya sa batas</u>. He violated the law.
labáha	n.	straight razor.
lában	prep.	against. <u>Laban sa kanya</u>. Anger against him.
	v.	/-um-/ to fight against. <u>Lumaban siya sa digmaan</u>. He fought in the war.
labandéra/o	n.	laundrywoman.
labanós	n.	radish.
labangán	n.	tub or trough feeding pigs and horses.
labás	n.	outside; exterior; out-of-doors.
	v.	/-um-/ to go out; to exit; to act in a show; to come out. <u>Lumabas siya sa eskuelahan</u>. He came out of the school.
		/mag-:i-/ to take out something; to put out something; to withdraw (money). <u>Ilabas mo ang plano</u>. Bring out the plan.

labatíba   n.   enema.

lábi'   n.   lips.

labíng   pref.   (from <u>labi</u> + <u>-ng</u>) excess over
                      the count of ten as <u>labíng-apat</u>
                      (fourteen).

labintadór n.   firecracker.

lábis   adj.   surplus; excessive.

labnót   v.   /mang-:-in/ pull out forcibly;
                      pluck; cut; uproot.

lábo   adj.   /ma-/ unclear; vague; hazy.

            v.   /-um-/ to become blurred.
                      <u>Lumabo ang kanyang paningin</u>.
                      His vision became blurred.

labóg   adj.   overcooked.

labóng   n.   bamboo shoots.

laboratóryo (Sp) n.   laboratory.

labúyo'   n.   wild chicken; jungle fowl.

labúyo   n.   chili pepper.

lákad   n.   a person's destination when pre-
                      paring to make a trip or when
                      preparing to leave.

            v.   /-um-/ to walk; to leave on a
                      trip; to set out for. <u>Lumakad</u>
                      <u>ka nang mabilis</u>. Walk fast.

                      /mag-/ to walk (not ride in a
                      vehicle). <u>Maglakád na lang tayo</u>.
                      Let's just walk.

                      /i-/ to peddle; to take care of.
                      <u>Ilakad mo ang pagtaas ng katungkulan</u>
                      <u>ko sa kaniya</u>. Have him take care
                      of my promotion.

/maka-/ to be able to walk.

lakás   adj.   /ma-/ strong; powerful; loud. **Malakas kumain**. He is great at eating. **Tumawa ng malakas**. He laughed aloud.

lakbáy   v.   /mag-:-in/ to travel; to take a trip. **Maglakbay tayo sa buong mundo**. Let's travel around the whole world.

lakí   adj.   big; large.

lakí   n.   size.

lakí   n.   high tide.

lákip   v.   /mag-:i-/ to enclose. **Maglákip ka ng abuloy mo sa sobre**. Enclose your contribution in the envelope.

láko'   v.   /mag-:i-/ to peddle (merchandise). **Iláko' mo ang tinda mo sa maraming tao**. Peddle your wares where there are many people.

laksá' (Sk) n.   ten thousand.

laksánte (Sp) adj.   laxative. --syn. purgá.

laktáw   n.   omission of step after making several consecutive ones.

             v.   /-um-:-an/ to skip or omit a few steps in a series supposed to be done consecutively. **Linaktawán niya ang tatlong pahina**. He skipped the three pages.

ladlád   v.   /i-/ to unfurl. **Iladlad mo ang bandila**. Unfurl the flag.

lága   v.   /mag-:i-, -in (ni)/ to boil food (fish, meat, vegetables).

lágak	v.	/mag-/ to deposit. <u>Maglagak ka</u> <u>ng pera sa bangko</u>. Deposit money in the bank.
lagalág	adj.	wandering; roving.
lagánap	adj.	scattered; well-known.
	v.	/-um-/ to be scattered; to be well-known.
lagári'	n.	saw.
lagás	adj.	fallen off; wilted.
lagaták	n.	indraft of rain through the roof.
lagáy	v.	/-um-/ to put oneself in a certain condition. <u>Lumagay ka</u> <u>sa aking lugar</u>. Put yourself in my place.
		/i-/ to put; to place (something); to lay down something. <u>Ilagay</u> <u>mo ang ulam sa kalan</u>. Put the main dish on the stove.
lagkít	adj.	/ma-/ sticky.
lagdá'	n.	signature.
lagíhay	adj.	/ma-/ somewhat dry; semi-dry.
lagím	n.	gloom. --syn. <u>lumbáy</u>, <u>lungkót</u>. Dread; terror. --syn. <u>pangambá</u>, <u>tákot</u>.
lagitík	n.	creak; creaking.
laglág	v.	/ma-/ to fall. <u>Nalaglag ang</u> <u>manggang hinog</u>. The ripe mango fell.
lagmák	adj.	helplessly prostrate.
lagnát	n.	fever.

lagó	adj.	/ma-/ luxuriant; bushy.
lagók	v.	to gulp. <u>Linagok niya ang tubig.</u> He gulped down the water.
lagót	v.	/ma-/ to snap. <u>Nalagót ang lubid</u>. The rope snapped.
lagpák	v.	/-um-/ to fall. <u>Lumagpak ang mangga</u>. The mango fell.
		/mag-:i-/ to fail, drop. <u>Ilagpak mo siya sa klase mo</u>. Fail him in your class. <u>Maglagpak ka ng estudiyanteng tamad</u>. Fail lazy students.
lagúsan	n.	mountain pass.
láhad	v.	/i-/ to present. <u>Ilahad mo ang katutuhanan</u>. Present the truth.
lahát	pro.	all.
	adj.	all; everyone; everything.
láhi'	n.	race.
lahók	n.	an ingredient.
	v.	/mag-/ to add to a mixture.
lahók	n.	entry in a contest.
	v.	/-um-/ to be a contestant; to butt in.
lalá'	adj.	/ma-/ serious; grave (illness).
laláki	n.	man; male.
	adj.	male.
lalamúnan	n.	throat.
lalawîgan	n.	province.

lálim	adj.	/ma-/ deep.

lálo'	adv.	more; excessive; especially; very. Lalu na kung madilim ang gabi... Especially when the night is dark...

lamán	n.	meat; contents.

lámang		only. Isa lamang ang mansanas na natira. Only one apple is left on the table.

lamáng	n.	advantage over others.
	v.	/mang-:-an/ to take advantage of others. Linamangán na naman niya ako. He took advantage of me again.

lámas	v.	/mag-:-in/ to mash or crush with the hand; to make dirty. Huwag mong lamásin ang tinda ko. Don't mash my goods for sale.
		/mang-:-in/ to mash or crush with the hand; to make dirty. Nanglamas siya ng mga prutas. He squashed the fruits.

lámat	n.	slight crack, especially on glass.

lámay	n.	funeral wake; vigil.
	v.	/mag-:-in/ to keep vigil; to stay awake all night. Lalamáyin ko ang trabaho ko. I'll stay up late with my work.

lambák	n.	valley.

lambát	n.	net.

lambîng	v.	/mag-/ to caress; to show fondness, affection, tenderness. Naglambing siya sa nanay niya. He showed affection for his mother.

lambót	adj.	/ma-/ soft; tender.
lamíg	adj.	/ma-/ cold; chilly; cool.
lamók	n.	mosquito.
lamóg	adj.	bruised; softened by over-handling.
lampá (Ch)	adj.	awkward and unsteady; unsure of footing.
lámpara	n.	lamp.
lampás	adj.	excessive; too much. --syn. labis, masyado, higít. Beyond limits; reaching beyond; penetrating beyond. Passing ahead of.
lampín	n.	diapers.
lamúkot	n.	fleshy part of fruit sticking to seeds.
lamyá'	n.	oozy or caressive manner of talking.
lána	n.	wool.
landás	n.	path; beaten path; trail. --syn. daán.
landí'	adj.	flirt, coquette
lansá	adj.	/ma-/ stench or taste of fish; fishy taste.
lanság	adj.	dismantled; broken into pieces (machinery or the like).
lansángan	n.	street (in a general sense).
lansónes	n.	lanzones.
lantá	adj.	wilted; withered; faded (decayed).
lantád	adj.	in full view; exposed.

lantík	n.	graceful bend or curve (of eye-lashes, hips, etc.).
	adj.	/ma-/ long, curved (eyelashes).
lantód	adj.	women indelicately dressed, or prone to be so; loose.
lántsa (Sp)	n.	launch.
lang	part.	only; just; representing little value; shortened form of lamang.
lángaw	n.	fly; housefly.
langká'	n.	jackfruit. --var. nangká'.
langgám	n.	ant.
langíb	n.	scab of wounds.
langís	n.	oil.
	adj.	/ma-/ oily.
lángit	n.	sky; heavens.
langitngít	n.	shrill, creaking sound (produced by rusty hinges or the rubbing of bamboo stalks, floor boards, etc., against each other).
langó'	adj.	tipsy; drunk. --syn. lasíng.
langóy	v.	/-um-:-in/ to swim. Lumangoy siya sa ilog. He swam the river.
laón	adj.	old, as grains and cereals.
laós	adj.	antiquated; outdated; obsolete.
lápa	n.	/pag-/ butchering; quartering (of animals).
	v.	/-in/ to butcher, slaughter. Linápa niya ang baka. He butch-ered the cow.

lápad	n.	width.
	adj.	/ma-/ wide.
lapág	v.	/mag-:i-/ to lay on floor or ground level. Ilapag mo ang palanggana. Put the basin on the floor/ground.
lapastángan	adj.	irreverent; disrespectful; discourteous.
lápat	adj.	adjusted; fit.
	v.	/mag-:i-/ to adjust; to fit. Ilapat mo ang pinto. Adjust the door.
lapída (Sp)	n.	gravestone (with inscription).
lapirót	adj.	mussed; crumpled (by tips of fingers).
lápis	n.	pencil.
lapisák	adj.	crushed broken such as eggs, fruits, tomatoes or the like.
lápit	adj.	/ma-/ near; close.
	v.	/-um-/ to approach or go near. Lumapit ka sa akin. Come near me.

/mag-/ to assume positions near each other. Maglapit kayo. Stay close together.

/mag-:i-/ to take something close to someone. Ilapit mo ang silya sa kaniya. Move the chair close to him. |
| lápu-lápu | n. | spotted rock bass. |

laráwan   n.   picture; portrait. --syn. <u>litrato</u>.

           v.   /i-/   to describe (someone or something); to portray.

laró'   n.   game.

           v.   /mag-/   to play (a game). <u>Maglaro kayo sa silong</u>. Play in the basement.

                    /-in/   to play with. <u>Laruin mo ang bata</u>. Play with the child.

láruan   n.   playground.

laruán   n.   toy; plaything.

lása   n.   taste.

          adj.   /ma-/   spicy; tasty.

           v.   /-um-:-in/   to taste; to have the taste of. <u>Ikaw ang lumasa ng ulam</u>. You taste the dish.

lasáp (Sk)   n.   fine taste; enjoyable taste.

           v.   /-um-:-in/   to relish the taste of food; by extension: to enjoy (something). <u>Lasapin mo ang simoy ng hangin</u>. Inhale (with relish) the (fresh) air.

laséta (Sp) n.   pocket knife.

lasíng   adj.   drunk; intoxicated.

láso (Sp)   n.   ribbon.

lástikó (Sp) n.   elastic rubber band.

láta   n.   tin; can.

látak   n.   residue; dregs; sediment (of liquids).

látag	v.	/mag-:i-/ to spread out; to unfold and lay on the ground. <u>Maglatag ka ng banig</u>. Roll out the mat.
látay (Ch)	n.	swollen lash or whip marks on the skin; welt.
latían	n.	swamp.
latík	n.	scum of coconut milk.
látiko	n.	whip.
láwa'	n.	lake; pool; lagoon.
láwak	n.	area.
	adj.	/ma-/ vast; very spacious.
láway	n.	saliva.
láwin	n.	hawk.
lawít	v.	/-um-/ to dangle; to hand down; to suspend. <u>Lumawit ang dila ng aso</u>. The dog's tongue hung down.
		/mag-:i-/ to dangle; to hang down; to suspend; to dangle (something). <u>Maglawit ka ng lubid</u>. Dangle the rope.
lawrél	n.	bay leaf.
láya'	n.	freedom.
	adj.	/ma-/ free; emancipated; independent.
layág	v.	/mag-/ to sail away; to rove. <u>Madalas siyang maglayag</u>. He roves most of the time.

láyas	v.	/-um-/ to go away; to run away. <u>Lumayas siya kahapon.</u> He ran away yesterday.

/mag-/ to travel around in vagabondage or wanderlust. <u>Mahilig siyang maglayas.</u> He loves to wander.

láyaw	n.	freedom.
láyo'	adj.	/ma-/ far distant.
	v.	/-um-/ to stay or keep away. <u>Lumayo ang mga kaibigan niya sa kaniya.</u> His friends kept away from him.

/mag-:i-/ to separate; to put something away from the reach of someone. <u>Maglayó kayo at nang huwag kayong magaway.</u> Separate from each other so you don't fight. <u>Ilayó mo ang baso sa bata.</u> Put the glass out of the child's reach.

láyon	n.	purpose; aim.
laybraryan	n.	librarian.
lebadúra (Sp)	n.	yeast.
leksiyón (Sp)	n.	lesson.
leég	n.	neck.
legál	adj.	lawful.
lénte (Sp)	n.	lens; flashlight; flood lights.
lentéhas (Sp)	n.	lentils.
león (Sp)	n.	lion. --var. <u>liyón.</u>

létra (Sp)   n.   alphabetic character; letter.

libág   n.   dirt of the skin.

líban   prep.   except. <u>Liban na lamang sa ilan</u>.
                       Except only for a few.

             n.   omission.

             adj.   absent (non-attendance).

libáng   v.   /mag-:-in/ to find some kind of
                       recreation; to provide distrac-
                       tion, amusement, or entertain-
                       ment. <u>Maglibang ka at baka ka
                       maloko</u>. Get some recreation or
                       you might crack up.

                       /mang-:-in/ to entertain; to
                       provide distraction, amusement
                       or entertainment; to console.
                       <u>Manglibang ka sa mga nagaantay</u>.
                       Entertain those who are waiting.
                       <u>Libangin mo ang mga nagaantay</u>.
                       Entertain those who are waiting.

Liberál   n.   Liberal Party (a major political
                       party in the Philippines).

libíng   n.   burial; internment.

             v.   /mag-:i-/ to bury; to inter.
                       <u>Inilibing nila ang patay</u>. They
                       buried the dead.

libíngan   n.   cemetery.

libís   n.   slope; hillside; valley.

liblíb   n.   hidden or unfrequented place.

libo   num.   a unit of thousand.

líbog   n.   /ka-:-an/ (<u>kalibúgan</u>) lust;
                       lascivious.

líbot	v.	/-um-/ to go around; to wander. **Lumibot siya sa paligid ng bahay.** He went around the outside of the house.
		/mag-/ to go around; to wander. **Maglibót ka sa bayan.** Go around town.
líbre (Sp)	adj.	free; gratis; free of responsibility.
libró	n.	book. --syn. **aklat**.
likás	adj.	natural; native; inborn; innate.
likhá'	v.	/-um-/ to create. **Lumikha si Nena ng malaking gulo.** Nena created great confusion.
líkido	adj.	liquid.
likó'	v.	/-um-/ to turn; to curve; to bend. **Lumiko ang kotse sa kanan.** The car turned to the right.
		/mag-:i-/ to turn something. **Iliko mo ang kotse sa kaliwa.** Turn the car to the left.
likód	n.	back; reverse side.
	adj.	back; rear; behind.
	adv.	used with **sa**.
likót	adj.	/ma-/ restless; fidgety; wriggly; mischievous.
liksî	adj.	/ma-/ active; fast.
liksyón	n.	lesson.
líder	n.	leader.

ligálig	n.	trouble; perturbation; pre-occupation; bother.
	adj.	perturbed; bothered; disturbed.
lígaw	n.	courtship.
	v.	/-um-/ to court; to woo. <u>Lumigaw</u> <u>siya sa magandang dalaga</u>. He courted a beautiful girl.
		/mang-:i-/ to court; to woo. <u>Lagi siyang nanliligaw ng mga</u> <u>babae</u>. He is always courting girls.
ligáw	v.	/ma-/ to get lost; to stray. <u>Naligáw siya sa lunsod</u>. He got lost in the city.
		/mang-:i-/ to guide to the wrong way. <u>Ilinigaw ng tsuper ang</u> <u>pasahero</u>. The driver took the passengers the wrong way.
ligáya	adj.	/ma-/ happy; merry.
ligíd	adj.	surrounded.
lígo'	n.	/pa-/ (<u>palígo'</u>) bathing.
		(rw. <u>ligó'</u>) (<u>páliguán</u>) bathroom; bathing place.
	v.	/ma-/ to take a bath or shower; to bathe. <u>Naligo siya sa ilog</u>. He went for a dip in the river.
ligpit	v.	/-in/ to clear; to put away (something).
ligtá'	v.	/maka-/ to omit or neglect inadvertently. <u>Nakaligtaan</u> <u>niyang isusi ang bahay</u>. He forgot to lock up the house.

ligtás	v.	/mag-:i-/ to save; to free. Iligtas mo po siya. Please help him.
líha'	n.	division of an orange fruit; a slice.
líham	n.	letter.
lihí	v.	/mag-:pag-, -an/ to show first signs of pregnancy. Naglihi siya sa mangga. She craved for mangoes (because she is conceiving).
líhim	n.	secret.
lihís	v.	/-um-/ to detour; to deviate from. Lumihis ang kotse sa putik. The car drove around the mud.
		/mag-:i-/ to deviate something from. Ilihis mo ang kotse sa mga bato. When driving the car avoid the rocks.
liít	adj.	/ma-/ small; little.
líla	adj.	violet; lavender. --syn. ube.
lílim	n.	shade.
lílip	n.	hemming (stitched, as on cloth).
lilís	v.	/mag-:i-/ to pull up the skirt or trousers; to roll up the sleeves. Naglilis siya ng damit dahil sa mataas ang tubig. She pulled up her skirt because of the high water.
lílo	adj.	unfaithful; disloyal; traitorous. --syn. taksíl, traidór.
limá	num.	five.

limbág   v.   /mag-:-in, i/ to print; to
                        write in block letters. <u>Linimbag</u>
                        <u>nila ang bagong libro</u>. They
                        printed the new book.

limós   v.   /mag-:i-/ to give alms. <u>Ilimos</u>
                        <u>mo ang baryang nasa iyo</u>. Give
                        the change you have to the poor.

                        /mang-/ to beg; to ask for alms.

                        /magpa-/ to beg; to ask for
                        alms. <u>Nagpalimós ang pulubi</u>.
                        The beggar begged for alms.

límot   v.   /-um-:-in/ to forget. <u>Lumimot</u>
                        <u>siya sa aming usapan</u>. He broke
                        our agreement.

                        /ka- -an/ to forget. <u>Huwag</u>
                        <u>mong kalimútan ang bilin ko</u>.
                        Don't forget my instruction.

limpiabóta   n.   bootblack; shoeshine boy.

limunáda (Sp) n.   lemonade.

linamnám   n.   deliciousness; exquisite taste
                        or savor.

              adj.   /ma-/ delicious.

línaw   adj.   /ma-/ clear.

lindól   n.   earthquake; tremor.

              v.   /-um-/ to shake (as in an earth-
                        quake). <u>Lumindol sa Pilipinas</u>.
                        There was an earthquake in the
                        Philippines.

línea (Sp)   n.   line. --syn. <u>guhit</u>.

línis   adj.   /ma-/ clean.

              v.   /mag-:-in/ to clean. <u>Linísin mo</u>
                        <u>ang bahay</u>. Clean the house.

168

linta'	n.	leech.
lintík	n.	lightning.
línga	n.	sesame seeds.
lingkód	v.	/mag-:pag- -an/ to serve; to give or offer service. <u>Maglingkod ka sa mga nangangailangan</u>. Help those who are in need.
Linggó	n.	Sunday. week.
lingg-linggo	adv.	every week.
lingíd	adj.	hidden; not known; secret.
lipád	v.	/-um-:-in/ to fly. <u>Lumipad ang ibon sa isang puno</u>. The bird flew to (or from) a tree.
lipás	adj.	out of fashion; obsolete; faded.
	v.	/-um-/ to lapse; to come to pass. <u>Lumipas ang mahabang panahon</u>. A long time passed.
lípat	v.	/-um-/ to transfer; to move to another place. <u>Lumipat na siya ng bahay</u>. He moved to a different house. /mag-:i-/ to transfer; to move to another place. <u>Ilipat mo ang aking mga kasangkapan</u>. Transfer my possessions.
lipistík	n.	lipstick.
lípon	n.	crowd, gathering; meeting. --syn. <u>pulong</u>, <u>miting</u>, <u>lupon</u>.
lipúnan	n.	(rw. <u>lípon</u>) society in general.

líryo	n.	lily.
lisá'	n.	nit, eggs of lice.
líso	adj.	plain; unadorned.
lislís	adj.	rolled up or blown up showing what is covered (usually skirts). --var. lilís.
listá	v.	/mag-:i-/ to list down. Maglista ka ng iyong mga kailangan. Make a list of those things you need.
lísto (Sp)	adj.	clever; quick; prompt.
litáw	v.	/-um-/ to emerge; to become visible. Lumitaw ang kanyang mga tagihawat. His pimples came out.
		/mag-:i-/ to bring out. Ilitaw mo ang iyong tunay na pagkatao. Bring out your own true nature. (Be yourself.)
lítid	n.	ligament.
litó	v.	/mang-:-in/ (lituhín) to confuse. Huwag mong lituhin ang bumibilang. Don't confuse the one counting.
litráto	n.	picture; photograph. --syn. larawan.
lítro	n./qnt.	liter.
litsîyas (Ch)	n.	cherimoyer; lychees.
litsón	n.	roast pig (usually a whole roasted pig).
litsúgas (Sp)	n.	lettuce.
liwánag	adj.	/ma-/ bright; clear; distinct.

liwaywáy	n.	dawning.
liyáb	v.	/mag-, -um-/ to blaze. <u>Lumiyáb</u> <u>ang kusina</u>. The kitchen was ablaze with fire. <u>Nagliyáb ang</u> <u>panggátong</u>. The firewood was ablaze.
liyábe	n.	wrench.
liyád	adj.	bent backward with stomach protruding.
liyémpo	n.	barbecued pork with much fat and little meat.
lóbo	n.	balloon.
lokál	adj.	local; not imported.
lóko/a	adj.	crazy; insane; mad.
	v.	/ma-/ to become crazy; to crack up; to be madly inclined; to do something.
lóla	n.	grandmother (term of address and reference).
lólo	n.	grandfather (term of address and reference).
lómo	n.	tenderloin.
longganísa (Sp) n.		pork sausage.
loób	n.	interior; interval part; the inside of something.
	adv.	used with <u>sa</u>, inside; within.
loók	n.	bay; gulf.
lóro	n.	parrot.
lóryat (Ch) n.		sumptuous dinner with a great number of Chinese dishes.

lubhá'   adj.   /ma-/ serious; grave; very ill.

lúbid   n.   rope.

lubóg   adj.   submerged.

             v.   /-um-/ to sink; to submerge.
                      <u>Lumubog ang bapor</u>. The boat
                      sank.

                      /mag-:i-/ to sink; to submerge.
                      <u>Huwag mo siyang ilubog sa ílog</u>.
                      Don't submerge him in the river.

lubós   adv.   total; entire; completely;
                      absolutely.

lukót   adj.   wrinkled; creased.

luksá'   adj.   in mourning; in black.

luksó   v.   /-um-:-in/ to jump; to hop.
                      <u>Luksuhin mo ang bakod</u>. Jump
                      over the fence.

luku-lukó   adj.   crazy. --var. <u>lóko</u>.

lúga'   n.   pus in ear.

lugár   n.   place. --var. <u>lugal</u>.

lugás   adj.   fallen off, as grains from the
                      stable, hair.

lúgaw   n.   porridge; gruel; watery rice.

lugáy   adj.   /naka-/ long hair hanging loosely
                      or freely.

lúgi   n./adj. loss in a business transaction.

luglóg (Ch) n.   a kind of noodle which is dipped
                      in boiling stock.

| | v. | /i-/ to rinse clothes by shaking in the water. --syn. banláw. Iluglog mo ang damit sa mainit na tubig. Rinse the clothes in hot water. |

lugmók   adj.   helplessly prostrate.

lugó   adj.   extremely weak due to sickness (fowls and birds).

lúha'   n.   tears.

lúla'   n.   /pagka-/ (pagkalúla') vertigo; seasickness. --syn. hílo, liyó.

     v.   /ma-/ to be dizzy due to seasickness or airsickness. Nalúla siya sa bapor. He got seasick in the boat.

lúlan   v.   /-um-/ to load; to ride. Lumulan siya sa tren. He rode a train.

     /mag-:i-/ to load; to ride. Maglulan ka ng mga gulay sa trak. You load the vegetables on the truck.

lulód   n.   shin.

lulón   v.   /-um-:-in/ to swallow. Lumulon siya ng buto ng santol. He swallowed the seed of the santol.

     /ma-/ to swallow. Nálulón ng bata ang imperdible. The child swallowed a safety pin.

     /mag-:-in, i-/ to roll up as paper money, mat or the like. Ilulon mo ang banig. Roll up the mat.

lúma'   adj.   old; not new; antiquated (used
                     for objects).

lumbáy   n.   sadness, downcast feeling; lone-
                     liness. --syn. lungkót.

lumpiyá' (Ch) n.   meat, shrimps and/or vegetables
                     packed in rice starch wrapper.

lúmot   n.   moss.

lumpó   adj.   crippled; partially or completely
                     paralyzed.

lúnas   n.   remedy; cure.

lundág   v.   /-um-:-in/ to leap; to jump.
                     Lumundag si Kardo sa bintana.
                     Kardo jumped out of the window.

Lúnes   n.   Monday.

lunók   v.   /-um-/ to swallow. Lumunok
                     siya bago magsalita. She swallow-
                     ed before she spoke.

                     /-in/ to swallow. Lunukin mo
                     ang gamot. Swallow the medicine.

lúnod   v.   /-in/ to overcome; to drown.
                     Lunurin mo sa alak ang iyong sama
                     ng loob. Drown your hurt feelings
                     in drink.

                     /ma-/ to drown. Nalúnod si
                     Josefa. Josepha drowned.

lunót   adj.   softened; overripe, referring
                     to fruits.

lunsád   n.   /-an/ (lunsaran) pier; unloading
                     port.

             v.   /-um:-an/ to alight from (a
                     vehicle).

lunsód   n.   city.

lungkót   adj.   sad; unhappy.

             v.   /ma-/ to become sad.

lunggá'   n.   hole for rats.

lúpa'   n.   earth soil; land; earth; ground; ground floor; downstairs.

lupálop   n.   any far-away place.

lupaypáy   adj.   with the wings or limbs weakened and drooping.

lupí'   n.   fold; folding. --syn. tupí', tiklóp.

             adj.   /naka-/ folded.

lupíg   adj.   vanquished; subjugated; conquered.

lupít   adj.   /ma-/ cruel.

lúpon   n.   committee; commission.

lurá'   n.   sputum.

             v.   /-um-:i-/ to spit. Lumura siya sa tabi ng daan. He spat on the side of the road (path).

                    /mang-/ to spit. Nanglúra siya sa mga nagdaraan. He spat on the passers-by.

luráy   adj.   mangled; destroyed.

luslós   n.   (Med) hernia; rupture.

             adj.   fallen; hanging down.

lúsob   v.   /-um-/ to attack; to assault. Lumusob ang mga masasamang loob sa bayan. The bandits attacked the town.

/mang-:-in/ to attack; to assault. Linusob nila ang mga kaaway. They assaulted their enemies.

lúsog   adj.   /ma-/ healthy.

lusóng   n.   mortar (for pounding rice).

lusót   v.   /-um-/ to pass through; to penetrate; to overtake. Lumusot ang paa niya sa butas. His foot passed through the opening.

/mag-:i-/ to smuggle. Inilusot nila ang mga kontrabando. They smuggled the contraband goods through.

lútang   n.   buoy.

    adj.   (lutáng) floating; adrift.

    v.   /-um-/ to rise above the surface (of liquids). Lumutang ang bankay sa ilog. The corpse floated in the river.

lutás   adj.   finished; terminated. --syn. tapós, yári', ganáp. Solved.

lutó'   adj.   cooked.

    v.   /mag-:-in, i-/ to cook. Magluto ka ng adobo. Cook adobo.

lutóng   adj.   /ma-/ crisp; brittle.

luwá'   adj.   bulging; sticking or protruding out.

    v.   /-um-/ to bulge; to stick out; to protrude. Lumuwa ang mata ni Tonia sa inggit. Toni's eyes bulged out with envy.

/mag-:i-/ to belch out; to spit out. <u>Iluwa mo ang buto ng kinakain mo</u>. Spit out the seeds of what you're eating.

luwág	adj.	loose.
luwál	v.	/mag-:i-/ to give birth. <u>Naglu-wál si Teria ng kambal</u>. Terry gave birth to twins.
luwalháti'	n.	glory.
luwáng	adj.	/ma-/ loose.
luwás	v.	/-um-/ to go from town to city. <u>Lumuwas siya sa Maynila</u>. She went to Manila (from the province).
		/mag-:i-/ to take to the city. <u>Iniluwas niya ang kanyang panauhin sa Maynila</u>. He brought his visitor to Manila.
luwát	adj.	/ma-/ long (in time); slow. <u>Maluwat matutuhan</u>. Takes a long time to learn. <u>Natutulog ako ng maluwat</u>. I sleep long (hours).
	adv.	for a long time.
lúya	n.	ginger.
luylóy	adj.	hanging loosely.

ma-	af.	indicates the possessor of a quality; ma- derivatives occasionally occur with absolute instead of conjunctive complements.
maaári'	p.v.	to make something possible; may; possibly. Maaari kang magtagumpay. You might become successful.
mabólo	n.	velvet apple.
maka-	pref.	a verb prefix meaning ability, permission or opportunity to act; an adjective prefix meaning 'for' or 'in favor of', as in maka-Rizal, 'for Rizal'.
makahiyá'	n.	mimosa pudica.
makapag-	pref.	a verb prefix meaning to have the chance or opportunity to do.
makapunó'	n.	freak coconut full of soft meat.
maki-	pref.	an actor-focus verb prefix which indicates a request; its goal-focus counterpart is paki.
mákina	n.	sewing machine; machine.
makinárya (Sp)	n.	machinery.
makinílya	n.	typewriter.
makíta	v.	to happen to see.
makópa	n.	mountain apple.
madaling-áraw	n.	dawn; sunrise.
madlá'	n.	the public; all the people.

mádre	n.	nun.
madrína (Sp)	n.	female sponsor at baptism, confirmation, wedding, or special celebration. --syn. ninang.
madyóng (Ch)	n.	the game of mahjong.
maéstra/o	n.	teacher.
magá'	adj.	swollen.
	v.	to become swollen.
mágasin	n.	magazine.
magkáno	int.	question word that means 'how much'.
magkasíng	aa.	of equal quality; as...as; same as.
magíng	v.	to be; to become. [Transient (active) particle word or phrase modified is something coming into being, arising at the time specified by the tense-form of the particle.] Siyay naging hukom. He became a judge. Naging bantog siya sa buong bayan. He became famous throughout the whole town.
magnéto	n.	magnet.
magsasaká	n.	farmer.
magúlang	n.	parents (term of reference).
mahál	adj.	dear; loved; costly; noble; well-esteemed; expensive.
	v.	/mag-:-in/ to hold dear; to love. Mahalín mo ang iyong mga magulang. Love your parents.

maís	n.	corn.
manás	n.	beriberi.
malagkít	n.	glutinous rice; a species of rice which is sticky when cooked.
	adj.	sticky.
maláman	v.	to know.
málas (Sp)	n.	bad luck.
	v.	/-in/ to suffer bad luck. <u>Minalas siya sa sabungan kahapon</u>. He had bad luck at the cockpit yesterday.
malasákit	n.	solicitude; protective concern.
malasádo (Sp)	adj.	half-cooked; cooked rare (or medium rare); soft-boiled (eggs).
malát	n.	hoarseness. --syn. <u>paós</u>.
málay	n.	knowledge; consciousness; awareness.
malay-táo	n.	consciousness.
maléta	n.	luggage.
malí'	n.	/ka- -an/ (kamalian) a blunder; a mistake, error.
	adj.	wrong.
malunggáy	n.	horseradish tree.
máma'	n.	mister.
mamayá'	adv.	after a while; soon; later on, as in <u>mamayang gabi</u>, later this evening.
mámamayan	n.	citizen.

mamón (Sp)   n.   a kind of sponge cupcake.

mán   pro.   with the interrogative pronouns
                     sino, kanino, ano, alin, kailan,
                     saan, etc. : ever, as, sino man
                     whoever; sa kanino man, whomever;
                     ano man, whatever; alin man, which-
                     ever; kailan man, whenever; saan
                     man, wherever; magkano man, what-
                     ever the cost (price); paano man
                     (papánuman), whatever the manner,
                     etc.

             adv.   also, too; as Ako man, I, too.
                     With lamang denotes minimum act
                     or the least to do, as Magluto
                     ka man lamang sana, the least
                     you could do is cook.

             conj.   although, despite; as Matalino
                     ka man ay dapat ding magaral.
                     Although you are intelligent
                     (you) need to study.

mána   n.   heritage; inheritance.

             v.   /mag-:-in/ to inherit; to receive
                     as inheritance; to take after.
                     Nagmana si Crisanta sa kanyang
                     ama. Crisanta inherited her
                     features from her father.

mananáyaw   n.   dancer.

manatíli'   v.   to stay; be permanent.

mandalá'   n.   haystack; stack of palay.

mándo (Sp)   n.   command. --syn. útos.

maného   v.   /mag-:-in/ to drive (a car);
                     to manage. Magmaneho ka ng kotse.
                     Drive a car.

manhíd   n.   cramp; numbness.

             adj.   numb.

maní'	n.	peanuts.
manibaláng	adj.	almost ripe; nearly ripe.
maníka'	n.	doll.
manikurísta	n.	manicurist.
mánidyer	n.	manager; employer; boss.
manlalápa'	n.	butcher.
máno	v.	/mag-/ to kiss an elder's hand in respect or greeting. Magmano ka sa iyong lola. Kiss the hand of your grandmother.
manók	n.	chicken.
mansánas	n.	apple.
mansanílya	n.	chrysanthemum.
mantekádo	adj.	buttered.
mantél	n.	table cloth.
mantíka'	n.	shortening; lard.
mantikílya	n.	butter.
mantsá	n.	stain.
manúgang	n.	daughter-in-law/son-in-law (term of reference).
mánunulat	n.	writer.
mang	adj.	a title of respect used with the first name of a man; contracted form of mama', mister. Mamang Pedro becomes Mang Pedro.
mángangalakál	n.	businessman.
mánganganta	n.	singer.

mangangátay	n.	butcher.
mangkók	n.	bowl.
manggá	n.	mango.
manggagámot	n.	doctor.
manggagáwa	n.	laborer.
manggás	n.	sleeve.
manggustín	n.	mangosteen.
manghuhúla'	n.	fortune-teller.
mangingisdá'	n.	fisherman.
mangmáng	adj.	illiterate; ignorant; stupid.
mangungúlot	n.	hairdresser; beautician.
mangyári	conj.	because.
	v.	to happen.
maóng	n.	denim.
máp	n.	mop.
mápa	n.	map.
maráhil	adv.	perhaps.
marálita'	adj.	(rw. dálitá') poor; indigent. --syn. dukhá'.
marámi	adj.	many; much; lots of; plenteous.
marká	v.	/mag-/ to mark; to stamp. Nagmarka ang sampal niya. His slap left a mark.
márgarin	n.	margarine.
margaríta	n.	zinnia (a kind of flower).

maríno	n.	serviceman in the navy or the marines.
maripósa (Sp)	n.	butterfly. --syn. paruparó.
marmól	n.	marble.
Márso	n.	March.
Martés	n.	Tuesday.
martílyo	n.	hammer.
martír (Sp)	n.	martyr.
mártsa (Sp)	n.	march.
	v.	/mag-/ to march. Nagmartsa siya sa parada. He marched in the parade.
mas	adv.	more, as in mas maganda, more beautiful.
mása (Sp)	n.	dough.
masáhe	n.	massage.
	v.	/mag-:in/ to give a massage.
masdán	v.	(rw. masíd) to observe or look at searchingly.
masétas (Sp)	n.	potted plants; plants in vases.
masetéra (Sp)	n.	flower pot; flower vase.
masíd	v.	/mag-:(-an)/ (masdán) to observe closely; to look at searchingly. Magmasid ka ng mga paligid mo. Observe your surroundings.
máso	n.	mallet; large hammer.
masustánsiya	adj.	nutritious.

masyádo	adv.	very; exceedingly.
matá	n.	eye.
matadéro (Sp)	n.	slaughterhouse.
matadór (Sp)	n.	bullfighter.
mata-póbre	adj.	snobbish.
matsíng	n.	monkey. --syn. unggóy.
máy	part.	to have; there is/are; to possess.
máya	n.	sparrow.
máya-máya	n.	malabar red snapper.
maybáhay	n.	wife (term of reference).
Máyo	n.	May.
mayonésa	n.	mayonnaise.
mayroón	part.	there is; there exists; to have (something); to possess.
mekániko	n.	mechanic.
medálya (Sp)	n.	medal.
medída	n.	tape measure.
medisína (Sp)	n.	medicine.
médya/o	adj.	half.
médya ágwa	n.	awning.
médyas	n.	socks; stockings.
médyo	adv.	somewhat; slightly; so-so.
melón (Sp)	n.	melon; cantaloupe.
ménos	adj.	less; of less degree or value; lacking; minus.

mensahéro (Sp) n.   messenger.

merienda   n.   snack.

            v.   /mag-/ to have a snack; to take
                     a snack.

mésa   n.   table.

mestíza   adj.   person of mixed blood usually
                     of Spanish-Filipino mixture.

métro   n.   meter; unit of length of the
                     metric system.

mgá   part.   (pronounced manga) particle that
                     pluralizes count nouns. Mga
                     guro' means 'teachers'.

méyor   n.   mayor of a city or town.

míki (Ch)   n.   noodles made from saline wheat
                     dough.

mikróbyo (Sp) n.   microbe; germ; bacterium.

mikrópono (Sp) n.   microphone. --syn. máik (fr.
                     'mike', English slang).

mikroskópyo (Sp) n. microscope.

Miérkoles   n.   Wednesday.

milágro (Sp) n.   miracle. --syn. himalá'.

mílya (Sp) n.   mile.

milyón (Sp) n.   million. --syn. ángaw.

milyonáryo n./adj. millionaire.

minerál   n.   mineral.

minindál   n.   snack.

minístro	n.	minister.
mínsan	adv.	once; once in a while.
mísa	n.	mass.
	v.	/mag-/ to say mass. <u>Nagmisa ang pare sa patay.</u> The priest said mass for the dead.
mísmo	pro.	himself/herself. <u>Siya mísmo.</u> He, himself.
misteryóso/a	adj.	mysterious.
míswa	n.	fine wheat noodle.
misyonáryo	n.	missionary.
míting	n.	a meeting.
	v.	/mag-/ to have a meeting.
Miyérkoles	n.	Wednesday.
mó	pro.	you; your; second person singular personal pronoun which is a member of the <u>ng</u> set of pronouns.
móda (Sp)	n.	fashion; style. --syn. <u>istílo</u>.
	adj.	with <u>nasa</u>.
modélo (Sp)	n.	model.
modérno/a	adj.	modern.
modísta	n.	modiste; dressmaker; seamstress; dress shop.
módo (Sp)	n.	manners; civility. --syn. <u>asal</u>, <u>ugáli</u>'.
molábe	n.	molave.
móngha	n.	nun.

morkón (Sp.) n.   a kind of meat dish; a meat roll stuffed with olives, pickles, sausage, hard-boiled eggs.

moréna/o (Sp) adj.   brown color; brown-skinned. --syn. kayumanggi, kulay-kapé, kastanyo.

móro/a (Sp) n.   moor; Mohammedan. --syn. muslim.

mortál (Sp) adj.   having the quality of dying or ending; fatal.

motorsíklo n.   motorcycle.

mukhá' n.   face.

mukhá adv.   seemingly; looks like; appears like.

mukmók v.   /mag-/ to sulk. Huwag kang magmukmok sa sulok. Don't sulk in the corner.

mulá' conj.   ever since; since.

prep.   from; derived from simulá', starting with or starting from.

múlat v.   /mag-:i-/ to open one's eyes; to educate; to nurture. Imulat mo ang iyong mga mata. Open your eyes.

mulí' adv.   again; once more; once again.

multá n.   fine; penalty.

v.   /mag-:i-/ to pay a fine. Nagmulta siya ng malaki. He paid a heavy fine.

multó n.   ghost.

múmo' n.   particles of cooked rice falling off the dish during the meal.

múmog   v.   /mag-:-in, i/   to gargle.
                  <u>Magmumug ka ng mainit na tubig</u>.
                  Gargle hot water.

múna   adv.   just a minute; before anything
                  else; for a while; first; before-
                  hand.   <u>Magawitan muna tayo bago</u>...
                  Let's sing a song first (before)...

mundó   n.   world.

munisípyo   n.   municipal building; townhall.

muntí'   adj.   small; little; diminutive.

mungkáhi'   v.   /mag-:-i-/   to suggest.   <u>Imungkahi'</u>
                  <u>mo na ang napagkayarian natin</u>.
                  Suggest what we have agreed upon.

munggó   n.   mongo beans.

múra   n.   curse; scolding reproach.

            v.   /mag-:-in/   to scold; to curse.
                  <u>Minura niya ang kaniyang mga</u>
                  <u>katulong</u>.   He scolded his helpers/
                  servants.

múra'   adj.   immature; unripe.

múra   adj.   cheap; inexpensive.

músa (Sp)   n.   muse.   --syn. <u>paraluman</u>, <u>diwatá'</u>,
                  <u>lakambini</u>, <u>reyna</u>.

muskáda/
   moskada (Sp) n.   nutmeg.   --var. <u>maskáda</u>.

muskitéro (Sp) n.   mosquito net.   --syn. <u>kulambó'</u>.

músiko   n.   musician.

musmós   adj.   innocent, as a child; immature,
                  as of mind.

mustása   n.   mustard.

múta'   n.   eyewash.

muwébles (Sp) n.   furniture.

na   adv.   now, already.
After nouns or pronouns: acts as an emphatic marker, as <u>Búkas na</u>, Let it be tomorrow; <u>Ako na</u>, It's my turn to do it now or I'll do it instead of someone else; <u>Si Maria na,</u> Let it be Maria's turn.
After verbs: If in the past tense form, denotes completion of action expressible in the past or present perfect in English, as <u>Nagsipilyo na siya</u>, He has already brushed (his teeth). If in the infinitive form or future form, denotes now, right away, immediately, soon, as <u>Magsipilyo ka na</u>, Brush (your teeth) now; <u>Papasok na ako</u>, I'm going to school now. If after verb roots, denotes completed action, as <u>Bukás na</u>, It's already open; <u>tapós na</u>, It's already finished.

na   lig.   connects modifier and word modified. Takes the form -<u>ng</u> when the word it follows ends in a vowel sound. <u>Mabait na bata</u> or <u>Batang mabait</u>, good child.

na   part.   with <u>sa/kay</u>, marks nouns indicating position, location, possession of something.

naka-   af.   an adjective prefix meaning state, position, or appearance.

nákaw   v.   /mag-:-in/ to steal; to pilfer. <u>Nagnakaw siya ng maraming salapi</u>. He stole a lot of money.

nakú!   intj.   oh, my! An interjection derived from <u>Nanay ko</u> or <u>Ina ko</u>, my mother!

nágwas   n.   half-slip. --var. hap slip.

náis   v.   /-in/ to desire; to wish.
Naísin man niyang sumama ay puno
na ang sasakyan. Even though he
wanted to come along, there wasn't
any room in the vehicle.

namán   part.   response marker; also; too; rather;
again; on the other hand.

    adv.   also; too.

    intj.   expression of gentle protest or
denial.

    id.   usually emphasizing the fact or
the feeling involved in the expression.

        expresses transition to another
subject hence also mild contrast.
Habang si Juana ay nagluluto si
Juan naman ay naglilinis ng
bahay. While Juana is cooking,
Huan cleans the house. Ano
ka ba namang tao? What sort of
person are you, anyway?

nána'   n.   pus.

nánay   n.   mother (term of address and
reference). --syn. inay.

nándito   adv.   it is here; here. --var. nárito.

nándiyan   adv.   it is there; there. --var. náriyan.

nándóon   adv.   it is over there; over there;
over in that place. --var. nároon.

nang   conj.   when (past reference). Nagaaral
kamí nang dumating siya. We were
studying when he arrived. So that
(in order that), usually with at,
and. Mag-aral ka at nang maka
pasa ka. You study so that you

will pass (your courses).

      adv.   when, in order to; particle added to an adjective to make an adverb of it. <u>Tumakbó siya nang matulin</u>. He ran swiftly. Used between repeated verbs to indicate intensity or continuity of the action. <u>Tumakbó siya nang tumakbo</u>. He kept on running.

nanganganínag adj.   transparent.

námin   pro.   we; our (exclusive, not including the person spoken to).

náog   v.   /ma-/ to go down; to descend.

nápaka-   af.   an adjective prefix meaning 'very'.

nára   n.   narra.

naranghíta   n.   native orange. --var. <u>dalanghíta</u>, <u>dalandán</u>.

nárit6   adv.   it's here (fr. <u>na</u> + <u>dito</u>). --var. <u>nándíto</u>.

náriyán   adv.   it's there (fr. <u>na</u> + <u>diyan</u>). --var. <u>nandiyán.</u>

náro6n   adv.   it's there; yonder (fr. <u>na</u> + <u>doon</u>). --var. <u>nándoon</u>.

nárs   n.   nurse.

nárses   n.   /pag-na-/ nursing (as a career or profession).

nása   part.   particle marking nouns indicating position or location of something.

násaan   int.   where?

Nasyonalista n.   Nacionalista Party (the political rival of the Liberal Party).

nátin   pron.   our (inclusive).

naturál   adj.   natural; inborn.

náyon   n.   village; country.

negríto (Sp) n.   dwarf negro of the Philippine mountains. --syn. ita, ayta, agta, balugá.

négro (Sp) n.   negro man.

    adj.   black. --syn. itím, maitím.

Néne'   n.   appellation for a small girl.

nérbiyos   n.   nerves.

ngá'   adv.   affirmative adverb 'indeed'. Siya nga ang duwag. He is indeed the coward. Polite particle. Pakiabot nga ang asin. (Please) pass the salt.

ní   part.   singular non-focus marker of proper nouns or names.

    mkr.   a proper noun (name) marker. Used before the actor of goal-focused sentences. Binili ni Luisa ang damit. The dress was bought by Luisa.

    part.   possessive marker. bahay ni Luisa. Luisa's house.

nikeládo (Sp) adj.   nickel plated.

nilá   pron.   they; their. Third person plural number, non-focus pronoun; shows possession, bahay nila, their house. Acts as non-focused actor in goal-focused sentences. Kinuha nila ang libro. They got the book.

nímpa (Sp) n.   nymph.

niná	mkr.	plural form of <u>ní</u>, the proper noun (name) marker.
níno	pron.	whose; post positive form of kanino. <u>Kaninong bahay</u> -- <u>bahay nino</u>, whose house.
nínang	n.	godmother (term of address and reference).
nínong	n.	godfather (term of address and reference).
ninyó	pron.	you; your (plural); used in the singular sense, it indicates a formal or polite form.
níngas	n.	flame. --var. <u>dingás</u>.
ningníng	adj.	/ma-/ shining; brilliant.
nípa	n.	cabo negro (palm).
nipís	adj.	/ma-/ thin.
nirí	dem.	of this; variant of <u>nitó</u>.
nisnís	adj.	unravelled.
nitó	dem.	of this; /ga-/ like this; (<u>ganitó</u>) in this manner of way. --var. <u>niré</u>, <u>ganiré</u>.
niyá	pron.	he; she; his; hers; her.
niyán	dem.	of that. /ga-/ like that; in that manner or way (<u>ganiyán</u>). --var. <u>ganyán</u>.
niyóg (Mal)	n.	coconut palm tree and fruit.
niyón	dem.	that over there; yonder; its; another variant is <u>noon</u>.
nobéla	n.	novel.
Nobyémbre	n.	November.

nóbyo/a	n.	fiance; sweetheart; betrothed.
noó	n.	forehead; brow.
noód	v.	/ma-/ to watch; to view.
noón	dem.	of that;yonder. /ga-/ (ganoón) like that yonder; in that manner or way.
noón	adv.	then; at that time.
normál	adj.	normal.
número (Sp)	n.	number.
nunál	n.	mole (skin).
núno'	n.	grandparents (term of reference). --var. ninúno'.
núnsiyo	n.	papal nuncio.
nuwébe (Sp)	num.	nine.

ng	mkr.	non-focus marking particle of actor or goal complements or noun phrases. Actor: <u>Kinain ng bata ang kendi</u>. The child ate the candy. Goal: <u>Kumain ang bata ng kendi</u>. The candy was eaten by the child.
	part.	possessive marker; a common noun marker which marks a possessive construction. <u>Direktor ng site</u>. Director of the site.
-ng	lig.	variant of <u>na</u>.
nga'	part.	emphatic particle; expressing confirmation; truly, really, certainly; request particle meaning 'please'; so, therefore, really (assertive and emphasizing) Oo, <u>nga'</u>. Yes, indeed. <u>Ikaw nga ang maysabi</u>. You, yourself. <u>Ituro nga ninyo</u> (polite requests). Please show me the way...
ngálan	n.	name.
ngala ngalá	n.	palate.
ngánga'	n.	a mixture of <u>buyo</u> for chewing.
	v.	/-um-:-in/ to chew <u>buyo</u>. <u>Ngumanganga' ba ang lola mo</u>? Does your grandmother chew beetle nut?
ngangá	v.	/-um-/ to open one's mouth. <u>Ngumanga si Cres para sa dentista</u>. Cres opened her mouth for the dentist.
ngatngát	v.	/-um-:-in/ to nibble; to gnaw. <u>Nginatngat ng daga ang mga damit</u>. The rat chewed on the dresses.

ngáwit	n.	numbness.	197
	adj.	tired; exhausted; numb.	
	v.	/mang-/ to become numb from exhaustion. <u>Nangawit siya sa kasusulat</u>. His hand felt tired and cramped from writing.	
ngayón	adv.	now; just now; today. <u>Siya ay nasa Maynila ngayon</u>. He is in Manila today. <u>Ngayong araw</u>... on this very day.	
ngíki	n.	chills; malaria.	
	v.	/mang-:-in/ to chill; to have the chills. <u>Nginíki si Cristina sa lamig</u>. Cristina chilled from the cold.	
ngiló	v.	/mang-/ to have tooth-edge pain. <u>Nangilo ang aking ngipin</u>. My teeth felt an edge-like pain.	
ngípin	n.	tooth.	
ngiti'	n.	smile.	
	v.	/-um-/ to smile. <u>Ngumiti siya nang palihim</u>. He smiled surreptitiously.	
ngiwí'	adj.	distorted; twisted; crooked (face).	
ngiyáw	n.	cry of cat or kitten.	
ngóngo'		speaking with a nasal twang; nasal defect.	
ngúnit	conj.	but. --syn. <u>datapwá't</u>, <u>pero</u>. <u>Ngunit sumagot siya kaagad</u>. But he answered at once.	
ngúso'	n.	upper lip.	

nguyá'   v.   /-um-:-in/   to chew; to masticate.
                    <u>Ngumuya siya ng babol gam</u>.   He
                    chewed bubble gum.

ó	conj.	alternate marker; or <u>Matanda ba siya o bata</u>? Is he old or young?
o	part.	used either as a sentence opener or closer which means 'now, see, please, okay.'
obíspo	n.	bishop.
obligádo	adj.	obliged; forced.
ókra	n.	okra.
Oktúbre	n.	October.
okupádo (Sp)	adj.	occupied; busy. --var. <u>ukupádo</u>.
oditóryum	n.	auditorium.
oháles (Sp)	n.	buttonhole. --var. <u>uháles</u>.
ónse	num.	eleven.
óo		yes; affirmative response.
operá	v.	/mag-:-an, -in/ to operate on (someone, something). <u>Inoperahán ang pasyente</u>. The patient was operated on.
operasyón (Sp)	n.	surgical operation; state of being operative.
opisína	n.	office.
ópo'	part.	yes (polite form); just like <u>po'</u> and <u>ho'</u>, the more colloquial or a little less formal form of <u>opo'</u> (although certainly not a less respectful form) is <u>óho'</u>.
oportunidád (Sp)	n.	opportunity.
óptiko (Sp)	n.	optician.

ópyo (Sp)   n.   opium.

óras   n.   hour; time.

orasán   n.   clock.

orasyón   n.   angelus.

órbita   n.   orbit.

orkéstra (Sp) n.   orchestra.

órkid   n.   orchid.

órder   n.   an order; a serving (of food).
                      --var. órden.

ordináryo   adj.   ordinary; usual; common.

orégano (Sp) n.   aromatic green herb cultivated
                      for spice and medicine.

órends   adj.   orange (color).

organdí (Sp) n.   organdy (kind of cloth).

organisasyón (Sp) n. organization.

organísmo   n.   organism.

órgano (Sp) n.   pipe organ.

o, siya   an expression meaning 'okay; all
                      right; well, etc.'

óso (Sp)   n.   bear.

ospitál   n.   hospital.

otél   n.   hotel.

ótmil   n.   oatmeal.

ótso (Sp)   num.   eight.

pa	af.	affix for verbs meaning 'to cause, get or allow someone to do what the root word indicates'.
pá	adv.	more; yet; still. Expresses the immaturity or continuance of a situation and stands in contrast with na. Mabuti pa... Better yet. Basá pa ang damit. The clothes are still wet.
paá	n.	foot.
paálam	intj.	(rw. alám) farewell.
	v.	/mag-/ to bid goodbye. Magpaalam ka sa iyong ina. Say goodbye to your mother.
pa'áno	int.	how.
páaralan	n.	(rw. áral) school. --syn. eskuwelahan.
pabagsák	n.	(rw. bagsák) bribery; tip.
	adv.	suddenly dropping something resoundingly.
pabangó	n.	perfume; lotion; cologne.
pabáon	n.	(rw. báon) provision (of money, food or supplies) allowed or given to someone making a trip.
pabayá'	adj.	careless; negligent.
pábo	n.	turkey.
pabór (Sp)	n.	favor.
paboríto/a	adj.	favorite.

201

pábrika (Sp) n.		factory.
pábula (Sp) n.		fable.
pakéte	n.	package.
pakí-	af.	a verbal prefix which indicates a request; pakiabot, please hand over, please get.
pakíling	n.	leaves used for scrubbing wooden floors and walls.
pakimkím	n.	(rw. kimkím) a sum of money given by a sponsor in baptism, confirmation or wedding, to the person being sponsored.
pakinábang	n.	profit; benefit; Holy Communion.
pakipkíp	n.	(rw. kipkíp) gift given by a ninong or ninang, specially in baptisms and confirmations.
paktoriyá (Sp) n.		baggage-master's office (railway); factory.
páko'	n.	nail.
pakó'	n.	fern.
pakpák	n.	wing.
paksá'	n.	topic; subject matter.
pákulútan	n.	beauty parlor.
pakundángan n.		reverence; respect (specially for age, holy things, traditions, honor, and the like).
pakwán	n.	watermelon.
pakyáw (Ch) n.		wholesale buying.

| | v. | /ma-/ to buy by wholesale. <u>Mamamakyaw siya sa Divisoria</u>. He's going to buy by wholesale at Divisoria (market).

/-in/ to buy something by whole-sale. <u>Pakyawín mong lahat ang tinda niya</u>. Buy all his goods. |

pád   n.   ruled paper.

padér   n.   wall or brick/stone wall.

padpád   v.   /ma-/ to be shipwrecked; to be driven or carried (by a storm or tide).

padríno (Sp) n.   male sponsor. --syn. <u>ninong</u> (colloq.).

padyák   v.   /-um-/ to stamp the feet. <u>Pumadyak siya sa inis</u>. He stamped his feet in irritation.

pádre   n.   a borrowing from Spanish which means 'father'; used as an appel-lation for a priest.

padýama   n.   pajamas.

pag   conj.   particle which means 'on, if, when'. <u>Pag ako ay pagod</u>... When I get tired...

pag-aári'   n.   property.

pagbabágo   n.   (rw. <u>bágo</u>) change.

pagkáin   n.   food.

pagkaraán   adv.   after; after passing.

pagkatáo   n.   upbringing.

pagkatápos   adv.   afterwards.

pagkít	n.	paste.
pagdáka	conj.	immediately; quickly. --var. pagkaráka. Pagdaháy tinangnan niya ang... He quickly seized the...
págod	n.	tiredness; exhaustion.
	adj.	(pagód) tired; exhausted.
	v.	/ma-/ to become tired.
pagóng	n.	turtle.
pagsasánay	n.	practice.
páhayagan	n.	newspaper.
páhid	v.	/mag-:i-:-an/ to wipe off; to apply on. Ipahid mo ang panyo sa mukha mo. Wipe your face with the handkerchief.
pahintúlot	n.	permission.
páhina (Sp)	n.	page.
pahingá	v.	/mag-/ to rest; to take a break. Magpahinga ka muna. You rest first.
páin	n.	bait.
paít	adj.	/ma-/ bitter.
pála	n.	shovel; spade.
palá	part.	so, as in Ikaw pala, so it is you; an exclamation of surprise.
palá	part.	when used after hindi, expresses contrast with one's expectation; a reversal. Ang isip ko'y balat lamang ng itlog ito, hindi pala,

kundi itlog na buo'. I thought
this was only an eggshell, but
no, it was a whole egg.

palabá	v.	/mag-/ to have clothes washed; to have someone wash one's clothes.
palabás	n.	show; film.
palaká'	n.	frog.
palákad	n.	policy; current practice.
palakól	n.	axe.
palakpák	n.	applause; sound of applause.
	v.	/-um-/ to applaud.
		/mag-:-an/ to applaud together simultaneously.
pálad	n.	palm of the hand.
palág	n.	wiggling, squirming; jerking of feet.
palagáy	n.	opinion; idea.
palági'	adv.	always; often. --var. lagi'.
palaisdáan	n.	fish pond.
palálo'	adj.	proud; boastful; high-hat; snobbish.
palanggána	n.	basin.
palapág	n.	(rw. lapág) floor or story of a building.
palará'	n.	tinsel; foil.
palaró'	n.	the games planned for an occasion.
palasó	n.	arrow.

palaspás	n.	fancily woven palm leaves blessed on Palm Sunday.
palásyo	n.	palace.
pálay	n.	unhusked rice; rice plant.
paláyaw	n.	nickname.
palayók	n.	pot (earthen).
pálda	n.	skirt.
paléngke	n.	marketplace.
palíban	n.	(rw. líban) postponement.
palibhása	conj.	expresses what follows is stated as a reason (parallel to halimbawa). --var. palibasa. ...palibhasa'y gawa rin. The reason being that they did it...
palíbot	n.	(rw. líbot) surroundings; environment.
palikéro	adj.	flirtatious (male).
palikpík	n.	fin of fish.
páligsáhan	n.	(rw. ligsá) contest; competition.
pálipáran	n.	(rw. lipád) airport.
palít	v.	/mag-:-an, i-/ to change; to replace; to exchange; to cash a check. Palitán mo ang kurtina. Change the curtain.
palitáw	n.	rice cake made of glutinous rice, sugar and coconut gratings.
palíto (Sp.)	n.	toothpick.

pálo'	v.	/mang-:-in/ to spank; to whip. <u>Namamalo siya ng mga bata</u>. He spanks children.
pálong	n.	cock's comb.
palós	n.	eel; large Bengal swamp eel. --syn. <u>igát</u>.
palsó (Sp)	adj.	spurious; counterfeit.
paltík	n.	crudely made native gun.
paltós	n.	blister.
palupálo'	n.	wooden paddle for beating laundry. --var. <u>palo-pálo'</u>.
palyók	n.	cooking pot. --var. <u>palayók</u>.
pamagát	n.	title of written work.
pamána	n.	inheritance; heritage.
pamangkín	n.	nephew or niece (term of reference).
pamburá	n.	eraser.
pamílya	n.	family.
pamintá	n.	black pepper; pepper.
páminggálan	n.	cupboard; pantry.
pamútas	n.	(fr. <u>pang</u> + <u>bútas</u>) perforator; hole borer. --var. <u>pambútas</u>.
pamútat	n.	(fr. <u>pang</u> + <u>pútat</u>) 'hors d'oeuvres', side dish.
pána'	n.	bow and arrow.
panadéro (Sp)	n.	baker.
panadérya	n.	bakery.

panaghóy	n.	(fr. pang + taghóy) lamentation.
panagínip	n.	dream.
panahón	n.	time; season; weather.
panalangin	n.	(rw. dalángin) prayer.
panálo	v.	/m-:-in/ to win. Nanalo siya sa sabong. He won in cockfighting.
panáog	v.	to go down. Nanaog siya sa matarik na hagdanan. He went down a steep stairway.
panáta'	n.	vow, usually religious.
panátag	adj.	(rw. tatág) tranquil; peaceful.
panátikó (Sp) adj.		fanatic.
panaúhin	n.	visitor; guest.
panáy	adj.	all; each and everyone (of a group).
pandák	adj.	short of stature.
pandánggo (Sp) n.		fandango dance.
pandáy	n.	blacksmith.
pandisál (Sp) n.		bread; a kind of french bread.
panhík	v.	/-um-/ to go upstairs; to come up the house.
		/mag-:i-/ to take upstairs. Ipanhik mo ang mga labada. Carry the washed clothes upstairs.
panibughó'	n.	jealousy.
paníki'	n.	bat.

pánig	n.	panel; side; party; page; section.
panís	adj.	stale and spoiled, referring especially to food.
paniwála'	n.	belief.
panoód	v.	to go and see. <u>Nanood si Belen ng sine kagabi</u>. Belen went to a movie last night.
panót	adj.	bald.
pánsamantalá	adj.	temporary; tentative; acting.
pansín	v.	/-um-:-in/ to give attention to; to take notice. <u>Huwag mong pansinin ang biro niya</u>. Don't pay any attention to his jokes.
pansít	n.	long rice; noodles.
pansitérya	n.	Chinese restaurant.
pantál	n.	welt.
pantalón	n.	pants; trousers.
pantáy	adj.	level; of the same length or height; even.
pantóg	n.	bladder.
pánty (Eng.)	n.	panties.
panúkat	n.	tape measure.
panutsá	n.	crude sugar.
panyó	n.	handkerchief. --var. <u>panyolíto</u>.
panyuélo (Sp)	n.	shawl; shoulder kerchief.
pangá	n.	jaw.
pangáko'	n.	promise.

pangahás	adj.	daring; bold; intrepid.
pang-áhit	n.	razor; shaver.
pangálan	n.	name.
pangambá	n.	fear; suspicion.
pangánay	n.	eldest in the family (term of reference).
pangánib	n.	danger.
pangárap	n.	daydream; ambition.
pangát	n.	fish cooked in vinegar and salt.
pangkát	n.	group; party.
pangkó'	adj.	carried in one's arms.
	v.	/-in/ to carry in one's arms. Pangkuín mo ang hinimatay na babae. Carry the woman who fainted.
pángil	n.	tusk.
panginoón	n.	master; lord.
pángit	adj.	ugly; not good.
pangláw	adj.	/ma-/ gloomy.
pangúlo'	n.	leader; president.
pangunáhin	adj.	leading; first; foremost.
paós	adj.	raucous; hoarse (voice).
Pápa	n.	Pope.
pápag	n.	bamboo bed; a wooden couch.
papáya	n.	papaya.
papél	n.	paper.

papél-de-líha n.   (rw. líha) sandpaper.

pára   adv.   like that of; in the manner of.

pára   conj.   so that; in order to.

           prep.   for; to; till; as in <u>menos singko</u>
                   <u>para alas tres</u>. Five minutes
                   before 3 o'clock.

pára   part.   non-focus benefactive phrase
                   marker. <u>Para sa iyo ang regalo</u>.
                   The gift is for you.

pára   mkr.   for; with <u>sa</u> benefactive noun
                   phrase marker; with <u>kay/kina</u>
                   used before proper nouns (names).

pára! (Sp) intj.   stop!

           v.   /-in/ to stop (a vehicle).
                   <u>Paráhin mo ang bus</u>. Stop the
                   bus.

                   /i-/ to cause a vehicle to stop.
                   <u>Ipara mo ang kotse</u>. (You) stop
                   the car.

paráda (Sp) n.   parade.

paráda   v.   /-um-/ to stop. <u>Pumarada ang</u>
                   <u>kotse</u>. The car stopped.

                   /i-/ to stop (a vehicle); to
                   park. <u>Iparada mo ang kotse sa</u>
                   <u>tabi ng daan</u>. Park the car on
                   the side of the road.

paraíso (Sp) n.   paradise.

parálisis (Sp) n. paralysis.

paralítiko (Sp) n./adj. paralytic person.

paralúman n.   muse.

párang   n.   meadow; prairie.

párang   conj.   as if.

parasítiko (Sp) adj.   parasitic.

parátang   n.   accusation.

paráti   adv.   always; all the time; again and again; perennial; often. Akóy parating nahahabol. I'm often pursued.

páre   n.   priest. --var. pári.

páre   appellation for a male friend; derived from kumpare or compadre; the feminine form is mare from kumare; sometimes used to address a man whose name one does not know.

parého   adj.   equal; similar; alike; identical.

páres   adj.   even; paired; similar; equal to; like.

parîlya (Sp) n.   broiler; toaster; grate of furnace.

páris (Sp pares)   n.   pair.

                 adj.   /ka-/ (one) of a pair; equal; similar; identical.

parîto   v.   /-um-/ to come here. --var. pumarîne. Pumarito ka bukas. You come here tomorrow.

pariyán   v.   /-um-/ (pumariyán) go there.

parmaseútiko/a (Sp) n. pharmacist. --var. parmasiyótiko.

parmásya   n.   pharmacy.

parokyáno (Sp) n.   parishioner; customer; client.

paról   n.   lantern.

paroón   v.   /-um-/ (pumaroón) go there, yonder.

párte   n.   part.

partído (Sp) n.   political party. --syn. lapían.

paruparó   n.   butterfly.

parúsa   n.   punishment.

pasá'   n.   contusion.

pasá   v.   /-um-/ to pass an academic course, an examination, an interview or the like. Pumasá si Linda sa eksamen. Linda passed the exam.

/mag-:i-/ to pass on. Ipása mo kay Dan ang bola. Pass on the ball to Dan.

pásak   n.   plug.

pasádo   adj.   past; passed.

pasadór (Sp) n.   sanitary napkin (used by women).

pasáhe (Sp) n.   passage; journey; fare.

pasahéro (Sp) n.   passenger.

pasalúbong   n.   a present (usually given by one arriving from a trip).

pasán   v.   /-um-/ to ride on one's back.

/mag-:-in/ to carry on one's back or shoulders. Pasanín mo ang isang sakong bigas. Carry the sack of rice on your shoulder.

pasapórte (Sp) n.   passport. --var. pásport.

pasaríng   n.   innuendo.

pásas (Sp) n.   raisin.

Pasasalámat n.   Thanksgiving.

Paskó   n.   Christmas.

páses (Sp) n.   pass; permit.

pasílyo (Sp) n.   corridor; aisle.

pasimáno   n.   window sill. --var. pasamáno.

pasimulá'   n.   beginning.

pasiyám   n.   nine-day novena after the burial.

pasiyénte   n.   a patient.

pasmá (Sp) n.   spasm.

pasmádo (Sp) adj.   suffering from spasm.

páso'   v.   /ma-/ to get burned. Napaso si Juan ng kumukulong tubig. John got scalded by the boiling water.

    /mang-:-in/ to burn or scald.

pások   v.   /-um-:(-in)/ to go to work; to go to school; to enter. Pumasok ka sa kuwarto ng ate mo. Enter your elder sister's room.

    /mag-:-i/ to enter; to go inside; to insert; to deposit (money). Ipasok mo ang mga plinantsa sa silid. Put the things you ironed in the room.

pásta   n.   filling (of tooth).

pastól	v.	/mag-:-in, i-/ to herd animals. <u>Ipastol mo ang mga kalabaw</u>. Herd the carabaos.
pastór	n.	pastor; minister.
pasyál	v.	/mag-:i-/ to go out for a walk; to take a walk; to stroll; to visit. <u>Magpasyal tayo sa Lizal Park</u>. Let's go to Rizal Park for an outing.
		/i-/ to take for a walk. <u>Ipasyal mo ang mga bata sa Linggo</u>. Take the children out for diversion this Sunday.
pasyénsiya (Sp) n.		patience. --var. <u>pasénsya</u>.
pasyénte (Sp) n.		patient.
pasyón (Sp) n.		the life of Christ in vernacular verse.
páta	n.	knuckles; feet (pork).
patabá'	n.	fertilizer.
paták	n.	drop of liquid.
pátakaran	n.	by-laws; basic or guiding principles.
pátag	n.	/ka-an/ (<u>kapatágan</u>) plain; lowland.
	adj.	smooth; level; even.
patáni'	n.	lima beans; kidney beans.
pátas	adj.	equal of the same level.
patátas	n.	potatoes.
patáwad	n.	forgiveness.
	v.	/-in/ to forgive (someone, something).

patáy	adj.	dead; not working; turned off.
	v.	/-um-:-in/ to kill; to turn off. Pumatay si Doming ng tao. Doming killed a man.
		/ma-/ to get killed.
		/mag-:-in/ to slaughter. Nagpatay sila ng tatlong baboy nang ikasal si Luisa. When Luisa got married, they killed/ slaughtered three pigs.
pataygútom	adj.	extremely hungry; tramp; destitute.
patí (Ch)	adv.	also; including.
patíd	v.	/mag-:-in/ to cut off.
		/mang-/
pátid	n.	tripping another's foot.
	v.	/-in/ to trip (someone). Huwag mo siyang patírin. Don't trip him.
patílya (Sp)	n.	side-whiskers; sideburns.
patíng	n.	shark.
patís	n.	fish sauce; native salty sauce.
patiwarík	adv.	(rw. tiwarík) upside down.
patláng (Ch)	n.	space between; interval.
patnúgot	n.	director; head of office.
páto	n.	duck.
patóla	n.	sponge gourd.
pátong	v.	/mag-:i-/ to put on top; to put over; to lay.

patpát	n.	piece of split bamboo.
patrón (Sp)	n.	patron saint.
patúbig	n.	irrigation.
patúngo	adj.	in the direction of; towards.
patútot	n.	prostitute.
pátyo	n.	churchyard.
paumanhín	n.	an apology; forgiveness or toleration of a fault committed.
paunáwa'	n.	notice; warning.
paús	adj.	hoarse. --var. paos.
páwid	n.	nipa palm, the leaves of which are used for thatching roof.
páwis	n.	perspiration; sweat.
	v.	/-an/ to perspire; to sweat.
páyag	v.	/-um-/ to agree; to conform.
payápa'	adj.	/ma-/ peaceful; calm; tranquil.
payát	adj.	thin; slim; lean; skinny.
páyo	n.	advice; counsel.
	v.	/mag-/ to give advice or counsel.
páyong	n.	umbrella.
paypáy	n.	fan. --var. pamaypáy.
	v.	/mag-:i-:-an/ to fan; to wave as to produce wind.
paypáy	n.	shoulder (Boston butt).
Pebréro	n.	February.

pékas (Sp) n.   freckles.

péklat   n.   scar.

pedál (Sp) n.   pedal; treadle.

pelíkula (Sp) n.   photo-film; movie-film.

pelígro (Sp) n.   danger. --var. piligro.

pelúka (Sp) n.   wig.

peniténsiya (Sp) n. penitence.

pénoy   n.   hard-boiled duck's egg.

pensïyón (Sp) n.   pension; allowance of expense
                        money.

péra   n.   money.

péras   n.   pear.

perhuwîsyo (Sp) n.   injury; damage; harm.

pérlas   n.   pearls.

péro   conj.   but; however.

personál   adj.   personal.

peryódiko (Sp) n.   newspaper; journal; periodical.

pésa'   n.   boiled fish spiced with pepper,
                        garlic, onion, ginger.

péste (Sp) n.   pest; plague; epidemic.

pétsa   n.   date (of the calendar).

pétsay   n.   Chinese cabbage (pechay).

pikî'   adj.   knock-kneed.

pikît   adj.   closed, referring to the eyes.

píknik (Eng)	v.	/mag-/ to go on a picnic.
píko	n.	pick.
piló'	n.	children's game of hop-scotch.
pikón	adj.	easily angered by jokes or jests; touchy.
píkot (Ch)	v.	/maka-:-ma/ to be forced into marriage. <u>Napikot siya ng isang bailarina.</u> He was forced to marry a taxi-dancer.
pigá'	v.	/mag-:-in/ to squeeze; to wring.
pigí'	n.	hips; rump.
pighatí'	n.	anguish; affliction.
pígil	v.	/-in/ to detain; to hold in hand; to prevent; to stop.
		/mag-/ to control; to hold back.
piglás	n.	effort to be freed from hold.
pigsá	n.	boil; tumor.
píhit	v.	/-um-/ to turn around.
		/mag-:-in:i/ to wind; to turn a crank or a shaft.
pího	adj.	sure; certain.
píla	n.	flashlight battery.
píla	n.	line; queue.
	v.	/-um-/ to fall in line.
		/mag-i-/ to aline.
pílak	n.	silver; money.
pilápil	n.	dike.

pílas	n.	rend; rip.
	adj.	(pilás) rent; ripped.
pílay	n.	lameness; sprain.
	adj.	(piláy) lame.
	v.	/ma-/ to become lame. Napilay siya nang madulas. He became lame when he slipped.
pildurás (Sp) n.		pill; pellet; medicine pill.
piléges	n.	pleats; fold; plait.
píli'	v.	/-um-/ to choose.
		/mang-:-in/ to select; to pick out (something).
píli	n.	pili nuts.
pilik matá	n.	eyelashes.
piligróso	adj.	dangerous.
píling	n.	side of.
pilíng	n.	bunch; cluster of fruits (bananas).
Pilipínas	n.	the Philippines.
Pilipíno/a	n.	Filipino.
pilípit	v.	/-um-/ to twist.
		/mag-:-in:i/ to coil; to twist (something).
pílit	adj.	/ma-/ forced; against one's will; insistent.
	v.	/mag-:-in/ to insist; to strive; to force.

pílyo/a	adj.	naughty; rascal; mischievous.
pín	n.	brooch.
pinaká	pref.	an affix to adjectives expressing superlative degree (of the quality).
pindót	v.	/-um-:-in/ to squeeze or crush with the fingers.
pínid	adj.	closed.
	v.	/mag-:i-/ to close; to shut.
		/i/ to close (door). <u>Ipinid mo ang pinto</u>. Close the door.
pinípig	n.	rice stamped flat.
píno	adj.	smooth; fine.
pinsála'	n.	damage; injury.
pínsan	n.	cousin (term of reference).
pintá	v.	/mag-:-an:i-/ to paint; to have (something) painted. <u>Magpinta tayo ng ating kuwarto</u>. Let's paint our room.
pintakási	n.	celebration of cockfighting.
pintás	v.	/mang-/ to find fault. <u>Huwag kang mamintas ng kapuwa</u>. Don't find fault with your fellowmen.
pintó'	n.	door. (<u>pintúan</u>) doorway.
pintór	n.	painter (artist).
pintúra	n.	paint.
pinyá	n.	pineapple.
pinggá	n.	pole for carrying weight across shoulder.

pinggán	n.	plate.
pípa	n.	pipe.
pípi	adj.	dumb; mute.
pipíno	n.	cucumber.
pipít (Mal)	n.	native sparrow.
piranggót	n.	a very small piece.
piráso	n.	a piece.

pi ráso v. /-um-/ to break a piece from. <u>Pumiraso ka sa tinapay ko</u>. Break a piece off from my bread.

/mag-:-in/ to break into pieces. <u>Pirasuhin mo ang tinapay</u>. Cut the bread into small pieces.

piríng	n.	blindfold.

piríto v. /mag-:in:i-/ to fry. --var. prîto. <u>Pritúhin mo ang bangus</u>. Fry the milkfish. <u>Magprito tayo ng isda</u>. Let's fry the fish.

pirmá n. signature.

v. /-um-:-an/ to affix one's signature. <u>Pumirma si Amalia sa aking otograp</u>. Amalia signed my autograph book. <u>Pirmahan mo ang aking report card</u>. Sign my report card.

pisá' v. /-um-:mag-:-in/ to crush; to compress; to hatch. <u>Pinisa' ng bata ang mga itlog</u>. The child crushed the egg.

pisák	adj.	blind of one eye.
pisára	n.	blackboard; chalkboard.

piskadór	n.	kingfisher.
piséta (Sp)	n.	a twenty-centavo piece or coin; twenty centavos.
písi'	n.	string; thread.
pisíl	n.	squeezing with the hand.
	v.	/-in/ to squeeze. <u>Pinisil niya ang bata</u>. He squeezed the child.
pisngí	n.	cheeks.
píso (Mex)	n.	peso; one peso (one hundred centavos).
pisón (Sp)	n.	steam-roller.
pispís	n.	remnants of what is eaten, specially fish bones (usually given as cat feed).
pistá	n.	fiesta; feast day.
pitáka' (Sp)	n.	wallet; purse; billfold.
pitás	v.	/-um-/ to pick.
		/mang-:-in/ (<u>mamitas</u>) to pick off (something) from a stem. <u>Pitasín mo ang mga rosas</u>. Pick the roses.
pitík	v.	/-um-/ to snap one's fingers; to topple or push with a flip of the fingers.
		/mang-:-in/ (<u>mamitik</u>).
pitís	adj.	tight-fitting (of clothes, dresses).
pitisyón (Sp)	n.	petition.
píto	n.	whistle.

	v.	/-um-/ to whistle.
pitó	num.	seven.
pitpít	adj.	flattened by pounding.
pítsa (Sp)	n.	chips (in checkers).
pitsél	n.	pitcher (water).
pitsó (Sp)	n.	breast of fowl or animal.
pitsón (Sp)	n.	young pigeon; spring chicken.
piyánsa (Sp)	n.	surety; bail; bond.
piyanísta	n.	pianist.
piyáno	n.	piano.
piyér	n.	pier.
piyérna	n.	chuck (of meat).
piyérna kórta	n.	round cut.
piyón	n.	laborer; unskilled or semi-skilled worker; pawn (in chess).
pláka	n.	record disc; a phonograph record.
plaís	n.	pliers.
planéta	n.	planet.
pláno	n.	a plan.
plánta (Sp)	n.	plant or site of a building; site or installation of a project.
plántsa	n.	flat iron.
	v.	/mag-/ to iron or to press clothes.
plantsadór/a	n.	one who irons clothes for a living.

plása	n.	plaza; the town park.
platapórma (Sp)	n.	platform.
platería (Sp)	n.	silversmithy; goldsmithy. --var. plateriyá.
platéro (Sp)	n.	silversmith; goldsmith.
platíto	n.	saucer.
pláto	n.	plate.
plása	n.	park; plaza.
pléma (Sp)	n.	phlegm.
ploréra	n.	flower vase.
plór waks	n.	floor wax.
plúma	n.	fountain pen.
po'	part.	a form that indicates respect or politeness; sir/ma'am. Opo' (oo + po) yes, sir.
póbre	adj.	poor.
pólbo	n.	powder. --var. pulbós.
polís (Eng)	n.	police. --var. pulis.
pólo	n.	polo shirt; sport shirt.
pólo baróng	n.	native-styled polo shirt; informal.
pomáda	n.	pomade.
populár	adj.	popular.
pormál	adj.	formal; serious.
portéro	n.	doorkeeper.

póso (Sp)   n.   a dug-out; well (of water).

poso-négro (Sp) n.   septic tank.

pósporo   n.   match.

póste   n.   post.

post ópis   n.   post office.

pranéla (Sp) n.   flannel.

prángka   adj.   frank; open; sincere.

práyle   n.   friar.

preparádo   adj.   prepared.

presidénte   n.   president.

préso (Sp)   n.   prisoner.

présyo (Sp) n.   price.

pribádo   adj.   private.

prinsipal/a n.   school principal.

primera/o (Sp) adj./adv.   first.

prinsésa (Sp) n.   princess.

prínsipe (Sp) n.   prince.

príto   adj.   fried.

             v.   /mag-:-in/ to fry. --var. <u>pirito</u>.

probínsiya (Sp) n.   province.

probinsiyána (Sp) n./adj.   female from the province;
                            provincial.

probléma   n.   problem.

prodúkto (Sp) n.   product.

programa n. program.

propaganda (Sp) n. propaganda; advertisement.

propesór/a n. professor.

propesyón n. profession.

prusisyón n. a religious procession.

prútas n. fruit.

pu' n./num. ten or tens.

púki n. vagina. --var. kíki'.

pukól v. /-um-/

/mag-:i-:-in/ to throw; to cast; to hurl.

puksá' v. /-um-:-in/

/mang-:-in/ (mamuksá') to exterminate; to overcome; to destroy.

pudpód adj. worn out; blunt.

púgad n. nest.

púgo' n. quail.

pugón n. oven. --var. óben.

pugót adj. decapitated; beheaded.

puhúnan n. capital in business.

pulá adj. /ma-/ red; rosy (cheeks).

púla' v. /-um-/

/mang-:-an/ to give adverse criticisms. (mamula').

pulbós	n.	powder.
pulgáda		twelve inches (measurement).
pulgás	n.	flea.
pulído	adj.	polished; refined; polite; neat.
pulís	n.	police; policeman.
pulitána (Sp) n.		flush score in a game of cards called <u>panggíngge</u>.
pulmunía (Sp) n.		pneumonia. --var. <u>pulmuniyá</u>.
puló'	n.	island; isolated place.
púlong	n.	meeting; conference. --syn. <u>miting</u>.
pulót	n.	honey; syrup.
púlot	v.	/-um-/
		/mang-:-in/ (<u>mamulot</u>) to pick up.
pulot-gatá' n.		honeymoon.
pulséras (Sp) n.		bracelet.
pulsó	n.	wrist.
pulúbi	adj.	mendicant; beggar.
pulpól	adj.	blunt; obtuse.
pulséras	n.	bracelet.
pulúpot	adj.	twisted; coiled around something.
	v.	/mag-:i-/ to twist around or to wind around something.
pulútan	n.	appetizer taken with wine.

púnas	v.	/mag-:(-an)/ to wipe; to mop; to dry, with a piece of cloth or rag.
pundá	n.	pillowcase.
pundído	adj.	burnt out (bulb).
punerárya	n.	funeral home.
púnit	n.	rip; tear.
	adj.	torn.
	v.	/-um-:-in/ to rip; to tear.
púno'	n.	head man.
púno'	n.	tree trunk; tree.
punó'	adj.	full; filled.
punsó'	n.	ant hill; hillock.
puntá	v.	/-um-/
		/mag-/ to go.
púnta y pétso	n.	brisket (of meat).
puntás (Sp)	n.	lace; lace-work.
púnto (Sp)	n.	period.
puntód	n.	mound; graveyard.
púnung-gúro	n.	head teacher; principal.
punyál (Sp)	n.	poniard; dagger.
púri	v.	/-um-/
		/mang-:-in/ (mamuri) to praise; to compliment; to flatter.
purgá (Sp)	n.	purgative.

	v.	/mag-/ to take purgative.
		/-in/ to give purgative.
púro	adj.	pure; clean; chaste.
puról	adj.	/ma-/ dull.
purtamunéda (Sp)	n.	bag; handbag.
púsa'	n.	cat.
pusáli'	n.	mire under the house.
pusít	n.	squid.
puslít	adj.	uninvited; illegal; contraband (sl).
púso'	n.	heart.
púso' ng ságing	n.	banana blossom.
púsod	n.	navel; umbilicus.
pusód	n.	hair-knot; coiffure that has a hair-knot.
pusón	n.	abdomen.
púspas	n.	dish of rice porridge and chicken. --syn. arrozcáldo. --var. póspas.
pustá	n.	bet.
	v.	/-um-:i/ to bet.
pustíso	adj.	false; artificial (teeth).
pustúra	adj.	dressed elegantly.
púta	n.	prostitute.
putaktí	n.	wasp.
putí'	adj.	/ma-/ fair (complexion); white.

pútik	n.	mud.
	adj.	/ma-/ muddy.
putlá'	adj.	/ma-/ light-colored or pale.
púto	n.	native rice cake.
putók	v.	/-um-/
		/mag-/ to explode; to blast; to erupt.
pútol	v.	/-um-:-in:-an/ to cut something.
		/mag-:-in:-an/ (magputól) to cut intensively, repeatedly.
		/mang-:-in/ (mamutol) to cut something say wood as a means of livelihood or to cut habitually.
putséro (Sp)	n.	dish of boiled meat and vegetables.
puwáng	n.	space; interval between.
puwéde	p.v.	can be; can; may; indicates possibility.
puwéra	adj.	not included.
puwérsa	v.	/mang-:-in/ (mamuwérsa) to force; to apply force or strength.
puwés (Sp)	conj.	therefore; then.
puwésto (Sp)	n.	place or space occupied; stall, stand (as in a market).
puwîng	n.	foreign body in the eye.
puwît	n.	buttocks.
puyát	adj.	night-long wakefulness.
puyó	n.	cowhide.

ráket (Eng) n.	racket (as of tennis or badminton); illicit or fraudulent scheme.
rádyo (Eng) n.	radio.
ráha n.	rajah.
ramí (Eng) n.	ramie.
rántso (Sp) n.	ranch (usually cattle ranch).
rasyón (Sp) n.	ration.
ratán n.	rattan.
ráyos (Sp) n.	spoke (of a wheel).
rayúma n.	rheumatism.
rebélde (Sp) n.	rebel; defaulter.
adj.	rebellious.
rebentadór (Sp) n.	firecracker. --var. labintador.
rebólber (Sp) n.	revolver.
rebolusyón (Sp) n.	revolution. --var. ribulusyón.
rekádo (Sp) n.	condiments.
rekîsa (Sp) n.	inspection by looking into containers (boxes or pockets).
reklámo (Sp) n.	complaint.
rekomendasyón (Sp) n.	recommendation.
rektánggulo (Sp) adj.	rectangle; rectangular.
rektór (Sp) n.	rector.
rekwérdo (Sp) n.	memory; remembrance; keepsake; momento; souvenir.

232

regálo	n.	gift; present.
	v.	/mag-/ to give gift.
regulár	adj.	regular; ordinary; moderate.
réhas (Sp)	n.	grating; railing; bars.
relasyón (Sp) n.		relation.
relihiyón	n.	religion.
reló	n.	watch; wrist watch; clock. --var. relós.
relohéro (Sp) n.		watch or clock maker; watch or clock dealer.
relós (Sp)	n.	watch; clock. --var. rilós.
relyéno	n.	a dish of stuffed chicken, stuffed fish, or stuffed crab.
rematádo (Sp) adj.		ended; finished; totally lost or sold (at auction or by default or by terms of commerce).
remédyo (Sp) n.		remedy.
rénda (Sp)	n.	reins.
rendído (Sp) adj.		fatigued; worn out; confused (in mind and body). --var. rindído.
repáso (Sp) n.		review.
repinádo	adj.	refined.
repólyo	n.	cabbage.
represko (Sp) n.		refreshment.
representánte n.		representative; congressman.
repridyiréytor/ pridyidér n.		refrigerator.

reputasyón (Sp) n.   reputation.

resérba (Sp) n.   something reserved for future use;
                      spare; spare tire.

reséta   n.   medical prescription.

resíbo (Sp) n.   receipt.

responsáble adj.   responsible.

restawrán   n.   restaurant.

resúlta (Sp) n.   result; loss in a transaction or
                      trust.

retáso   n.   remnants of cloth.

retratísta n.   photographer.

réyna   n.   queen.

reynds   n.   range.

rikádo   n.   condiments.

rigudón (Sp) n.   rigadoon, quadrille (dance).

ríles   n.   railway.

rimárim   v.   /ma-/ to feel disgust; loathing.

rímas   n.   breadfruit.

rindído   adj.   fatigued; tired out; confused.
                      (rindé) exhausted. --var.
                      rendído.

rípa   n.   a kind of lottery.

rólyo (Sp) n.   roll; bundle (of cloth or paper).

románsa (Sp) n.   romance.

romántiká/o adj.   romantic.

rondálya (Sp) n.	string orchestra.
ropéro (Sp) n.	dirty linen basket.
rosál n.	gardenia.
rosáryo (Sp) n.	rosary.
rósas n.	roses.
rósas adj.	rose; pink (color).
róskas (Sp) n.	screw thread.
rotónda (Sp) n.	rotunda.
rubí (Sp) n.	ruby.
ruléta (Sp) n.	roulette.
Rúsya (Sp) n.	Russia.
ruwéda (Sp) n.	wheel.

S

sa	mkr.	location or direction marker: to, from, in, on, etc.
sá	part.	non-focus locative phrase marker.
saán	int.	where? in what place?
sabá	n.	bananas (cooking variety).
Sábado	n.	Saturday.
sabáw	n.	soup broth.

sabáy v. /-um-:-an/ to go with; to go at the same time. Sumabay ka sa aming pagsisimba. Go to church with us at the same time.

/mag-/

sábi v. /mag-:-in/ to say; to ask permission; to tell; to relate. Magsabi ka sa nanay at nang hindi tayo pagalitan... Tell mother (ask mother's permission) so we won't be scolded.

sabík adj. eager; anxious.

sábit v. /-um-/ to hang; to suspend.

/mag-:i-/ to hang. Isabit mo ang bago mong litrato sa kuwarto. Hang your new picture in the room.

sábog v. /-um-/ to explode. Sumabog ang bomba. The bomb exploded.

/mag-:i-/ to strew; to scatter; to spill. Isabog mo ang mga butong ito sa hardin. Scatter the seeds in the garden.

sabón	n.	soap.

sábong   n.   cockfight.

/-an/ (sabungán) cockpit.

v.   /mag-/ to engage in cockfighting; to play or bet in a cockfight. Magsabong tayo sa linggo. Let's go bet at the cockfight.

/i-/

sabúnot   n.   pulling of hair; uprooting of hair.

v.   /-an/ to pull (someone's hair) by the roots. Sinabunútan siya ng Nanay niya. Her hair was pulled by her Mother.

sabungán   n.   cockpit.

saká'   conj.   also; in addition; and. --var. atsaká'.

saká   after that; then. Saka pa lamang. Only then, not till then...

(+ na) next time; another time. Saka na tayo manood ng sine. Let's go to the movies another time.

sakál   v.   /-in/ to strangle (someone).

/mang-:-in/ (manakál) to strangle. Nanakal siya ng tao. He strangled a person.

sakáli'   conj.   in case; if it should.

sakáng   adj.   bow-legged.

sakáy	v.	/-um-/ to ride in a vehicle; to board a vehicle; to take/ board a plane. <u>Sumakáy ako sa eroplano nang pumunta ako sa San Francisco</u>. I took a plane when I went to San Francisco.
		/mag-:i-/ to load in a vehicle.
sakdál	adj./adv.	(superlative degree) very; most; -est as <u>sakdál ganda</u>, most beautiful.
sakím	adj.	greedy; selfish.
sakít	n.	sickness; physical suffering; pain.
	adj.	/ma-/ painful.
	v.	/-um-/ to ache; to be in pain; to be ill.
saklát	adj.	/ma-/ bitter; acrid.
saklólo	v.	/-um-/ to aid; to succor; to help.
sáko	n./qnt.	a sack.
sákong	n.	heel.
sakristán	n.	altar boy.
saksák	v.	/-um-:-in/ to stab; to pierce. <u>Sinaksak ang isang lalaki kagabi</u>. A man got/was stabbed last night.
		/mag-:i-/ to stuff; to cram in clothes as in packing.
		/mang-/ (<u>manaksak</u>).
saksî	n.	witness.

v. /-um-/ to witness; to testify; to witness against. <u>Sumaksi siya laban sa nasasakdal</u>. He witnessed against the accused.

sakuná' n. accident; misfortune.

sadsád adj. anchored; grounded (boats).

sadyá' n. purpose; aim.

v. /-um-/ to go to a place with a definite intention. <u>Sumadya sila sa Hapuna</u>. They went to Hapuna.

/mag-:-in/

/mang-/ (<u>manadya</u>') to do intentionally.

sagábal n. obstruction.

adj. full of impediment.

sagád adj. sunk to the hilt; down to the bottom.

sagála (Sp) n. maiden in costume joining the Lenten Procession or the <u>Santacruzan</u>.

sagána adj. /ma-/ bountiful; plentiful; abundant.

ságap n. something scooped from just below the surface of water.

ságap v. /maka-:ma-/ to inhale something (fig.) to pick up a rumor unintentionally. <u>Nakasagap siya ng mabuting balita</u>. He was able to pick up some good news.

ságing n. banana.

sagísag	n.	emblem; insignia; pen-name; pseudonym.
sagitsít	n.	hissing or whizzing sound.
saglít	n.	instant; moment; second (time).
sagó	n.	palm tree of medium height bearing globular fruits that have globular seeds of white bony albumen.
sagót	n.	answer; response; reply.
	v.	/-um-:-in/ to answer; to reply. Sagutin mo ang tanong ko. Answer my question.
sagrádo	adj.	sacred; consecrated.
sagúpa'	v.	/-um-/ to encounter; to combat; to collide. Sinagupa nila ang mga bandido. They encountered the bandits.
		/mang-:-in/ (managupa').
sagwá'	adj.	/ma-/ not in good taste.
sagwán	n.	paddle.
sáha'	n.	sheathing leafstalks of banana.
sahíg	n.	floor.
sáhod	n.	salary.
	v.	/-um-/ to catch the flow of something with a receptacle; to receive a salary or wage. Sumahod ako kahapon. I got/received my pay yesterday.
		/mag-:-in/
		/in/ to catch the dripping. Sahúrin mo ang tumutulong tubig

<table>
<tbody>
<tr><td></td><td></td><td><u>sa gripo</u>. Catch the dripping water from the faucet (in a receptacle).</td></tr>
<tr><td>sahóg</td><td>n.</td><td>mixture for taste.</td></tr>
<tr><td>sahól</td><td>adj.</td><td>/ma-/ worse; less good; lacking; falling short.</td></tr>
<tr><td>saíd</td><td>adj.</td><td>consumed; used up; exhausted.</td></tr>
<tr><td>sáing</td><td>v.</td><td>/mag-:i-/ to cook by steam as in rice. <u>Magsaing ka mamayang gabi</u>. Cook rice later tonight.</td></tr>
<tr><td>saís (Sp)</td><td>num.</td><td>six.</td></tr>
<tr><td>sála</td><td>n.</td><td>error; sin; fault.</td></tr>
<tr><td>sála</td><td>n.</td><td>living room.</td></tr>
<tr><td>salaán</td><td>n.</td><td>colander; strainer; sifter.</td></tr>
<tr><td>salabát</td><td>n.</td><td>ginger drink; ginger tea.</td></tr>
<tr><td>salákay</td><td>n.</td><td>assault; invasion.</td></tr>
<tr><td></td><td>v.</td><td>/-in/ to invade (a place).</td></tr>
<tr><td>salakót</td><td>n.</td><td>native hat made of nipa palm.</td></tr>
<tr><td>salagúbang</td><td>n.</td><td>beetle.</td></tr>
<tr><td>salámat</td><td>n.</td><td>thanks; thank you.</td></tr>
<tr><td>salamín</td><td>n.</td><td>mirror; looking-glass; eye glasses.</td></tr>
<tr><td>salansán</td><td>v.</td><td>/mag-:-in:i-/ to file orderly; to put in an orderly stack. <u>Salansanín mo ang mga importanteng papel</u>. File the important papers.</td></tr>
<tr><td>salantá'</td><td>v.</td><td>/mag-:-in/ badly injured or damaged; weakened.</td></tr>
<tr><td>salapí'</td><td>n.</td><td>money.</td></tr>
</tbody>
</table>

salarín   n.   villain; criminal.

sálawáhan   adj.   fickle.

salawál   n.   panties; underwear; undergarments;
                     trousers.   --var. pánty.

salaysáy   n.   narration; story.

             v.   /mag-:i-/ to narrate; to relate;
                     to tell a story. Isalaysay mo
                     ang nangyari. Narrate what hap-
                     pened.

salbabída (Sp) n.   life-preserver.

salbáhe   adj.   rude; unkind; bad.

sáli   v.   /-um-/ to participate; to join.
                     Sumali si Terry sa mga palaro.
                     Terry joined in with the parlor
                     games.

                     /mag-:i-/ to allow one to parti-
                     cipate; to include in a group or
                     group work. Isali ninyo si Sandra
                     sa inyong laro. Include Sandra
                     in your game.

saliksík   n.   detailed; minute search; research.

sálin   v.   /mag-:i-/ to pour into another
                     receptacle; to copy; to translate;
                     to transcribe.

salitá'   n.   word.

             v.   /mag-/ to speak; to talk; to
                     speak out.

salítre   n.   saltpeter.

salmón   n.   salmon.

saló   v.   /-um-/ to catch.

sálok	v.	/-um-/ to fetch, as in fetching water.
salóp	n.	ganta.
sálot	n.	epidemic; pest; plague.
salpók	n.	collision; impact; bump.
sálsa (Sp)	n.	sauce; gravy. --var. sarsa.
sálsa périn	n.	worchestershire sauce.
sálu-sálo	n.	a get-together.
salúbong	v.	/-um-:-in/ to meet or receive someone who has just come.
		/mag-/ to meet along the way.
samá'	adj.	/ma-/ bad.
	v.	/-um-/ to become bad; to become ill.
samá ng loób	n.	ill feelings.
sáma	v.	/-um-/ to go with; to join the company.
		/mag-:i-/ to take along with.
samakatuwíd	conj.	therefore.
samantála	adv./conj.	while; in the meantime.
sambá	v.	/-um-:-in/ to adore; to worship. Sambahin mo ang Dios. Worship God.
sampagíta	n.	Hawaiian pikake; Arabian jasmine.
sampál	v.	/mang-:-in/ (manampál) to slap on the face.
sampalatáya	n.	act of faith.
	v.	/-um-/ to believe.

sampálok   n.   tamarind.

sampáy   v.   /mag-:i-/ to hang clothes on a line.

sampú'   num.   ten; derived from isang pu', one ten.

sána   with; hope. Expresses unreal futurity in the past or doubtful futurity in the present. In the latter sense it expresses modesty in a request: Ipaglalaba sana kita ng damit ngunit wala akong sabon. I would have washed your clothes for you, but I didn't have any soap.

sanáy   adj.   skilled; experienced.

            v.   /mag-:-in/ to practice; to exercise; to rehearse; to get used to. Magsanay kang lumakad nang mabilis. You better get used to walking fast.

sandál   n.   act of reclining against an object.

            v.   /mag-:i-/ to place (something or someone) in a reclining or leaning position against a support.

sandálan   n.   (rw. sandál) back of a seat; something used to lean or recline against.

sandalî   adv.   a moment; a minute; a short time; lang, wait a minute.

sandályas   n.   sandals.

sandáta'   n.   weapon; arms.

sandíg (Mal/Sk) v. /-um-/ to recline.

sándo	n.	undershirt.
sandók	n.	ladle.
	v.	/mag-:-um-:-in/ to scoop; to take with a ladle. <u>Magsandok ka ng kanin</u>. Scoop out the rice.
sanidád	n.	health inspector.
sanlá'	v.	/mag-:i-/ to pawn; to mortgage. <u>Isanla mo ang singsing ko</u>. Pawn my ring.
sanlibután	n.	(fr. <u>sang</u> + <u>libot</u> + <u>an</u>) universe.
sansála'	n.	interdiction; injunction; pro- hibition. --syn. <u>pígil</u>, <u>sawáy</u>.
sansé (Ch)	n.	appellation for third eldest sister.
santacrúsan	n.	May flower festival.
santán	n.	iscora; shrub with white (<u>santang putí'</u>), red (<u>santang pulá</u>) or pink (<u>santang rosas</u>) flowers.
sánto/a	n.	saint.
	adj.	saintly; holy; sacred.
santól	n.	santol.
sang-	af.	the whole; the whole unit; one, in its entirety, as <u>sang-angaw</u>, one million.
sangá	n.	stem; branch; twig.
sangkálan	n.	chopping block.
sangkáp	n.	belongings; implements; contents; ingredients.

sanggá	v.	/-um-/ to shield; to obstruct for protection.
		/mang-:-in/ (manangga)
		/in/ to block (boxing) Sanggahín mo ang suntok niya. Block his punch (boxing).
sánggano	n.	gangster.
sanggól	n.	baby; infant.
sanglá' (Ch)	n.	pledge (as in pawning); mortgage. --var. sanlá'.
sangsáng	n.	strong agreeable odor. --var. sansáng.
sápa'	n.	brook; creek; stream.
sapák (Ch)	adj.	dovetailed very well; inserted fully.
	intj.	expressing full satisfaction.
sapagká(t)	conj.	because.
sápal	n.	residue; e.g. of coconut meat after it has been squeezed.
sápalarán	n.	(rw. pálad) taking of chances or risks; venturing.
sapantáha'	n.	presumption; suspicion.
sapát	adj.	enough; sufficient.
sapatéro	n.	shoemaker.
sapatîlyas	n.	slippers (for dress wear); step-in.
sapátos	n.	shoes.
sápi'	n.	member (of a society); organization.

sapín	n.	underlayer; protective under-layer.
	v.	/mag-:i-/ to put or use an under-layer. <u>Isapin mo ang panyo ko.</u> Use my handkerchief as an under-cover.
sapók	n.	a straight box at the face.
sapól	adv.	at the very beginning; at the very root.
sapsáp	n.	a species of slipmouth fish.
sará	v.	/-um-/ to close. <u>Sumara ang bintana sa lakas ng hangin.</u> The window closed in the strong wind.
		/mag-:-an:i-/ to close (something); to shut; to turn off. <u>Sarahán (sarhán) mo ang pinto.</u> Close the door.
sarádo	adj.	closed; shut; turned off.
saráp	adj.	/ma-/ delicious; good.
sarát	adj.	flat (of nose).
sardínas	n.	sardines.
saríli	n.	self; oneself.
	adj.	private.
sári-sári'	n.	variety store.
sari'sari'	adj.	diverse.
saríwa'	adj.	fresh; new; recent (food).
sársa (Sp)	n.	sauce.
sarsaparílya (Sp)	n.	sarsaparilla, a kind of beverage.

sartén (Sp) n.   frying pan; tin cup for drinking.

sasakyán   n.   vehicle for transportation.

sastré   n.   tailor; tailor shop.

saúli'   v.   /mag-:i-/ to return what was borrowed. <u>Isauli mo ang libro sa aklatan</u>. Return the book to the library.

saúlo   v.   /mag-:-in/ to memorize. <u>Saulúhin mo ang leksiyon</u>. Memorize the lesson.

sawá   n.   boa constrictor.

sawá'   adj.   satiated; sated; satisfied; tired.

sawáli'   n.   interwoven splits of bamboo for walling.

sawáy   n.   /pag-/ prohibition; act of prohibiting; stopping.

             v.   /-in/ to prohibit; to stop; to forbid. <u>Sawayín mo siya sa masamang gawain</u>. Stop him from doing bad things.

sawî'   adj.   ill-fated.

sawsáw   v.   /-um-/ to dip food in liquid, e.g. sauce.

                   /mag-:i-/ <u>Isawsaw mo ang langgonisa sa suka'</u>. Dip the (native) sausage in vinegar.

sáya   n.   long skirt.

sayá   adj.   /ma-/ happy; cheerful; merry; gay.

             v.   /mag-/ to be happy; to be cheerful; to be gay.

sayád   adj.   touching or dragging on floor at bottom, or on the sides.

sáyang! (Mal) intj. what a pity!

                 v.   /ma-/ to be wasted. <u>Nasayang ang pagod ko</u>. My efforts were wasted.

sayáw   n.   /-an/ a dance; a social gathering for dancing; a ball.

                 v.   /-um-/ to dance. <u>Sumayaw kami kagabi</u>. We went dancing last night.

                       /mag-:i-, -in/ <u>Sayawín mo ang tinikling</u>. Dance the tinikling.

sayóte   n.   pear-shaped vegetable.

saysáy   n.   value; worth.

sébo (Sp)   n.   tallow; fat.

sekréta (Sp) n.   detective; plainclothesman.

sekretárya/o n.   secretary.

secréto (Sp) n.   secret.

                adj.   /ma-/ secretive.

séda (Sp)   n.   silk.

segúro (Sp)   n.   insurance.

sélan   adj.   /ma-/ fastidious; meticulous; particular.

sélos   v.   /mag-/ to be jealous. <u>Huwag kang magselos</u>. Don't be jealous.

sélula   n.   cell.

sélyo   n.   stamp.

selyádo   adj.   sealed; stamped.

sementéryo   n.   cemetery.

senador/a   n.   senator.

sentído (Sp) n.   sense (of an expression). --var. sintído.

sentído-komún (Sp) n. common sense. --var. sintido-komún.

sentimentál adj.   sentimental.

sentimyénto (Sp) n. sentiment.

            v.   /mag-/ Nagsentimyento siya sa akin. He harbored hurt feelings against me.

senyál (Sp) n.   mark; sign. --var. sinyál.

sényas (Sp) n.   sign; signal; mark. --var. sinyás.

            v.   /-um-/ Sumenyas siya sa weyter. He signaled to the waiter.

senyór (Sp) n.   sir; mister; lord; master. --var. sinyór.

senyóra (Sp) n.   madam; mistress; aristocratic lady. --var. sinyóra.

senyoríta (Sp) n. little miss; miss; little mistress; (deprecatingly) girl who dislikes work. --var. sinyuríta.

sepilyo   n.   toothbrush; brush. --var. sipílyo.

Septiyémbre n.   September. --var. Setyémbre.

serbésa   n.   beer.

serbidór/a n   waiter/waitress.

serbilyéta n.   table napkin.

serbísyo (Sp) n.   service.

seréno (Sp) n.   night watchman; night breeze; nocturnal coolness causing chill.

sérmon   n.   sermon.

seténta (Sp) num.   seventy.

            n.   seventy centavos.

sí   part.   singular focus marker of proper nouns or names.

sibák (Ch) v.   /-in/ to split (wood) with hatchet. <u>Sinibak niya ang punungkahoy</u>. He chopped down the tree.

sibád   n.   sudden burst of flight.

sibát   n.   spear.

síbi   n.   shed attached to side of house; balcony; portico.

siból   n.   growth; bud; sprout; spring of water.

            v.   /-um-/ to grow, sprout.

sibúyas   n.   onions.

            (<u>na múra</u>) green onions.

síkad   n.   backward kick; energy; force; potency.

            v.   /-um-:i-/ to kick backward.

síkap	adj.	/ma-/ diligent; active; assiduous.
	v.	/mag-/ to strive; to persevere; to work diligently.
síkat	n.	rays.
sikíp	adj.	/ma-/ tight; crowded; narrow; snug.
siklót	n.	a game of skill consisting of throwing up a given number of seeds (or <u>sigay</u>, small shells or small stones) and catching them with the back of the hand.
sikmúra'	n.	stomach.
síko	n.	elbow.
siksík	v.	/-um-/ to cram in; to force into; to crowd in.
		/mag-:i-/
sikuláte	n.	chocolate. --var. <u>tsokoláte</u>.
sidhí'	adj.	/ma-/ assiduous; intensive.
sigá'	n.	bonfire.
	v.	/mag-:-an/ to build a bonfire. <u>Magsigá ka na</u>. Build a bonfire.
sigáng	v.	/mag-:in:i-/ to cook with broth and condiments; to stew.
sigarîlyas	n.	winged <u>seguidillas</u> beans.
sigarîlyo	n.	cigarette.
	v.	/mag-/ to smoke a cigarette.
sigásig	n.	assiduity; persistence.

síga-síga'	adj.	showing-off as able to take it easy (with a feeling of security and pride); being such a show-off. (S1)
sigáw	v.	/-um-/ to shout; to call out loud; to scream.
		/i-/
sígay	n.	shells of small snails.
síge	intj.	go on; go ahead; proceed; continue.
	part.	go on; proceed; continue. O sige: okay then; well; okay; all right. Sige na: come on.
siglá	adj.	/ma-/ lively; enthusiastic.
signós (Sp)	n.	fatal sign; fate.
sigsag	adj.	zigzag.
sigúndo (Sp)	n.	second (of time).
sigurádo	adj.	sure; certain.
sigúro	adv.	maybe; perhaps; probably.
siít	n.	branchlets of bamboo.
silá	pron.	they.
siláb	n.	blaze of burning garbage; fire; conflagration.
	v.	/-an/ Silabán mo ang basura. Burn the garbage.
siláhis (Sp)	n.	rays of the sun breaking through clouds.

siláng	n.	mountain pass; narrow path along mountain sides.
Silángan	n.	East; Orient.
silát	n.	slit between strips of bamboo floor; break on the floor.
sílaw	n.	glare.
	adj.	(siláw) dazzled.
	v.	/ma-/ to be dazzled. <u>Nasilaw siya sa salapi</u>. He was blinded by the money.
silbáto	n.	whistle; sound of whistle or siren.
silbí	v.	/mag-:i-/ to serve.
síli	n.	pepper.
silíd	n.	room; bedroom. --var. <u>kuwárto</u>.
silid-aralan	n.	classroom; study room.
silíndro	n.	harmonica.
sílip	v.	/-um-/ to peep.
		/mang-:-in/ (<u>manilip</u>).
sílo'	n.	loop; lariat.
sílong	n.	basement; space below the house; ground floor.
sílya	n.	chair.
simbá	n.	/-an/ (<u>simbáhan</u>) church.
	v.	/-um-:mag-/ to go to church.
siménto	n.	cement.

sími'	n.	refuse or remnants of fish fallen on the dining table.
simót	adj.	picked up to the last grain or piece (from floor, soil, dish or container) entirely consumed, taken, or used.
	v.	/-in/ <u>Sinimot niya ang natirang kanin sa pinggan</u>. He consumed all of the rice left on the plate.
símoy	n.	breeze.
simpátika	adj.	charming.
símple (Sp)	adj.	simple.
simsím	n.	trying the taste of something; slow enjoyment of something pleasant.
simulá'	n.	beginning.
	v.	/mag-:-an/ to start; to begin.
simyénto	n.	concrete.
siná	mkr.	plural focus marker of <u>si</u>, used before names of persons to mean 'and company' as <u>siná Luis</u>, Luis and his companions.
sínag	n.	rays or light (from sun, moon, stars, lamp); halo around heads of images of saints.
sínat	n.	slight fever.
sinangág	n.	fried rice.
	adj.	fried.
sinkáw	v.	/mag-:i-/ to harness.

sindí	v.	/-um-/ to light up.
		/mag-:-an:i-/ to kindle; to light. <u>Sindihán mo ang sigarilyo ko</u>. Light my cigarette.
síne	n.	movie theatre; cinema.
	v.	/mag-/ (to see a) movie.
sinélas	n.	slippers.
sinibúyas	n.	bulb (plant).
sinigwélas	n.	variety of plum.
síno	int.	who?
sinók	n.	hiccough.
sínop	adj.	/ma-/ economical; thrifty; frugal; careful.
sinsílyo (Sp) n.		loose change.
sinsín	adj.	/ma-/ close.
sintá (Mal) n.		love between man and woman; love of man for the diety; love for country.
		/ka-, -an/ (<u>kasintáhan</u>) sweetheart.
sintás (Sp) n.		lace; lacing; shoestring.
sintído (Sp) n.		the temples.
sintído komun (Sp) n.		common sense. --var. <u>sentído komún</u>.
sintúnis (Sp) n.		term common in the Batangas area for Mandarin type or tangerine orange; native orange.

sinúlid	n.	thread.
sínuman	pro.	whoever. --var. <u>sino</u> <u>man</u>.
sinturón	n.	belt.
sinungáling	adj.	dishonest; liar.
	v.	/mag-/ to tell a lie or a false-hood. <u>Nagsinungaling siya sa</u> <u>akin</u>. He lied to me.
sinu-sino	int.	who (plural).
singá	v.	/-um-:i-/ to expel mucus from the nose. <u>Suminga ka</u>. Blow your nose. <u>Isinga mo ang sipon mo</u>. Blow out the mucus from your cold.
singáw	n.	vapor; steam.
singkamás	n.	yam bean (native turnip).
singkáw	n.	yoke.
	v.	/i-/ to harness. <u>Isingkaw mo</u> <u>ang mga kalabaw</u>. Harness the carabaos.
síngko (Sp)	num.	five.
singkuwénta	num.	fifty; a native term for 'fifty centavos' is <u>isang salapí</u>.
singhál	n.	local vocal outburst of anger; angry snap.
singíl	n.	price quoted; charge; collection of payment of debt.
	v.	/-um-:-in/ to collect payment for accounts. <u>Siningil niya</u> <u>ang mga may utang sa kaniya</u>. He collected the debts of all those who owed him.

singit	v.	/-um-/ to stand in between; to cut into. <u>Sumingit siya sa pila</u>. He cut into the line.
		/mag-:i-/ to insert in slits or chinks. <u>Isingit mo ito sa unang talata</u>. Insert this in the first paragraph.
singsíng	n.	ring.
sipa'	v.	/-um-/ to kick.
		/ma-/ to kick. <u>Nanipa ang kabayo</u>. The horse kicked.
		/mang-:-in/ (<u>manipa</u>).
		/-in/ <u>Sinipa ng bata ang bola</u>. The child kicked the ball.
sipag	adj.	/ma-/ diligent; hard-working; industrious.
siper	n.	zipper.
sipi'	n.	copy; number of issue.
	v.	/-um-/ to copy; to quote.
sipilyo	n.	brush, usually toothbrush.
	v.	/mag-:-in/ to brush (one's teeth). <u>Magsipilyo ka pagkatapus mong kumain</u>. Brush your teeth after eating.
siping	v.	/-um-/ to lie down beside; to place by the side. <u>Sumiping si Dina sa akin</u>. Dina laid down beside me.
sipit	n.	tongs; pincers; chopsticks.

sípol (Sp) n.   whistling; sound of whistling or of a siren.

            v.   /-um-/ to whistle.

sipón n.   cold; catarrh.

sipsíp v.   /-um-:-in/ to sip; to suck. **Sumipsip siya sa iniinom ko.** She sipped from my drink.

síra' n.   a tear (as in clothing); a defect.

           adj.   (<u>sirá</u>) destroyed; broken.

            v.   /-um-/ to destroy; to break; to rip; to tear. <u>Sumira siya sa aming usapan.</u> She broke our verbal agreement.

               /mang-:-in/ (<u>manira</u>). <u>Huwag mong siráin ang laruan.</u> Don't break the toy.

sírko (Sp) n.   circus; acrobatics.

siréna (Sp) n.   mermaid; siren; foghorn.

sisánte (Sp) adj.   dismissed from office.

            v.   /ma-/ to be fired; to lose one's job.

               /mag-:-in/ to fire (someone); to dismiss from the office.

sísi v.   /mag-/ to repent; to regret. <u>Baka magsisi ka lang.</u> You might just regret it.

               /mang-:-in/ (<u>manísi</u>) to lay the blame on someone. <u>Sisihin mo si Bert sa nangyari.</u> Blame Bert for what happened.

sísid	n.	diving head first into the water; swimming under water.
	v.	/-um-:-in/ <u>Sumisid siya sa dagat</u>. He dove into the sea.
sisidlán	n.	(rw. <u>silíd</u>) comparatively small covered container.
sisíl	n.	brush (native).
sísiw	n.	chick.
sisté	adj.	/ma-/ entertaining; full of jokes.
sítaw	n.	string-beans or longbean.
sítsaro	n.	snow pea; pea pod.
sitsarón	n.	pork rind; cracklings (pork).
sitsiríka	n.	Madagascar periwinkle.
sitsít (Ch)	n.	gossip; the sound of a call: 'pssst'.
síwang	n.	slit; crevice; space of a small opening (as of window or door).
siyá	pro.	he/she.
siyám	num.	nine.
siyansí	n.	kitchen turner (spatula).
siyánga' (+ <u>ba</u>)	adv.	really; honestly; is that so? --syn. <u>talagá</u>.
siyémpre	adv.	always; of course; surely; naturally. ...<u>ay syempre sa kaiklian ng bangka</u>. Is always along the short axis of a boat...
siyénse	n.	spatula.
siyéte (Sp)		seven.

siyópaw (Ch) n.   steamed rice cake with meat and
                   condiments inside.

siyudád   n.   city.

sóbra   adj./adv. in excess of.

sóbre (Sp) n.   envelope.

sólo   n.   single; alone.

            adj.   solo; alone; solitary.

            v.   /mag-/ to be by oneself; to be
                   alone. Magsolo ka na lang sa
                   kwarto. Just stay alone in the
                   room.

solomílyo   n.   tenderloin.

sombréro (Sp) n.   hat. --var. sumbréro, sumbléro,
                   sumbalílo.

sopá   n.   sofa; couch.

sópas (Sp) n.   soup.

sorbétes   n.   ice cream.

sosyál   adj.   social; socialite; friendly.

sotanghón   n.   transparent bean noodle; long
                   rice.

stépin   n.   slippers.

sú!   intj. shoo! Sound used for driving
                   away fowls or animals.

subáli't   conj. but; less common than ngunit
                   and datapwat.

subásta (Sp) n.   auction.

            v.   /mag-:i-/ to sell or offer for
                   sale at auction.

subaybáy	n.	attentive and careful observation made by following up the progress of the objective.
súbo'	v.	/-um-:i-/ to get into trouble. <u>Sumubo siya sa gulo</u>. He got into trouble.
		/mag-:i-/ to feed or put food into the mouth. <u>Isubo mo ito sa bata</u>. Put this into the child's mouth.
súbok	v.	/mag-:-in/ to try; to test. <u>Subúkin mong magsalita ng Tagalog</u>. Try speaking in Tagalog.
		/mang-/ (<u>manúbok</u>) to spy on.
subsób	v.	/-um-/ to fall on the face. <u>Sumubsob siya sa pagmamadali</u>. He fell on his face in the rush.
		/mag-:i-/ to get intensely involved. <u>Isubsob mo ang sarili mo sa iyong ginagawa</u>. Involve yourself intensely in what you're doing.
súka'	n.	vinegar.
súka	n.	vomit.
	v.	/-um-:i-/ to vomit; to throw up. <u>Sumuka siya kanina</u>. He vomitted a little while ago.
		/mag-/ <u>Baka magsuká ka</u>. You might vomit.
súkal	n.	dirt; refuse.
súkat	n.	/-an/ (<u>sukatán</u>) a measure.

	p.v.	fitting; right. <u>Hindi mo sukat ikagalit</u>. It is not right for you to get angry.

| | v. | /-um-:-in/ to measure; to try on. <u>Sukátin mo ang haba ng kwarto</u>. Measure the length of the room.

/mag-:i-/ <u>Isukat mo ang bagong damit</u>. Try on the new dress.

sukbît v. /mag-:i-/ to let something hang from the waistline; to hook on to one's belt, skirt, or trousers. <u>Isukbit mo ang itak</u>. Let the bolo hang from your side.

súki' n. customer of long standing.

suklám n. aversion; repugnance; loathing; disgust.

v. /ma-/ to be disgusted.

suklây n. comb.

v. /mag-:-in/ to comb the hair. <u>Magsuklay ka</u>. Comb your hair. <u>Suklayín mo ang buhok ng bata</u>. Comb the child's hair.

suklî' n. change (from a purchase).

v. /mag-:i-/ to change money. <u>Isukli mo itong diyes sa bata</u>. Give this ten cents change to the child.

suklób v. /mag-:i-/ to cover completely; to cover with encasing around sides. <u>Isuklob mo ito nang di ka mabasa ng ulan</u>. Use this for a cover so you won't get wet from the rain.

súko'   v.   /-um-/ to surrender; to give up; to succumb. <u>Sumuko ang kriminal</u>. The criminal surrendered.

/i-/ <u>Isuko mo ang baril na ginamit mo</u>. Give up the gun you used.

súkob   v.   /-um-/ to share a cover or shelter; e.g. umbrella. <u>Sumukob si Rosita sa payong ko</u>. Rosita shared my umbrella (with me).

/mag-:i-/ <u>Isukob mo ang bata sa payong mo</u>. Let the child share your umbrella.

suksók   v.   /mag-:i-/ to insert in between layers; to keep away; to push down in a container. <u>Isuksok mo ang natirang pera</u>. Set aside the money that's left.

súga   v.   /mag-:i-/ to tether. <u>Isuga mo ang kabayo</u>. Tether the horse.

sugál   n.   gambling; any game (usually a game of cards) that involves a bet or wager.

/-an/ (<u>sugálan</u>) gambling den.

v.   /mag-/ to gamble. <u>Huwag kang magsugal</u>. Don't gamble.

sugapá'   adj.   inveterate drunkard who reels around habitually when drunk.

sugaról   n.   gambler.

súgat   n.   wound.

v.   /-um-/ to hurt. <u>Sumugat sa kanyang damdamin ang alaala ng lumipas</u>. His feelings became hurt in remembering the past.

/mag-/ to develop into a wound. <u>Baka magsugat iyan sa kakakamot mo</u>. That might develop into a wound from your scratching it.

/mang-:-an/ (<u>manugat</u>) to inflict pain.

Sugbuánon   n.   the Cebuano language. --var. <u>Sugbuhanon</u>, <u>Sibuhanon</u>, <u>Sebwano</u>.

sugpóng   n.   connection; juncture; joint; welding.

súgo'   n.   representative.

súgod   v.   /-um-/ to advance or rush into a forward attack. <u>Sumugod ang mga kaaway</u>. The enemies rushed in together in an attack.

/mang-:-in/ (<u>manugod</u>).

sugpó'   v.   /-um-/ to suppress or check the progress of something developing, swelling or rising.

/mang-:-in/ (<u>manugpó'</u>). <u>Sugpuin natin ang kasamaan</u>. Let's stop (the progress of) evil.

sugpó'   n.   prawn.

súha'   n.   pomelo.

suhî'   adj.   born in abnormal position (i.e. feet first).

súhol   n.   bribery.

         v.   /mag-:i-/ to bribe. <u>Huwag kang magsuhol</u>. Don't bribe.

/mang-/ (<u>manuhol</u>). <u>Nanuhol ang dayuhan</u>. The alien engaged in bribery.

sulár (Sp) n.   small fenced lot with plants and trees, usually surrounding a residence.

súlat   n.   letter.

         v.   /-um-/ to write. <u>Sumulat si Tony sa akin</u>. Tony wrote to me.

               /mag-:-in:i-/ <u>Isulat mo ang tula sa pisara</u>. Write the poem on the blackboard.

suló'   n.   torch.

súlok   n.   corner (of room).

súlong!   intj.   go ahead! go away!; push forward; scram.

         v.   /i-/ to push forward.

sulsî   v.   /mag-:-an/ to mend clothes. <u>Nanulsi kami ng mga sirang damit kahapon</u>. We mended the torn dresses yesterday.

               /mang-:-an/ (<u>manulsi</u>) <u>Sulsihán mo ang medyas ko</u>. Mend my socks.

sulsól   v.   /-um-/ to prod; to incite someone to do something usually not good; to instigate.

               /mang-:-an/ (<u>manulsól</u>) to prod; to incite someone to do something usually not good; to instigate. <u>Nanulsol siya sa mga manggagawa'</u>. He incited the laborers.

sulyáp   v.   /-um-/ to glance; to give a side-glance. <u>Sumulyap siya sa aking ginagawa</u>. He gave a side-glance at what I was doing.

súma   v.   /mag-:-in/ to sum up. <u>Sumahin</u>
<u>mo ang ating nagasta</u>. Add up
our expenditures.

súman   n.   native rice cake wrapped in
banana or palm leaves.

sumbát   v.   /mang-/ (<u>manumbát</u>) to upbraid.
<u>Nanumbat ang prinsipal kahapon</u>.
The principal was upbraiding
people yesterday.

sumbóng   v.   /mag-:i-/ to accuse; to tell
on; to complain about. <u>Nag-</u>
<u>sumbong ang bata sa kanyang ina</u>.
The child turned tattle tale to
his mother. <u>Isumbong mo sa</u>
<u>kanyang ama ang mga kalukohan</u>
<u>niya</u>. Tell his father what
nonsense he has done.

sumbréro   n.   hat. --var. <u>sombréro</u>.

sumpa'   v.   /-um-/ to promise; to make an
oath; to curse. <u>Sumumpa kang</u>
<u>darating ka sa oras</u>. Promise to
come on time.

                     /-in/ to curse a person.

sumpít   n.   blow gun.

sumpóng   adj.   /-in/ (<u>sumpúngin</u>) moody.

sundálo   n.   soldier.

sundo'   v.   /mang-:-in/ (<u>manundo'</u>) to
fetch a person; to pass by a
person; to meet. <u>Sinundo namin</u>
<u>si Tessie kahapon</u>. We went by
and picked up Tessie yesterday.

sundót   v.   /-um-/ to poke (with the point
of a finger, stick, spear or the
like).

/mang-/ (<u>manundót</u>) to poke
(with the point of a finger,
stick, spear or the like).
<u>Sinundot niya si Juanita</u>. He
poked Juanita.

/-in/ to poke (with the point
of a finger, stick, spear or
the like). <u>Sundutin mo ang hindi
naka-upo nang maayos</u>. Poke the
ones that aren't sitting properly.

sunód   adj.   /ma-:-in/ (<u>masunúrin</u>) obedient.
<u>Sundin natin ang ating guro</u>.
Let's obey our teacher.

              v.   /-um-:-in/ to follow; to obey.
<u>Sumunod ka sa iyong magulang</u>.
Follow/Obey your parents.

/i-/ to follow with something
left behind for someone.

súnog   n.   a fire.

              v.   /-in/ (<u>sunúgin</u>) to set on fire;
to burn.

súnong   v.   /mag-:-in, i/ to carry on the
head. <u>Sunungin mo ang isang
bilaong puto</u>. Carry the tray of
rice cakes on your head.

suntók   v.   /-um-/ to box; to hit with the
fist. <u>Nanuntok ang lasing</u>. The
drunken man began swinging at
people.

/mang-:-in/ (<u>manuntók</u>) to box;
to hit with the fist. <u>Sinuntok
niya ang dingding sa galit</u>. He
banged his fist against the wall
in anger.

súngay   n.   horn(s) of an animal.

sungká'   n.   native game.

sungkí' (Ch) n.   acute angled corner; abnormal tooth growth.

sungkít   v.   /-um-/ to pick fruit by means of a hook attached to the end of a pole.

/mang-:-in/ (manungkít) to pick fruit by means of a hook attached to the end of a pole. Sungkitín natin ang mga hinog na prutas. Let's get the ripe fruit from the tree by means of a pole.

sunggáb   v.   /-um-/ to grab, to grasp, clutch, seize with the hands. Sinunggabán ng mga bata ang mga prutas. The children grabbed the fruits.

/mang-:-an/ (manunggáb) to grab, grasp, clutch, seize with the hands.

súngit   adj.   /ma-/ ill-tempered; short-tempered; sulky; irritable.

suót   n.   refers to clothes worn by a person.

v.   /-um-/ to go inside or to go through. Sumuot sila sa isang madilim na kuweba. They entered a dark cave.

/mag-:i-/ to wear an apparel. Magsuot ka ng magandang damit. Wear an attractive dress. Isuot mo ang bago mong damit. Wear your new dress.

supá (Sp)   n.   sofa.

supalpál   n.   something covering the mouth; something forced into the mouth.

superbisór   n.   supervisor.

superintindénte n.   superintendent.

supládo/a   adj.   conceited.

supleménto (Sp) n.   supplement.

supling   n.   sprout; shoots.

supók   adj.   carbonized.

súpot   n.   small bag; a paper bag; pouch.

súri'   v.   /-um-/ to analyze; to examine.

                       /mag-:-in/ to analyze; to examine;
                       to diagnose. Sinuri ng doktor
                       ang kanyang pasyente. The doctor
                       examined his patient.

súrot   n.   bedbug.

surtído (Sp) adj.   assorted.

sús!   intj.   an exclamation of surprise or
                       disapproval; abbreviation for
                       Hesús, Jesus.

súsi'   n.   key.

             v.   /-an/ to lock. Susian mo ang
                       iyong aparador. Lock your cabi-
                       net.

susó'   n.   snail.

súso   n.   breasts.

             v.   /-um-:-in/ to suck milk; to
                       nurse. Sumuso ang bata sa ina.
                       The child was nursed by his
                       mother.

susón   n.   second layer; reinforcing layer.

            adj.   /magka-/ one layer over another.

suspendído (Sp) adj.   suspended.

susténto   n.   allowance; support.

            v.   /mag-:-an, in/ to support; to finance. <u>Nagsusustento si Nonong sa kanyang kapatid</u>. Nonong is supporting his brother (or sister). <u>Sustentuhan mo ang aking pagaaral</u>. Support me in my studies.

sutíl   adj.   stubborn; disobedient.

sutlá'   n.   silk.

sutsót   v.   /-um-/ sssst!; a sibilant sound produced to call someone or to urge silence. <u>Sumutsot ang dalaga</u>. The young girl called with a hissing sound.

suwábe   adj.   soft; smooth; mild; gentle.

suwág   v.   /-um-/ to butt with the horns.

            /ma-/ to butt with horns. <u>Baka manuwag ang baka</u>. The cow might butt someone with his horns.

            /mang-:-in/ (<u>manuwag</u>).

            /-in/ to butt with horns. <u>Sinuwag ng kalabaw ang magsasaka</u>. The carabao butted the farmer with his horns.

suwaíl   adj.   rebellious; disobedient; insolent.

suwáy   v.   /-um-:-in/ to disobey; to violate; to go against; to go against the wishes of somebody. <u>Sumuway si Edna sa kanyang magulang</u>. Edna went against her parents. <u>Sinuway niya ang utos ng magulang niya</u>. She disobeyed her parents' wishes.

suwélas (Sp) n.   sole (of footwear).

suwéldo   n.   pay; salary; wage.

           v.   /-um-/ to receive one's pay or salary. <u>Sumuweldo ako kahapon</u>. I got paid yesterday.

                    /mag-:i-/

suwérte (Sp) n.   luck; good luck; good fortune.

suwí (Mal) n.   shoot (of plants, as bananas).

suwítik   adj.   tricky; crafty; cunning; knavish; sly.

suyá'   adj.   fed up.

súyo'   v.   /mang-:-in/ (<u>manuyo'</u>) to win one's affection. <u>Nanuyo si Remigio kay Tessie</u>. Remigio tried to win Tessie's affection.

súyod   n.   lice comb; fine toothed comb; farmer's harrow.

           v.   /mag-:-in/ to comb one's hair with a fine nit comb; to catch lice; to harrow the soil; to make an intensive search in a place. <u>Magsuyod ka at baka may kuto ka</u>. Comb your hair with a fine tooth comb because you might have lice. <u>Suyúrin mo ang lugar nang makuha mo ang nawala mo</u>. Comb the area to find what you have lost.

swéter   n.   sweater.

swîpistik   n.   sweepstakes.

T

taál	adj.	genuine; legitimate; native; inborn; innate.
taán	v.	/mag-:i-/ to reserve; to save for other people for some future time. Magtaan ka ng pagkain para mamayang gabi. Set aside food for later this evening. Itaan mo ito para bukas. Save this for tomorrow.
taás	n.	height.
		/ka-, -an/ (kataásan) upland.
	adj.	high; tall; height; altitude; superiority.
	v.	/-um-/ to become higher or taller.. Tumaas si Angel. Angel has gotten taller.
		/mag-:i-/ to put up; to carry up a height; to hoist. Itaas mo ang ating bandila. Raise our flag.
tabá'	adj.	stout; fat.
	v.	/-um-/ to become stout.
tabák (Mal)	n.	cutlass.
tabáko	n.	cigar.
tában	n.	holder or support (so as to keep something in position).
tabáng	adj.	/ma-/ bland; tasteless; lack of seasoning or spices.
tábas	n.	cut for a dress.

274

	v.	/-um-/ to cut the design or according to a design or pattern, as of cloth, paper, etc; to hack. <u>Tumabas ako ng damit kagabi.</u> I cut a dress last night for sewing. <u>Tabasin mo ang mga sanga ng puno ng mangga.</u> Hack off the branches of the mango tree.

/mag-:-in/ to cut down plant growth by hacking away.

tabí	n.	side; brim; border.
	adv.	beside; by the side of.
	v.	/mag-:-i/ to save up or to store.

tabí	v.	/-um-/ to stand beside or aside; to get out of the way; to go to the side of. <u>Tumabi si Belen sa akin.</u> Belen came beside me.

/mag-:i-/ to keep away something for future use. <u>Itabi mo ang kaunting salapi para sa hinaharap.</u> Set aside a little money for the future.

tabíke (Sp)	n.	partition wall.

tábig	v.	/mang-:-in/ (<u>manábig</u>) to shove violently with the elbow. <u>Tinabig ng lasing ang baso.</u> The drunken man pushed the glass aside violently with his elbow.

tabíl	n.	glibness of tongue; talkativeness.
	adj.	/ma-/
	v.	/-um-/

tábing	n.	screen; covering screen.

tabíng-dágat	n.	beach; seashore.

tabingí'   adj.   not symmetrical; disproportional; unbalanced.

             v.   /-um-/ to be or to become unsymmetrical; to become crooked. Tumabingi ang nakasabit na litratro. The picture hanging on the wall was crooked.

                    /i-, -in/ to make unsymmetrical.

tablá   n.   wood board; lumber.

tablétas (Sp) n.   tablet (med).

tábo'   n.   a dipper; scoop; usually a coconut shell or an empty can.

             v.   /-um-:mag-:-in/ to scoop water with a coconut shell or an empty can; to use a dipper, a coconut shell or an empty can. Tumabo siya ng tubig sa tapayan. He scooped out water from the glass jar.

tábon   v.   /ma-, -an/ to be covered with. Natabunan siya ng buhangin. He was covered with sand.

                    /mag-:i-/ to cover with earth.

                    /-an/ (tabúnan) to cover with soil. Tabunan mo ng lupa ang siga'. Cover the bonfire with soil.

tabóy   n.   statement, admonition or shout given to urge or drive a person to go away, leave, or do something that should be done right away or earlier.

             v.   /mag-:i-/ to drive away; to drive out of. Itaboy mo ang mga baboy na nasa halamanan. Drive the pigs out of the garden.

tábing	n.	curtain; screen.
tákal	n.	/-an/ (takalán) a measure.
	v.	/-um-/ to measure by volume of liquids, grains or powder.
		/mag-:-in/ to measure. Magtakal ka ng bigas. Measure the uncooked rice.
tákas	v.	/-um-/ to escape; to run away. Tumakas ang bilanggo. The prisoner escaped.
		/mag-:i-/ to run away with something.
tákaw	adj.	/ma-/ greedy; voracious; gluttonous.
takbó	v.	/-um-/ to run. Tumakbo siya nang matulin. He ran rapidly.
		/mag-:i-/ to run with something.
takdá'	n.	limitation, determination or fixing of time; provision (of rule, ordinance, law).
takílya (Sp)	n.	ticket-booth; ticket office.
takilyéra	n.	ticket girl (in theatres).
takíp	n.	cover.
	v.	/mag-:-an/ to cover. Nagtakíp siya ng kaniyang mga mata. He covered his eyes. Takpán mo ang ulam. Put a cover on the food (main dish).
takípsilim	n.	twilight; sunset.

taklób	v.	/mag-:i-:-an/ to cover, usually provided with overlapping sides; to put one side over on the other as in a sandwich.

Itaklob mo itong kumot. Use the blanket for a cover. Takluban mo ng lona ang binilad na palay. Cover the dried rice grains with a canvas.

takóng (Sp)	n.	shoe or boot heel.
tákot	n.	fear; fright.
	adj.	/nakaka-/ frightening; formidable.
	v.	/ma-/ to be frightened, scared or afraid. Natakot siya sa nakita niya. He was afraid of what he saw.

/-in/ to frighten; to scare. Takútin natin si Vida mamayang gabi. Let's frighten Vida later this evening.

táksi	n.	taxi; cab.
taksîl	adj.	treacherous; unfaithful.
takwîl	v.	/mag-:i-/ to disown; to deny; to repudiate. Baka itakwil ka ng iyong ama. You might be disowned by your father.
tadhána'	n.	nature; fate.
tadtád	v.	/mag-:-in/ to chop to pieces; Magtadtad ka ng sibuyas. Chop the onions into small pieces. Tadtarín mo ang karne. Chop the meat.

tadyák   v.   /-um-/ to kick backwards; to kick violently. <u>Tumadyak ang kabayo</u>. The horse kicked back violently.

/mang-:-an/ (<u>manadyák</u>)

/-an/ to kick. <u>Tadyakan kita riyan, nakita mo</u>. I'll kick you...you'll see.

tadyáng   n.   ribs; spareribs.

táe   n.   excreta.

       v.   /-um-:i-/ to defecate; to have a bowel movement. <u>Tumae ang bata sa sala</u>. The child had a bowel movement in the living room.

/mag-/ to have diarrhea. <u>Baka magtaé ka</u>. You might get diarrhea.

tagá'   v.   /mang-:-in/ to hack with a cutting instrument. <u>Tagaín mo ang mga panggatong</u>. Hack/chop the firewood.

       af.   a noun-forming prefix meaning 'native of' or 'coming from'; with verb roots, it means 'regular performer of'.

tagakták   n.   rapid dropping (of tears or sweat).

       v.   /-um-/ to perspire profusely or to cry with tears falling rapidly.

tagál   adj.   /ma-/ late; that takes a long time; for a long period of time.

       v.   /-um-/ to endure; to withstand. <u>Tumagal siya sa hirap</u>. He withstood the hardship.

/mag-/ to take a long time;
to stay long. <u>Huwag kang mag-
tagal</u>. Don't be long.

taga-saán   int.   from where.

taga-tanggap   n.   receiver.

taghóy   n.   lament; lamentation.

tagiktík   n.   light sound of consecutive drops;
ticking of clocks and watches.

tagiháwat   n.   pimples.

tagílid   v.   /-um-/ to become tilt; to become slanted; to become lop-
sided. <u>Tumagilid ang bahay dahil
sa lindol</u>. The house became
lopsided because of the earthquake.

/mag-:i-/ to tilt; to slant.
<u>Itagilid mo ang mesa</u>. Tilt the
table.

tagilíran   n.   side.

taglamíg   n.   (rw. <u>lamíg</u>) cold season; winter.

tagláy   v.   /mag-:-in/ to bear; to possess.
<u>Nagtataglay si Amalia ng pambi-
hirang kagandahan</u>. Amalia
possesses extraordinary beauty.

tágo'   v.   /mag-:i-/ to keep; to hide; to
put away. <u>Nagtago si Maria sa
hiya</u>. Maria hid from shame.
<u>Itago mo ang natirang pagkain</u>.
Put away the leftover food.

tagós   v.   /-um-:-an/ to penetrate, reach
through a whole width, thickness
or length. <u>Tumagos ang lanseta
sa kanyang katawan</u>. The pocket-
knife penetrated his body.

tagpí'	n.	patch; patching (of cloth); to cover a tear or break.
tagpó'	v.	/mag-:-in/ to meet; to agree to meet; to meet each other. <u>Magtagpo tayo bukas sa paaralan.</u> Let's meet each other at school tomorrow. <u>Tagpuin mo ako sa opisina.</u> Meet me at the office.
tag-ulán	n.	rainy or wet season.
tagumpáy	n.	victory. /mag-/ to win.
táhan	v.	/-um-/ to cease or stop crying. <u>Tumahan ang bata sa pag-iiyak.</u> The child stopped crying.
tahánan	n.	home.
tahí'	v.	/-um-/ to sew. <u>Tumahi si Kelly ng damit ko.</u> Kelly sewed my dress. /mang-:-in/ (<u>manahi'</u>). <u>Nanahi ako kagabi.</u> I sewed last night. /-in/ to sew. <u>Tahiin mo ang damit ng bata.</u> Sew the child's dress.
tahímik	adj.	quiet; peaceful; tranquil.
tahíp	n.	up and down movement of rice grains being winnowed on a flat basket; rapid palpitation or throbbing (of heartbeat).
	v. .	/-um-/ to beat rapidly (heart). /mag-/ to winnow (cereals).
tahó	n.	Chinese mongo bean jelly or meal with syrup sold by Chinese peddlers; bean curd.

tahól	v.	/-um-/ to bark. <u>Tumahol ang</u> <u>aso</u>. The dog barked.
tahóng	n.	salt water mussel; a species of clam.
táhuri (Ch)	n.	fermented salted soybean curd.
taimtím	adj.	/ma-/ sincere.
tainga	n.	ear.
tála'	n.	bright star.
taláb	v.	/-um-/ to cut through; to be effective, i.e. medicine, instruction, etc. <u>Tumalab din</u> <u>ang pangaral mo</u>. Your advice was effective.
talabá	n.	oyster.
talakítok	n.	cavalla; a species of fish.
talagá	adv.	truly; really; honestly. --syn. <u>siyangá'</u>.
taláhib	n.	a species of tall grass.
talampákan	n.	sole of foot; a foot long. --syn. <u>piyé</u>.
talangká'	n.	small crab.
tálas	adj.	/ma-/ sharp; acute.
táli'	n./qnt.	a bundle (tied with a string).
	v.	/mag-:i-/ to tie. <u>Itali mo</u> <u>ang aso</u>. Tie the dog.
talíkod	v.	/-um-/ to turn one's back to; to renounce, forsake.
talílong	n.	mullet (immature).

talím	adj.	/ma-/ sharp.
talíno	adj.	/ma-/ intelligent; wise; sharp.
táling	n.	mole.
talinghága'	n.	allegory; figure of speech, metaphor. --var. talinhága'.
talipapá'	n.	fish-market with temporary stalls under flat sheds.
tálo	adj.	defeated; beaten; surpassed.
	v.	/ma-/ to be defeated; to lose. Natalo sila sa basketbol. They lost the basketball game. /mang-:-in/ (manalo) to defeat; to surpass; to win over. Baka talunin ka ni Juan. John might defeat you.
talón	n.	waterfall.
talón	v.	/-um-:-in/ to jump; to leap. Tumalon si Linda. Linda jumped. Tinalon niya ang kanal. He jumped over the canal.
talóng	n.	eggplant.
tálop	n.	act of peeling.
	adj.	(talóp) peeled; decorticated.
talós	adj.	comprehended; perfectly understood.
talúkab	n.	carapace (of crabs).
talúkap	n.	sheath of palm leaves or banana stalk; eyelid.
talukbóng	n.	head covering.
talúlot	n.	petals of flowers.

talyér (Sp) n.   mill; factory; workshop.

talumpáti   n.   speech.

              v.   /mag-/ to give a speech. Nag-
talumpati ang senador. The
senator gave a speech.

talyási'   n.   vat; medium sized iron vat (for
cooking).

táma'   adj.   correct; right; true.

              v.   /-um-/ to hit the mark; to be
right or correct. Tumama sa
ulo niya ang bola. The ball hit
him right on the head.

                     /mag-:-i/ to put correctly.

tamák   adj.   impregnated.

tama ka na   an expression which is a mild or
affectionate way of saying 'Oh,
stop it; Oh, shut up'.

tamád   adj.   lazy, idle, indolent.

tambák   n.   a heap; a pile; filler (soil).

              v.   /mag-:-i/ to pile; to dump into;
to fill up with rubbish, earth
or stones. Itambak mo ang mga
basura sa isang tabi. Pile the
garbage in one corner.

tambád   adj.   exposed to view.

tambál   v.   /mag-/ to pair up; to be billed
together. Nagtambal ang dalawang
sikat na artista. The two famous
film stars paired up/billed together (in a film).

                     /i-/ to pair. Itambal mo si
Tessie kay Remigio. Pair Tessie
with Remigio.

tambán	n.	herring.
tambó	n.	soft broom.
tamból	n.	drum.
	v.	/mag-:-i/ to drum; to pound as a drum. Magtambol ka. Beat the drum.
tambúli'	n.	bugle made of horn.
tamís	n.	sweet; sweets; dessert.
	adj.	/ma-/ sweet (food).
tamó'	v.	/mag-:i-/ to obtain; to acquire; to be awarded. Nagtamo si Jose ng isang karangalan. Joe attained an honor.
tampál	v.	/mang-:-in/ to slap with the hand; cf. sampal (manampál). Baka tampalín ka niya. He might slap you.
tampalásan	adj.	wicked; perverse; destructive.
tampípi'	n.	chest or trunk made of palm leaves.
tampisáw	v.	/mag-/ to wade in the water. Nagtampisaw kami sa tabing dagat. We waded at the seashore.
tampó	v.	/mag-/ to sulk. Nagtampo si Dolores. Dolores sulked.
tánan	v.	/mag-:i-/ to elope; to elope with. Nagtanan sina Celia at Senen. Celia and Senen eloped. Itanan mo ang iyong kasintahan. Elope with your sweetheart.

tanáw	n.	/-in/ (<u>tanawin</u>) scenery; landscape; view.
	v.	/-um-:-in/ to view; to look. <u>Tumanaw ka sa dakong silangan.</u> View the easterly direction. <u>Tanawin mo ang dagat at bundok.</u> View the ocean and the mountain.
tandá'	n.	mark or sign.
tanda'	n.	age.
	adj.	/ma-/ elderly; old.
	v.	/-um-/ to age; to get older. <u>Tumanda agad ang presidente.</u> The president aged quickly.
tandá	v.	/mag-:-an/ to remember; to retain. <u>Tandaan mo ang sinabi ko.</u> Mark my words. <u>Uli uli magtanda ka.</u> Next time learn from your experience.
tandáng	n.	rooster.
tanikalá'	n.	chain.
taním	n.	plants.
	v.	/mag-:i-/ to plant. <u>Nagtanim kami ng kamote sa bakuran.</u> We planted sweet potatoes in the backyard. <u>Itanim mo ang mustasa.</u> Plant the mustard.
táning	n.	a time limit.
	v.	/mag-:-an/ to give a time limit. <u>Nagtaning ng buhay ng pasyente ang doktor.</u> The doctor said the patient had a limited time to live.
tánod	n.	sentinel; guard.

tanóng	n.	a question.
	v.	/mag-:-in, i-/ to ask; to question; to inquire. <u>Nagtanong siya sa akin</u>. He asked me. <u>Itanong mo sa kanya kung anong oras ang miting</u>. Ask him what time the meeting is. <u>Tinanong niya ako</u>. He asked me.
tansó'	n.	copper.
tantó'	adj.	realized.
tanyág	adj.	popular; known; famous.
tangá	adj.	stupid; ignorant; idiot.
tángan	v.	/-um-/ to hold in hand; to hold onto. <u>Tumangan ka sa akin</u>. Hold on to me.
		/mag-:-an/ to hold in hand; to hold onto. <u>Tangánan mo ang iyong kapatid</u>. Hold onto your brother (sister).
tangáy	adj.	carried away (by seizure, force, mouth).
tangká'	v.	/mag-:-in/ to premeditate; to plan; to intend. <u>Nagtangka siyang magpakamatay</u>. He planned to commit suicide. <u>Baka tangkain niyang ako ay patayin</u>. He might plan to kill me.
tangkád	adj.	/ma-/ 'tall and slender of stature.
tangkál	n.	cage for chickens.
tangké	n.	tank.

tanggál	v.	/mag-:-in/ to unfasten; to dismantle; to remove; to take off. <u>Nagtanggal si Rosita ng sapatos niya.</u> Rosita took off her shoes. <u>Tinanggal ni Nita ang kanyang salamin.</u> Nita took off her glasses.
tanggap	v.	/-um-:-in/ to receive; to accept; to admit. <u>Tumanggap ako ng sulat kahapon.</u> I got a letter yesterday. <u>Tanggapin mo ang aking pakikiramay.</u> Accept my condolence.
tanggápan	n.	office.
tanggi'	v.	/-um-:-an/ to refuse; to deny. <u>Tumanggi ako sa alok niya.</u> I refused his offer. <u>Tinanggihan ko ang mga bintang niya.</u> I refused his accusations.
tánggo	n.	tango (dance).
tanggól	n.	defense.
	v.	/mag-:i-/ to defend.
		/ipag-/ to defend. <u>Ipagtanggol mo ang inyong bayan.</u> Defend your country.
tanghál	n.	/-an/ (<u>tanghálan</u>) place where the show or program is exhibited.
	adj.	exalted; prominent.
	v.	/mag-:-in/ to exalt; to exhibit.
tangháli'	n.	/-an/ (<u>tanghalían</u>) lunch; noon meal.
	adj.	late (time); not early.
	adv.	late; high noon; midday.

	v.	/mang-/ (mananghali') to have lunch.
tángi'	adj.	special; favorite; one and only.
tangó'	v.	/-um-:i-/ to nod; to say yes. Tumango siya. He nodded. Itango mo ang iyong ulo. Nod your head.
tángos	n.	(Geog) cape; promontory; peninsula.
tángos	n.	prominence (physically, as of nose or forehead); high-bridged nose.
	adj.	/ma-/ high-bridged nose.
táo	n.	person.
Tao pó'!		a phrase used by a caller to announce his presence at the entrance of a home. (Lit. There is a person here.)
taób	v.	/-um-/ to capsize; to put face down; to overturn. Tumaob ang bangka. The canoe turned over.
		/mag-:i-/ to capsize; to put face down; to overturn. Itaob mo ang mga plato. Turn the plates over.
taón	n.	year.
taóng	n.	kerosene can (approximately five gallons).
táong-báhay	n.	housekeeper; housewife.
tápa	n.	jerked beef or pork; dried meat.
tápak	v.	/-um-:-an/ to tread on; to lay the foot on; to step on. Tapákan mo ito. Step on this.

/mag-/ (<u>magtapák</u>) to go barefoot. <u>Magtapák tayo bukas</u>.
Let's go barefoot tomorrow.

tápal   v.   /mag-:i-/ to patch; to apply.
<u>Itapal mo ito kung masakit ang
iyong ulo</u>. Apply this if your
head aches.

tápang   adj.   /ma-/ brave; courageous.

tapát   n.   the place in front; that which
is across.

    adv.   in front of.

    v.   /-um-/ to stand in front of.
<u>Tumapat si Pedro sa akin</u>. Pedro
stood in front of me.

               /mag-:i-/ to put directly in
front; to tell the truth.
<u>Magtapat ka sa akin</u>. Tell me
the truth. <u>Itapat mo ang mesa
ko sa mesa ni Alma</u>. Put my
table in front of Alma's.

tapát   adj.   /ma-/ honest; truthful;
sincere; loyal.

    v.   /mag-/ to tell the truth; to
be frank, sincere, honest.

tapáyan   n.   large earthen jar for water
storage.

tapéte   n.   tablecloth.

tápi'   n.   a piece of cloth usually wrapped around the body or wrapped
from the waist down.

    v.   /mag-, i-/ to wrap a piece of
cloth around the body. <u>Itapi mo
ang tuwalya</u>. Wrap the towel
around yourself.

tapiyóka   n.   tapioca.

tapón   n.   cork; stopper; plug.

tápon   v.   /-um-/ to be spilled. <u>Tumapon</u> <u>ang gatas</u>. The milk got spilled.

/mag-:i/ to throw away; to cart aside something. <u>Nagtapon ako</u> <u>ng basura kagabi</u>. I threw out the garbage last night. <u>Itapon</u> <u>mo ang mga hindi na kailangan.</u> Throw out what you don't need.

tápos   n.   ending; conclusion.

          adv.   afterwards.

          v.   /mag-/ to graduate. <u>Nagtapos</u> <u>ako sa Dalubhasaang Normal ng</u> <u>Pilipinas</u>. I graduated from Philippine Normal College.

/-in/ to finish. <u>Tapusin mo</u> <u>ang ipinagagawa ko sa iyo.</u> Finish up what I've asked you to do.

tapyás   n.   facet (as on a precious stone) resulting from shipping or shaping.

          adj.   chipped; trimmed.

tarabáho   n.   work. --var. <u>trabáho</u>.

tárak   n.   knife or dagger sticking out with sharp end embedded.

          adj.   /naka-/ plunged in as of a dagger.

          v.   /i-/ to stab with (a knife or dagger).

/-an/ to stab (someone or animal) with a knife or dagger.

tarantádo (Sp) adj. a person with misdirected acts.

taráng   n.   stamping of feet (in pain or anger).

tarangká (Sp) n.   bar or closing-peg across a door or window. --var. trangká.

tarhéta (Sp) n.   calling or visiting card.

tartanílya (Sp) n.   round-top two wheeled horse-drawn carriage.

tása   n.   cup.

tastás   adj.   unstitched; detached; ripped.

              v.   /mag-:-in/ to rip what has been sewn. Tastasin mo ang tahi ng damit. Rip the sewing of the dress.

taták   n.   imprint; stamp, seal; mark, trademark.

tatág   adj.   /ma-/ stable; solvent.

tatág   v.   /mag-:i-/ to found; to organize; to establish. Nagtatag si Cres ng isang samahan. Cres organized a club.

tatás   adj.   /ma-/ fluent.

tátay   n.   father (term of address and reference).

tatló   num.   three.

tatsúlok   n.   triangle.

tatú (Eng)   n.   tattoo. --var. tató.

táwa   v.   /-um-/ to laugh. Tumawa si Rogelio nang malakas. Roger laughed loudly.

/mag-/ (<u>magtawá</u>) to laugh
continuously.

táwad   n.   a discount; reduction in price.

      v.   /-um-:-in; i-:-an/ to bargain;
to ask for a discount. <u>Tumawad</u>
<u>ako</u>. I bargained. <u>Tawáran mo</u>
<u>ng uno singkuwenta</u>. Try to
buy it for one fifty.

táwag   v.   /-um-:-in/ to call. <u>Tumawag</u>
<u>ang tatay mo kanina</u>. Your
father called a few minutes
ago. <u>Tawágin mo si Ernesto</u>.
Call Ernesto.

         /mag-/ (<u>magtawág</u>) to call.
<u>Magtawag ka ng makakasama sa</u>
<u>atin</u>. Call (the people) that
could go with us.

tuwálya n.   towel.

táwas   n.   alum.

tawíd   n.   crossing; act of crossing or
going across (a street, river,
stretch of country).

      v.   /-um-:-in/ to cross, as a
street or a river. <u>Tumawid ka</u>
<u>kung walang sasakyang dumarating</u>.
Cross the street if there aren't
any vehicles coming.

         /mag-, i-/ to take across; to
help someone cross the street.
<u>Itawid mo ang bulag</u>. Help the
blind man across the street.

tawsî (Ch) n.   beans preserved in soy sauce.

tayá'	n.	the 'it' in a game.

                 v.   /-um-/ to wager; to bet on.
Tumaya kami sa kabayong itim.
We bet on the black horse.

/mag-:i-/ to wager; to bet.
Itaya mo ang lahat mong salapi.
Bet all the money you have.

tayó'   v.   /-um-/ to stand; to build;
to let stand. Tumayo ka Pedro.
Stand up Pedro.

/mag-:i-/ to stand; to construct;
to build; to let stand. Nagtayo
sila ng bahay. They built a
house. Itayo mo ang halaman.
Straighten up the plant.

táyo   pro.   we (inclusive, you and I or
you, I and others).

táyog   adj.   /ma-/ high; altitude; elevation.

táypis (Eng) n.   typist.

téka   part.   an expression which means 'just
a minute', or 'by the way'; de-
rived from hintay ka.

téla   n.   cloth; clothing material.

telebísyon n.   television, television set.

telegráma n.   telegram; cable.

telépono   n.   telephone.

temperatúra n.   temperature.

téna   part.   an expression which means 'let's
go' or 'come on'; a contraction
of tayo na.

ténis (Eng) n.   tennis.

tentasyón (Sp) n.   temptation.

tenyénte (Sp) n.   lieutenant. --var. tininté.

ténga   n.   ear; originally pronounced
                   tainga or taynga.

tengang-dagá' n.   dried black mushroom.

teríble (Sp) adj.   terrible.

térmos (Sp) n.   thermos bottle.

térno   n.   woman's native costume with
                   butterfly sleeves, formal; see
                   saya.

tesuréro/a   n.   treasurer. --var. tesoréro.

tétano (Sp) n.   tetanus.

tiának   n.   folkloric elf or goblin.

tibay   adj. /ma-/ durable; sturdy; lasting.

tibí   n.   constipation; costiveness.

tibo'   n.   splinter of glass.

             v.   /ma-/ be splintered by glass.

tibók   v.   /-um-/ to throb; to pulsate;
                   to beat. Tumibok ang kanyang
                   puso nang nakita niya ang kanyang
                   mahal. Her heart beat fast
                   when she saw her lover.

tiket   n.   ticket.

tikím   v.   /-um-:-an/ to taste; to sample
                   food. Tumikim si Loly sa
                   niluluto ko. Loly tasted my
                   cooking. Tikman mo itong adobo.
                   Taste this adobo.

tikís	adv.	on purpose; intentionally.
tiklíng	n.	rail bird with long legs.
tiklóp	n.	fold.
	v.	/-um-/ to fold.

/mag-:-in/ to fold. Tiklupín mo ang mga kumot. Fold the blankets.

tiktík	n.	spy.
tigáng	adj.	extremely dry (soil).
tigás	adj.	/ma-/ hard; tough; tenacious.
tigdás	n.	measles.
tigíb	adj.	filled; overburdened; over-loaded.
tígil	v.	/-um-/ to stop; to discontinue; to suspend. Tumigil si Rosy sa kanyang pag-aaral. Rosy stopped her studies.

/mag-:i-/ to stop; to discon-tinue; to suspend. Itigil ang makina. Stop the machine.

tigmák	adj.	soaked; drenched; thoroughly immersed.
tígre (Sp)	n.	tiger.
tihéras	n.	cot.
tiháya'	v.	/-um-/ to lie with face or ventral side up; to lie on ne's back. Tumihaya siya pagka apos kumain. He lay on his back after eating.

/mag-:i-/ (<u>tihayá'</u>) to lie
with face or ventral side up.

tiís   v.   /mag-:-in/ to bear; to suffer;
to endure. <u>Nagtiis siya ng
katakut-takot na hirap</u>. He
endured a great deal of hardship. <u>Tiisin mo ang hapdi</u>.
Endure the stinging pain.

tíla'   adj.   ended; ceased.

tilád   n.   small pieces or bits (from
cutting or chopping).

tilapíya   n.   tilapia.

tilamsík   n.   splash (of water); spark (of
fire, specially from the forge).

tiláok   n.   crowing of rooster.

tilí   n.   sudden shrill cry (from fright
or pain); the cry of the deer.

tílin   n.   clitoris.

timáwa'   n.   freeman; emancipated slave.

timbá'   n.   pail; bucket.

timbáng   n.   weights.

    v.   /-um-:-in/ to weigh. <u>Timbangín mo ang mga dadalhin ko</u>.
Weigh what I'm going to carry.

       /mag-/ to weigh. <u>Nagtimbang
kami kahapon</u>. We weighed
(ourselves) yesterday.

tímog   n.   south.

timplá (Sp)   n.   ingredients added or mixed to
fill a prescription (in drug
stores); seasoning (in cooking);
mixture.

timpládo (Sp)	adj.	moderate; tempered.
timtíman	adj.	/ma-/ constant; faithful.
timpí'	v.	/mag-:-in/ to control oneself. <u>Magtimpi ka</u>. Control yourself.
tína'	n.	dye; indigo.
tinapá	n.	smoked fish.
tinápay	n.	bread.
tindá	n.	goods for sale; merchandise.
		/-an/ (<u>tindáhan</u>) store.
	v.	/mag-:i-/ to sell. <u>Nagtinda si Nenita ng kamatis</u>. Nenita sold tomatoes. <u>Itinda mo ang puto</u>. Sell the rice cake.
tindéro/a	n.	storekeeper; shop-owner.
tindí	n.	ponderousness; intensity; gravity; heaviness.
	adj.	/ma-/ grave; intense ponderous; heavy.
tindíg	v.	/-um-/ to stand up. <u>Tumindig ka</u>. Stand up.
		/mag-:i-/ to put in an upright position. <u>Itindig mo ang plorera</u>. Stand the flower vase up.
tiník	n.	thorn; fishbone.
	adj.	/ma-/ thorny.
tiniklíng	n.	a native dance in which the dancer steps in and out of two clapping bamboo poles.
tinidór	n.	fork.

tínig	n.	voice. --syn. boses.
tinó'	adj.	/ma-/ sane; full of common sense; sensible.
tínta	n.	ink.
tintúra (Sp)	n.	tincture.
tinyénte	n.	lieutenant.
tingá (Ch)	n.	foreign matter lodged between the teeth.
tingalá'	adj.	with face looking upward.
	adv.	/pa-/ looking upward, with face or front in the upward position.
tingkád	adj.	/ma-/ bright (colored).
tinggá'	n.	lead; tin.
tingí' (Ch)	n.	selling or sold at retail.
tingín	v.	/-um-:-an/ to look at; to view. Tumigin ka sa kaliwa. Look to the left. Tingnan mo ang langit. Look at the sky.
tingtíng	n.	stickbroom; ribs of palms. (walis na) tingting.
tipák	v.	/-um-/ to hit; win a fortune. Tumipak sina Delfin sa karera. Delfin and his group made a fortune off the race.
		/mag-:-in/ to chop off a piece or portion of matter. Tipakin mo ang isang bloke ng yelo. Chop off a block of ice.
tipaklóng	n.	species of grasshopper.

tipíd   adj.   /ma-/ economical; thrifty; frugal.

            v.   /mag-:-in/ to use economically; to be thrifty. Magtipid tayo. Let's spend our money carefully.

típon   v.   /mag-:-in/ to collect; to gather together; to store away. Tipúnin mo ang mga lumang selyo. Gather the old stamps together.

tirá   adj.   /naka-/ staying at; residing in.

            v.   /-um-/ to reside; to dwell. Tumira ako sa kalye Merced. I lived on Merced Street.

tirá   n.   leftover; remainder.

            v.   /mag-:i-/ to set aside, as food, for someone. Nagtira ako ng makakain para kay Teria. I left some food for Teria to eat. Itira mo ang pritong isda kay Emma. Leave some of the fried fish for Emma.

tiradór (Sp) n.   Y-slingshot.

tiránte (Sp) n.   suspenders; reins.

tírik   v.   /-um-/ to look straight upward, as in a state of delirium. Tumirik ang mata ng naghihingalong matanda. The delirious old man's eyes rolled back in his head.

                  /mag-:i-/ to set upright (as of candles).

tirintás (Sp) n.   braid; pigtail. --var. trintás.

tirís (Sp) n.   crushing (of lice between thumbnails).

tísa' (Sp)	n.	roof tile; chalk.
tísis (Sp)	n.	tuberculosis.
títi'	n.	penis.
títik	n.	letter of alphabet or <u>abakada</u>; writing; handwriting; penmanship.
títig	v.	/-um-/ to stare at. <u>Tumitig siya sa akin</u>. He stared at me.
títser	n.	teacher. --syn. <u>guró</u>, <u>mestro/a</u>.
título (Sp)	n.	title; degree (academic); torrens title (for land ownership).
tíwa	n.	intestinal worm.
tiwakál	v.	/mag-/ to commit suicide.
tiwála'	n.	trust; faith; hope.
	v.	/mag-/ to have trust or confidence in someone. <u>Magtiwala ka sa akin</u>. Trust me.
tiwalág	v.	/-um-/ to separate; to resign from. <u>Tumiwalag si Arturo sa aming samahan</u>. Arturo resigned from our club.
		/mag-:i-/ to dismiss; to expel; to remove from. <u>Itiwalag mo si Ruben sa ating grupo</u>. Expel Ruben from our group.
tiwangwáng	adj.	/naka-/ widely open; totally exposed (to wind and sun).
tiwarík	adj.	upside down, head down, feet up.
tiwasáy	adj.	tranquil.
tiyá	n.	aunt (term of address and reference).

tiyák	adj.	specific; direct; to the point.
tiyagá'	adj.	/ma-/ constant; patient; persevering.
tiyán	n.	stomach; belly.
tiyáni'	n.	tweezers.
tiyémpo (Sp)	n.	timing; cadence; rhythm (specially in music).
	v.	/ma-:-an/ (<u>matiyémpuhan</u>) to find or do something at the precise moment.
tiyó (Sp)	n.	uncle (term of address and reference).
tokadór (Sp)	n.	ladies dressing table with large mirror; a dresser. --var. <u>tukadór</u>.
tokáyo (Sp)	n.	namesake; person having the same first name as self. --var. <u>tukáyo</u>.
tókwa (Ch)	n.	pressed soybean curd.
tódo (Sp)	adj.	all.
tóga (Sp)	n.	academic gown; judicial robe; cap and gown (for graduation).
tóge	n.	bean sprouts; mongo shoot.
tólda (Sp)	n.	canvas (cloth); tent.
tóno (Sp)	n.	tone; tune.
tónsil (Lat)	n.	tonsil.
topograpiyá (Sp)	n.	topography.
tornílyo (Sp)	n.	screw.
tóro (Sp)	n.	bull.

tórpe (Sp)   adj.   dull; stupid.

tórta (Sp)   n.   omelet.

totoó   adj.   true; as an expression, it means 'Honestly?; Really?'. --syn. talaga, siyanga'.

tótoy   n.   appellation for a small boy.

tótso (Ch)   n.   sauteed fish with táhuri (soy bean curd).

tóyo'   n.   soy sauce.

trabáho   n.   work; job; occupation.

   v.   /mag-:-in/ to work. Magtrabaho tayo hanggang alas nuwebe ng gabi. Let's work until nine at night.

trák   n.   truck. --var. tarák.

traktór (Eng) n.   tractor.

tráhe (Sp)   n.   suit of clothes.

transístor (Eng) n.   transistor radio.

tránsper (Eng) n.   transfer.

trangkáso (Sp) n.   grippe; influenza.

trápo (Sp)   n.   cleaning rag; rag.

tráto. (Sp)   n.   agreement; contract.

trayánggulo (Sp) adj.   triangle; triangular.

traysíkle/ (Eng) n.   tricycle; pedicabs.
  pedikab

treínta (Sp) adj.   thirty. --var. trénta.

trén   n.   train.

trés (Sp)   num.   three.

trígo (Sp)   n.   wheat.

tróno (Sp)   n.   throne.

trópa (Sp)   n.   troop.

tsá/tsáa (Ch) n.   tea.

tsampáka (Sp) n.   white or orange champak.

tsampurádo (Sp) n.   chocolate-flavored porridge.

tsápa (Sp)   n.   badge.

tsáperon (Eng) n.   chaperon.

tséke (Sp)   n.   a bank check.

tsíko   n.   chico.

tsinélas (Sp) n.   slippers.

tsíp (Eng)   n.   chief.

tsísmis   n.   gossip.

tsismóso/a (Sp) adj.   tale-bearing person; a gossip;
                        tattletail.

tsók (Eng)   n.   chalk.

tsóke (Sp)   n.   impact; collision.

               v.   /mag-/ to collide.

tsokoláte (Sp) n.   chocolate.

               adj.   brown. --syn. kape, kayumanggi.

tsónggo   n.   monkey.

tsupér (Fr) n.   driver of a motor vehicle; chauffeur.

tsupládo/a adj. snobbish; haughty.

T-syert n.   T-shirt.

tubá' n.   native drink; palm sap.

tubéro n.   plumber.

túbig n.   water.

tubó n.   sugarcane.

túbo' n.   gain; profit; benefit.

v.   /-um-/ to grow (plants).
Tumubo ang itinanim kong rosas.
The roses I planted grew.

/mag-/ to gain, profit, earn
interest; to grow. Nagtubo ang
pera ko sa bangko. My money in
the bank earned interest.

tubós v.   /mang-:-in/ to redeem. Tubusín
mo ang isinangla kong relo.
Redeem the watch that I pawned.

tubó n.   /-an/ (tubuhán) sugarcane
plantation or field.

tuká' n.   bill of a fowl; peck.

v.   /-um-:-in/ to peck. Tinuka
ng ibon ang bayabas. The bird
pecked at the guava.

/mang-:-in/ (manuká') to peck.

tukláp v.   /mag-:-in/ to detach; to remove
the skin or covering; to pry.
Tuklapin mo ang balat ng sampalok.
Remove the covering on the
tamarind.

túkod	n.	prop.

tuksó	v.	/mang-:-in/ (manukso) to tease; to joke; to jest; to tempt. Baka manukso sila. They might tease. Tuksuhín natin si Marcia. Let's tease Marcia.

tuktók	n.	tap; knock.
		top, tip, peak (of head); mountain peak.

tugón	n.	answer.

tugtóg	v.	/-um-:-in/ to play music; to play on an instrument. Tumugtog ang banda ng mabilis na musika. The band played fast music. Tugtugín mo sa piyano ang 'Dahil sa Iyo'. Play 'Dahil sa Iyo' on the piano.

túhod	n.	knee.

túhog	v.	/mag-:-in, i-/ to string together; to thread. Magtuhog kayo ng bulaklak. String flowers together. Tuhúgin mo ang mga bulaklak. String the flowers together.

tulá'	n.	poem.
	v.	/-um-/ to recite a poem.

túlak	v.	/-um-/ to leave by boat; to depart by boat. Tumulak na ang barko noong kami ay dumating. The boat departed when we came.
		/mag-:i-/ to shove; to push. Nagtulak kami ng kotse ni Roger. We pushed Roger's car. Itulak mo ang kariton. Push the cart.

túlad	adj.	same as; similar to; like that of.
tulalá'	adj.	stupid; ignorant.
tuláy	n.	bridge.
tulíg	adj.	stunned; bewildered; stupefied; deafened.
túlin	adj.	/ma-/ fast; swift; rapid.
tulíngan	n.	tuna.
tulís	adj.	/ma-/ sharp-pointed.
tuldók	n.	period mark.
túli' (Ch)	n.	circumcision.
	adj.	(tulí') circumised.
tulíg	adj.	so deafened by noise as to be confused.
	v.	/ma-/ to be deafened by noise.
tulisán	n.	highwayman; brigand.
túlo'	v.	/-um-/ to drip. Tumulo ang gripo. The faucet dripped.
tulóg	adj.	asleep; sluggard.
túlog	v.	/ma-/ to sleep; to go to bed. Matulog ka nang maaga. Go to bed early.
túlong	v.	/-um-/ to help; to aid. Tumulong ka sa mga nangangailangan. Help those who are in need.
		/-an/ to help. tulungan mo siya. Help her.

tulóy   v.   /-um-/ to come in; to enter; to stay in a place temporarily. Tumuloy kami kina Lorna noong pumunta kami sa Pangasinan. We stayed in Lorna's house when we went to Pangasinan.

/mag-:i-/ to continue; to go ahead. Ituloy mo ang sinabi mo. Go ahead with what you were saying.

tulyá   n.   a species of clam.

túmag   n./adj.   dunce; dolt; blockhead.

túmal   n.   slowness or dullness (in sales or market activity).

adj.   /ma-/ slow in sales.

tumána'   n.   wide, level highland (above water level).

tumbá   v.   /-um-/ to fall down; to topple; to tumble. Tumumba ang kahoy sa lakas ng hangin. The tree fell down in the strong wind.

/mag-:i-/ to cause something to tumble or be overturned or upset; to push over. Itumba mo ang mga bote. Push the bottles over (on their sides).

tumbalík   adj.   inverted; upside down; reverse.

tumbás   adj.   /ka-/ equal.

v.   /-um-:-an/ to equal; to counterbalance; to match. Tumbasan mo ang kanyang kakayahan. Match him for ability.

tumbók	adj.	hit right smack on (center or near center); i.e., a bull's-eye hit.
	v.	/ma-/ to be hit.
tumbóng	n.	rectum.
tumpák	adj.	correct; right; proper.
tumór (Sp)	n.	tumor.
tumpók	n.	a heap; a pile; usually serving as a unit of measure for tomatoes, garlic, shrimps, etc.
	v.	/mag-:i-/ to make a heap or pile; to pile up. Nagtumpok siya ng mga panggatong. He piled up the firewood. Itumpok mo ang mga kamatis. Pile up the tomatoes.
tunáw	adj.	melted; liquefied.
túnaw	v.	/ma-/ to melt. Natunaw ang yelo. The ice melted.
		/mag-:-in/ to melt; to dissolve; to digest. Tunawin mo ang gulaman. Melt the gelatin.
túnay	adj.	genuine; true; real.
tunóg	n.	sound; noise.
	adj.	resounding; alert.
tunsóy	n.	adult fimbriated herring.
tuntóng	v.	/-um-/ to step on; to tread on. Tumuntong ka sa batong iyon. Step on that stone.
tuntóng	n.	pot cover made of clay.

tungangá'	adj.	/naka-/ open-mouthed, as when one is curious or surprised.
tungkód	n.	cane; a walking stick; a staff.
	v.	/mag-:i-/ to walk with a cane. <u>Nagtungkod ang matanda</u>. The old man walked with a cane.
tungkól	prep.	(+ <u>sa</u>) regarding; about; referring to; concerning. <u>Tungkol sa kanilang usap</u>. (about...).
tungkós	n.	something wrapped, specially in cloth or leaves; bouquet (of flowers); bundle (of leaves, sticks, vegetables).
tungkulin	n.	duty; obligation.
tunggá'	v.	/-um-:-in/ to drink in gulps (drinking wine). <u>Tinungga ni Berting ang alak</u>. Bert gulped down the wine.
tunggák	adj.	doltish.
túngo	v.	/-um-/ to go to.
		/mag-/ to go. <u>Nagtungo kami sa aklatan</u>. We went to the library.
tungó	v.	/-um-/ to bow. <u>Tumango siya</u>. He bowed his head.
		/i-/ to bow one's head. <u>Itungo mo ang iyong ulo</u>. Bow your head.
tuós	v.	/mag-:-in/ to make an accounting of; to settle differences. <u>Magtuos tayo ng ating gastos</u>. Let's make an accounting of our expenditures.

Tuusin natin ang pinamili.
Let's settle our accounts on
what we bought.

túpa   n.   sheep.

tupád   v.   /-um-:-in/ to comply with; to
                     accomplish what is required or
                     agreed upon. Tumupad si Tonio
                     sa kanyang mga pangako. Tonio
                     complied with his promises.
                     Tuparin mo ang sinabi mo.
                     Comply with what you said.

tupáda (Sp)   n.   picnic; illegal cockfighting.

tupí'   n.   fcld; plait.

tupók   adj.   completely burned; burnt to
                     ashes.

turísta (Sp) n.   tourist.

turnílyo (Sp) n.   screw.

túrno (Sp)   n.   turn; alternation.

túro'   v.   /mag-:i-/ to teach; to point
                     to; to point at. Nagturo ako
                     ng sayaw sa mga trainees. I
                     taught a dance to the trainees.
                     Ituro mo ang gusto mo. Teach
                     whatever you like. Point to
                     whatever you like.

turók   v.   /mag-:-an/ to be pierced (by
                     a pointed instrument, as a
                     pin, needle or the like).

                     /mag-:i-/ to pierce (with a
                     needle); to give hypodermic
                     injection.

turón (Sp)   n.   fritters in lumpiyá' (egg roll)
                     wrapper.
turumpó   n.   toy top.

tusíno	n.	bacon.
túso	adj.	shrewd; astute; cunning.
túsok (Mal)	n.	piercing or perforating with a pointed object.
tustádo	adj.	toasted.
tustós	v.	/mag-:i-/ to support financially, e.g., sending someone to school; giving some kind of allowance or pension; regular support. Nagtustos ako sa pag-aaral ng kapatid ko. I supported my brother's (sister's) studies.
tutá'	n.	puppy.
túto	v.	/ma-/ to learn; to become skillful. Matuto kang magsalita ng Tagalog. Learn to speak Tagalog.
tútok	n.	direction of a point or the business end of a weapon.
	v.	/-an/ to stick up (as in a holdup). Tinutúkan niya ako ng baril. He held me up (with a gun).
tútol (Mal)	n.	objection; protest.
	v.	/-um-/ to object; to protest; to disagree. Tumutol ang guro sa balak ng mga estudyante. The teacher disagreed with the students' plan.
tutóng	n.	burnt rice sticking to the bottom of the pot.
tutsáng (Ch)	n.	short hair on a woman's head.
tutubî	n.	dragonfly.
tutulî	n.	ear wax.

tuwá'	n.	joy; pleasure; gladness.
	v.	/ma-/ to become glad; to be pleased; to be joyful; to be amused.
tuwálya	n.	towel.
tuwí'	adv.	every; each time; always.
	conj.	whenever.
tuwí	conj.	(+ ng) whenever; every time. Tuwing umaga... Every morning...
tuwíd	adj.	/ma-/ straight; direct; correct; to the point.
	v.	/-um-/ to become straight; to straighten out. Tumuwid ang bakal. The iron straightened out.
		/mag-:-in, i-/ to straighten; to straighten out. Ituwid mo ang alambre. Straighten out the wire.
tuyá'	v.	/ma-/ to be sarcastic. Nanuya na naman si Gina. Gina became sarcastic again.
		/mang-:-in/ (manuya') to be sarcastic or ironical.
		/-in/ to ridicule. Tinuya ng komentarista ang opisyal ng pamahalaan. The commentator ridiculed the officials of the government.
tuyó'	n.	dried herring or fish.
tuyó'	adj.	(tuyót) dry; extremely dry; dehydrated; dried.

v.   /ma-/ to dry. <u>Natuyo na ang mga linabhan</u>. The clothes that were washed are dry now.

/mag-:-in/ to dry up.

tuyót   adj.   extremely dry.

U

úban	n.	gray hair.
úbas	n.	grapes.
úbi	n.	yam.
ubó	n.	cough.
	v.	/-um-:-in/ to cough. <u>Umubo</u> <u>ang bata</u>. The child coughed. <u>Baka ubuhin ka</u>. You might start to cough.
úbod	n.	soft pith of palm; path of coconut trunk.
úbos	v.	/-in/ to consume; to eat up; to finish off. <u>Inubos namin</u> <u>ang ulam</u>. We finished off the main dish.
uká'	adj.	dent; hollowed out.
úkit	v.	/mag-:-in/ to carve; to engrave, as in sculpture. <u>Ukitin mo</u> <u>ang mukha ni Susana sa kahoy</u>. Carve Susana's face in wood.
úkol	n.	what the thing is intended for; what is proper for something else.
ukupádo (Sp)	adj.	occupied; taken; busy.
udyók	v.	/mag-:-an/ to induce; to incite; to prod. <u>Udyukan mo si Joseng</u> <u>bumili ng telebisyon</u>. Prod Jose into buying a T.V. set.
		/mang-:-an/ to induce. <u>Nang-</u> <u>udyuk si Luisa na biruin si</u> <u>Berto</u>. Luisa was inducing people to joke with Bert.

ugá'   v.   /-um-/ to shake. <u>Umuga ang</u>
                        <u>bahay dahil sa lindol</u>. The
                        house shook from the earthquake.

                        /mag-:-in, i-/ to shake some-
                        thing. <u>Ugain mo ang mesa</u>.
                        Shake the table.

ugáli'   n.   custom; habit; ways.

ugát   n.   root.

                        vein. <u>Malaking ugat</u> 'artery'.

ugnáy   n.   /ka-:-an/ connection; relation.

                adj.   /ka-/ connected; related (to
                        each other).

                v.   /mag-/ to relate, connect.

ugók   adj.   stupid; silly.

ugod-ugód   adj.   extremely weak or feeble due
                        to sickness or old age.

ug-óg   v.   /-um-/ to shake, vibrate.

                        /mag-:-in/ to shake (a tree
                        or the like) so that fruits
                        (or contents) should fall out.

ugóy   v.   /mag-:-in, i-/ to swing as
                        done to cradles or swings; to
                        rock. <u>Iugoy mo ang duyan</u>.
                        Rock the cradle.

uháles   n.   button hole.

úhaw   n.   thirst.

                v.   /ma-/ to become thirsty. <u>auhaw</u>
                        <u>ako sa init ng panahon</u>. The hot
                        weather made me thirsty.

                        /-in/ to be thirsty.

úhog	n.	mucous from nose.
úlam	n.	main dish of a meal (<u>viand</u>, as used in the Philippines).
ulán	n.	rain.
	adj.	/ma-/ rainy.
	v.	/-um-:-in/ to rain. <u>Umulan kaninang umaga</u>. It rained this morning.
uláng	n.	lobster.
úlap	n.	cloud; fog; mist.
	adj.	/ma-/ cloudy.
úlat	n.	report; reckoning given; explanation.
uláyaw	n.	/pag-/ (<u>pag-uulayaw</u>) keeping together in pleasant and intimate companionship.
		/ka-/ one's pleasant and intimate companion or friend.
ulí'	adv.	again; once more. <u>Nahulog siya uli</u> 'he fell again'. <u>Nang magdaan siya uli sa</u>... 'when he again walked on this...'.
	v.	/mag-:i-/ to revert to a former state.
uliánip	adj.	forgetful (due to senility); absent-minded.
ulîla	n.	orphan.
úling	n.	charcoal.
úli-ulí'	n.	whirlpool.

uli'/úlit   adv.   again; once more.

          v.   /-um-/ to repeat; to renew the action.

               /mag-:-in/ to repeat something. Nag-ulit kami ng sayaw. We repeated the dance. Ulitin mo ang ginawa mo. Do your work over again.

ulirát   n.   consciousness; sense.

úlo   n.   head.

ulól   adj.   crazy; foolish; fool; mad.

úlserá (Sp)   n.   ulcer. --var. úlser.

último (Sp)   adj.   last; final.

ulupóng   n.   poisonous snake.

umága   n.   morning.

umalkíla (Sp)   v.   to rent; to hire. --var. umarkíla'.

umpisá   v.   /mag-:-an/ to start; to begin. Nag-umpisa ang programa nang maaga. The program began early. Umpisahan mo na ang dapat mong gawin. Start what you're supposed to do.

umpóg   v.   /ma-/ to bump one's head against something hard unintentionally. Naumpog ang bata sa mesa. The child bumped his head on the table.

               /mang-:-in/ to bump one's head against another intentionally or deliberately.

               /i-/ to bump another's head against something hard.

úna (Sp) num. first; prior; earliest.

     v. /ma-/ to go ahead; to go first.

únan   n. pillow.

unát   adj. straightened out; stretched out.

     v. /um-/ to stretch out.

      /mag-:-in, i-/ to straigten or smooth out; to press; to iron. Nag-unát siya pagkagising kanina. He stretched when he woke up.

unawaín adj. /ma-/ understanding.

     v. /-um-:-in/ to understand; to grasp mentally; to get the idea of. Unawain niyo ang nilalaman ng kwento. Get the central idea of the story.

unibersidád (Sp) n. university.

únikó (Sp) adj. only; sole; the only one.

unipórme (Sp) n. uniform.

ungkát v. /mag-:-in/ to bring up again. Ungkatin mo ang pinag-usapan kahapon. Bring up what was being talked about yesterday.

      /mang-:-in/

unggóy n. monkey.

úno (Sp) num. one.

unós   n. thunderstorm.

untóg   n. head bump. --var. umpóg.

úngal   n. howl; cry of cattle in pain, hunger or anger.

úngol	n.	grumble; growl.
úod	n.	worm.
úpa	n.	rent; payment for work done; wages; renumeration.
	v.	/-um-:-an/ to rent. Umupa kami ng kotse noong isang linggo. We rented a car last week. Upahan mo ang bahay nina Edna. Rent Edna's house.
úpang	conj.	in order to; so that. upang mananghali. In order to eat the noon meal. upang siya'y malibang. So that he may be cheered.
úpo	n.	white squash; bottle gourd.
upó'	v.	/-um-/ to sit down; to sit on. Umupo kami sa bato. We sat on a rock.
		/ma-/ to sit down. Maupo ka. Sit down.
		/mag-:i-/ to lay something in a sitting position.
upós	n.	cigarette stub or butt.
	adj.	consumed; down to the butt (as candles, cigarettes, cigars); submerged.
urbanidád (Sp) n.		good manners.
úri'	n.	kind; type; class; classification.
úrong	v.	/-um-/ to step back; to retreat. Umurong ang mga kalaban. The enemies retreated.
		/mag-:i-/ to take away the dishes from the table.

		/i-/ to move. <u>Iurong mo ang mesa sa tabi</u>. Move the table back to the side.
usá	n.	deer.
úsad	n.	brief movement along the floor by dragging the buttocks.
úsap	v.	/mag-/ to talk with another; to converse. <u>Mag-usap tayo ng masinsinan</u>. Let's talk heart to heart.
usbóng	n.	young leaves.
usbóng	v.	/-um-/ to sprout; to grow. <u>Umusbong na ang monggo</u>. The monggo beans sprouted.
		/mag-/ to develop.
úsig	n.	persecution; assiduous inquiry.
	v.	/-in/ to inquire; interrogate.
usísa'	v.	/mag-:-in/ to inquire. <u>Usisain mo si Florencio tungkol sa nangyari</u>. Inquire from Florencio about what happened.
uslí'	adj.	protruding; projecting.
úso (Sp)	n.	vogue; style.
	v.	/ma-/ to be in vogue.
úsok	n.	fume; smoke.
	v.	/-um-/ to smoke; to give off fume. <u>Umusok ang kalan</u>. The stove smoked.
us-ós	n.	slipping; sliding down.
útak	n.	brain.

utál	adj.	stammering.
útang	n.	debt.
	v.	/-um-/ to owe somebody a debt or an account; to borrow; to ask for a loan. <u>Umutang ka kay Fina</u>. Borrow money from Fina.
		/mang-:-in/ to get on credit. <u>Nangutang ako sa tindahan</u>. I got credit from the store.
utang na loob		an expression which means 'a debt of gratitude'.
utás	v.	/ma-/ to have ended or terminated, consummated. <u>Nautas din ang kriminal</u>. The criminal's life came at last to an end.
utóng	n.	nipple.
útos	n.	order; command.
	v.	/mag-:i-:-an/ to command; to give an order.
utót	n.	break wind; fart.
uto-utó'	adj.	foolish; silly; gullible.
útos	n.	/-an/ (utusán) houseboy; servant; helper; maid.
	v.	/mag-:-an/ to give a command or order to someone. <u>Utúsan mo si Sabel sa palengke</u>. Send Sabel to the market (to buy something).
uwák	n.	crow.
uwáng	n.	coconut beetle.

uwí'   v.   /-um-/ to return home. <u>Umuwi</u>
                         <u>ka agad</u>. Go home (as) early
                         (as possible).

                         /mag-:i-/ to take something
                         home. <u>Mag-uwi ka ng makakain</u>.
                         Bring home something to eat.
                         <u>Iuwi mo na ang bata</u>. Take the
                         child home.

úy!   intj.   say! (an expression of admira-
                         tion); wow!

wakás	adj.	end; conclusion.
	v.	/mag-:-an/ to end; the final end; to conclude. Nagwakas na ang pinakikinggan kong drama. The drama I was listening to ended. Wakasan mo na ang iyong talumpati. Finish your speech.
waksí	v.	/i-/ to get rid of something by jerking away the hand, foot or body; to renounce.
wakwák	adj.	ripped or torn violently (disclosing inner structures).
wagás	adj.	pure; sincere; genuine; endless; unfeigned; true.
wagí'	v.	/mag-/ to attain victory; to triumph. Nagwagi ang aking kandidato. My candidate won.
waglít	v.	/ma-/ to be misplaced or mislaid. Baka mawaglit na naman ang relos mo. Your watch might get lost/misplaced again.
wagwág	n.	a species of rice grain; first class rice.
	v.	/mag-:i-/ to dry (wet cloth) by shaking up; to shake the dust off (clothes, floor rugs, etc.); to clean (cloth) of dust, soap suds by shaking in water without rubbing.
walá'	part.	not any; absent; nothing.
	p.v.	there is none.
	v.	/ma-/ to be lost (missing); to disappear.

waláng anumán		you're welcome; not at all.
walang-bísa'	adj.	void; ineffective.
walang-hanggán	adj.	everlasting; eternal.
walanghiyá'	adj.	shameless.
waláng lamán	adj.	empty.
walang-muwáng	adj.	without sense or understanding; ignorant; innocent.
waláng-pakundángan	adj.	irreverent; disrespectful.
waláng-pahintúlot	adj.	without permission.
walang táwad		an expression in sales meaning 'fixed price' (lit. no discount/ bargain).
waláng-tígil	adj.	without stopping.
waláy (Ch)	adj.	/hi-/ separated.
wálay	v.	/i-/ to separate from; to wean (a baby) from the mother's breast.
wálet (Eng)	n.	wallet.
walís	n.	broom.
	v.	/mag-:-in/ to sweep (with a broom). <u>Magwalis ka ng bahay</u>. Sweep the house. <u>Walisin mo ang dumi sa balkon</u>. Sweep up the dirt on the balcony.
waló	num.	eight.
Waráy	n.	familiar reference to Samar-Leyte language or the people who speak it.

wasák	v.	/mag-:-in/ to destroy completely; to tear down. <u>Wasakin mo ang pintuan</u>. Smash down the door.
wastó'	adj.	correct; right; proper.
	v.	/mag-:-in/ to correct; to make right. <u>Wastuịn mo ang mga mali ni Petra</u>. Correct Petra's errors.
watak-waták	adj.	scattered; not united; separated; isolated; dispersed.
wélga	n.	a (labor) strike.
wéyter (Eng)	n.	waiter.
wíka' (Mal)	n.	language.
wíli	adj.	fondness; accustomed; fond of.
		<u>wiling-wili</u> 'very much at home'.
	v.	/ma-/ to become engrossed or interested; to desire to continue with an experience because of its pleasantness, attractiveness or profit. <u>Nawili ako sa pagtutugtog ng gitara</u>. I got wrapped up in the guitar music.
wilíg	v.	/mag-:-an/ to sprinkle water (on clothes to be pressed). <u>Wiligán mo ang mga paplantsahin</u>. Sprinkle the clothes to be ironed.
wisík	v.	/mag-:-an/ to spray liquid or to sprinkle it lightly. <u>Wisikán mo ng tubig ang mga bulaklak nang di malanta</u>. Sprinkle the flowers with water so they won't wilt.

Y

y	conj.	and (a Spanish borrowing used only with time and sometimes with middle names).
'y		contraction of 'ay' in writing, as in <u>ako' y guró'</u> (<u>ako ay guró'</u>).
yabág	n.	sound of footstep.
yábang	adj.	/ma-/ pride; arrogance; proud; snob; boastful; conceited.
yabóng	adj.	/ma-/ luxuriant.
yákag	n.	/pag-/ vocal invitation.
	v.	/mag-/ (<u>magyakág</u>) to invite people vocally (to go somewhere). <u>Magyakág tayo ng mga makakasama.</u> Let's invite persons who will be able to go with us.
		/-in/ to invite or induce (someone) to come along or do something. <u>Yakágin mo siyang sumama.</u> Ask him to come along.
		/mang-:-in/ to invite on the spur of the moment. <u>Yinakag nila ako sa bolingan.</u> They invited me to go bowling.
yakál	n.	yacca tree.
yákap	v.	/-um-/ to embrace; to hug. <u>Yumakap siya sa akin.</u> She/he embraced me.
		/mang-:-in/ to embrace; to hug. <u>Nangyakap ang lasing.</u> The drunken (person) began embracing (people). <u>Yakápin mo ang iyong ina.</u> Embrace your mother.

yáman	n.	treasure; wealth; richness.
		/ka-:-an/ (kayamánan).
	adj.	/ma-/ rich; wealthy.
yámang	conj.	while; as. Yamang ang sa pagong ay lumaki... While that of the turtle grew...
yá'o	v.	/-um-/ to leave; depart; to die.
ya'ón	pron./adj.	that (which is far from both speaker and addressed and usually out of sight).
yápak	n.	tread; footstep; footprint. --syn. tapak.
	adj.	/naka-/ barefoot.
yapós	v.	/-um-/ to embrace; to hug. Yumapos si Lina sa kaibigan niya. Lina embraced her friend.
		/mang-:-in/ to embrace; to hug. Yapusín mo ang iyong kalaro. Embrace your playmate.
yamót	n.	annoyance; boredom.
	v.	/ma-/ to be annoyed with.
yaníg	n.	tremor.
yantók	n.	a species of rattan.
yárda	n./qnt.	yard.
yári'	v.	/ma-/ to be finished; to be made.
		/mag-:-in/ to make; to construct; to manufacture. Yariin mo na ang tinatahi mo. Finish your sewing.

yata'	adv.	maybe; it seems; perhaps; in emphatic form, it connotes definiteness as in "<u>Johnson yata' iyan</u>", "it's Johnson (brand) (so it definitely is good)."
yáya	n.	nurse; nursemaid; wet nurse; governess.
yáya'	v.	/mag-:-in/ to invite; to induce. <u>Nagyaya silang magboling</u>. They invited (us) to go bowling. /mang-:-in/ <u>Yayain mo sina Nina</u>. Invite Nina and her group.
yelo	n.	ice.
yéma (Sp)	n.	yolk (of egg).
yéro	n.	galvanized iron sheets.
yódo (Sp)	n.	tincture of iodine.
yóyo'	n.	yoyo toy.
yukó'	v.	/-um-/ to bow. <u>Yumuko siya bilang tanda ng kanyang paggalang</u>. He bowed his head as a sign of respect. /i-/ to bow one's head.
yukód	n.	bowing one's head in respect or in salute; in humiliation.
yungîb	n.	cave.
yúpi'	n.	dent (as on automobile fenders, guards or bodies).
	adj.	(<u>yupî'</u>) dented.
	v.	/ma-/ to be dented.

yúrak   v.   /-um-:-an/ (yurákan) to trample upon (something or someone) with disregard or disrespect.

yúta'   n.   a hundred thousand.